DATE DUE

MR 20 '97			
FE 19'99			
MY 1 1'01			
JE 1 1'01			
OC 2 9 '01			
NO 28 '01			
DE 15 03			
AG 3 '04			
JA 31 '04			
FE 10 '05			

DEMCO 38-296

WOMEN IN
WORLD POLITICS

WOMEN IN WORLD POLITICS

An Introduction

Edited by

Francine D'Amico and
Peter R. Beckman

BERGIN & GARVEY
Westport, Connecticut • London

Library of Congress Cataloging-in-Publication Data

Women in world politics : an introduction / edited by Francine D'Amico
and Peter R. Beckman.
    p.   cm.
   Includes bibliographical references and index.
   ISBN 0–89789–410–3 (alk. paper). — ISBN 0–89789–411–1 (pbk. :
alk. paper)
    1. Feminist theory. 2. World politics. 3. International
relations. I. D'Amico, Francine. II. Beckman, Peter R.
  HQ1190.W687   1995
  305.42—dc20   94–21994

British Library Cataloguing in Publication Data is available.

Library of Congress Catalog Card Number: 94–21994
ISBN: 0–89789–410–3
    0–89789–411–1 (pbk.)

First published in 1995

Bergin & Garvey, 88 Post Road West, Westport, CT 06881
An imprint of Greenwood Publishing Group, Inc.

Printed in the United States of America

The paper used in this book complies with the
Permanent Paper Standard issued by the National
Information Standards Organization (Z39.48–1984).

10 9 8 7 6 5 4 3 2 1

We dedicate this volume to Petra Kelly
(November 29, 1947–October 19, 1992) and to the
many women like her around the world who
envision a better future and struggle to make
it so.

Contents

Illustrations   ix

Preface   xi

Introduction   1
      Francine D'Amico and Peter R. Beckman

1. Women National Leaders   15
      Francine D'Amico

2. Violeta Barrios de Chamorro   31
      Harvey Williams

3. Indira Gandhi: Gender and Foreign Policy   45
      Mary C. Carras

4. Prime Minister Margaret Thatcher: The Influence of Her Gender on Her Foreign Policy   59
      Kenneth Harris

5. Corazon Aquino: Gender, Class, and the People Power President   71
      Vincent G. Boudreau

6. Women as Insiders: The Glass Ceiling at the United Nations   85
      Kristen Timothy

7. In Their Own Words 95

    Margaret Anstee, *UN Undersecretary General* 95
    Benazir Bhutto, *Pakistan* 102
    Jeane J. Kirkpatrick, *U.S. Representative to UN* 105
    Golda Meir, *Israel* 108

8. Gender and the Political Beliefs of American
Opinion Leaders 113
    Ole R. Holsti and James N. Rosenau

9. Organizing for Change: International Women's
Movements and World Politics 143
    Deborah Stienstra

10. Jane Addams: The Chance the World Missed 155
    Sybil Oldfield

11. Women and the Global Green Movement 169
    Petra Kelly

12. Women in Revolutionary Movements: Cuba and
Nicaragua 183
    Margaret Randall

    Conclusion: An End and a Beginning 199
    Peter R. Beckman and Francine D'Amico

    Selected Bibliography 215

    Index 221

    About the Editors and Contributors 229

Margaret Thatcher

Illustrations

TABLES

1.1	Women National Leaders since World War II	20
1.2	Paths to Power	24
8.1	Gender and Political Beliefs among American Leaders, 1984–1988: Causes of War	116
8.2	Gender and Political Beliefs among American Leaders, 1984–1988: Approaches to World Peace	117
8.3	Gender and Political Beliefs among American Leaders, 1980–1988: Future Threats to American National Security	119
8.4	Gender and Political Beliefs among American Leaders, 1984–1988: Soviet Foreign Policy	120
8.5	Gender and Political Beliefs among American Leaders, 1976–1988: Hard-Liners, Internationalists, Isolationists, and Accommodationists	122
8.6	The Militant Internationalism Scale: Responses by Gender in the 1976, 1980, 1984, and 1988 Foreign Policy Leadership Surveys	123
8.7	The Cooperative Internationalism Scale: Responses by Gender in the 1976, 1980, 1984, and 1988 Foreign Policy Leadership Surveys	124
8.8	Gender and Political Beliefs among American Leaders, 1976–1988: Foreign Policy Goals	126

8.9   Gender and Political Beliefs among American Leaders,
        1976–1988: Military Power and the Use of Force   129

8.10   Gender and Political Beliefs among American Leaders,
        1984: U.S. Actions   132

8.11   Gender and Political Beliefs among American Leaders,
        1988: U.S. Actions   133

8.12   The Effect of Gender on Leadership Survey Responses,
        1988, Controlling for Ideology, Party, Occupation,
        and Age   136

FIGURE

6.1   Staff by Gender and Grade in Geographical Posts, June
        30, 1992   87

PHOTOGRAPHS

Violeta Barrios de Chamorro   32
Indira Gandhi   46
Margaret Thatcher   60
Corazon Aquino   72
Jane Addams   156
Petra Kelly   170

Preface

This project started in a classroom many years ago when a student in an introductory course on world politics asked her instructor what role women played in world politics and why there was no discussion of gender in the textbook. The perplexed teacher, after tossing out the names of several women policy makers, allowed that it was a good question. A dialogue began and developed as the student went on to become a teacher in the same field. A decade later, the two of us found ourselves in conversation, regretting the fact that while some academics had begun to work with this "good question," there were no books on the subject written explicitly for "beginners," that is, people who were new both to the study of world politics and to gender analysis, as were the students in our courses. So we decided to write our own.

We talked with dozens of individuals interested in this question, asking them to take part in the project. Eventually, the project grew to two volumes, with chapters by academics, journalists, diplomats, and political activists from six nations. We asked them to write with three groups of people in mind: beginning students of world politics, teachers new to gender analysis, and general readers interested in the question, Where are the women in world politics?

The contributors to this volume and to its companion, *Women, Gender, and World Politics: Perspectives, Policies, and Prospects*, bring a diversity of perspectives to their subjects. Some of the authors write from feminist perspectives, but this book is not exclusively a feminist treatment of the issues. We leave it to you to decide which perspectives seem most valuable in helping to raise and to answer three questions that inform this book: (1) How have women participated in world politics? (2) How has women's participation affected world politics? (3) Is gender a useful concept for understanding world politics? There are a number of reasons for asking these questions. First, more women are participating directly in the making of world politics (and of all politics). More women number among the informed publics that help shape policies or set limits on officials' behaviors. And we expect that, in the not-too-distant future, even more women will occupy decision-making positions in governmental offices.

Second, as Cynthia Enloe has so compellingly suggested, women have always been involved in world politics. The real challenge is to see how they have been so and what that involvement has meant. Thus, we offer this hypothesis: If one doesn't look for women and their effect on world politics, one's understanding of world politics might be significantly distorted or shortsighted.

And third, as the cold war ends and some new future waits to be created, it is important that everyone have a voice in shaping that future, not only for justice's sake (although that alone is persuasive), but also because we cannot afford to continue to overlook the ideas and hopes of half the human race.

As editors, we have incurred many debts in the pursuit of this project. Francine D'Amico wishes to express her gratitude to her colleagues in the International Studies Association, particularly Geeta Chowdhry, Mark Neufeld, Steve Niva, V. Spike Peterson, Anne Sisson Runyan, Simona Sharoni, Deborah Stienstra, Christine Sylvester, J. Ann Tickner, and Sandra Whitworth, for their courage and energy in moving feminist scholarship in international relations "from margin to center" and for their commitment in creating a caring community for scholars working in this area. She also wishes to acknowledge her indebtedness to Carol Cohn, Jean Bethke Elshtain, and Cynthia Enloe, whose work has helped her focus and expand her own analyses, and to Zillah Eisenstein, whose thoughtful criticism, encouragement, and friendship have helped her to grow as a scholar, teacher, and parent.

Peter Beckman thanks Iva Deutchman, Jack Harris, Rocco Capraro, and other members of the Gender Workshop at Hobart and William Smith Colleges for their encouragement and suggestions.

We both wish to thank all the contributors to this volume and to its companion, *Women, Gender, and World Politics: Perspectives, Policies, and Prospects*, for their insights and hard work, their enthusiasm for the project, and their patience with the process. We are grateful for the support and encouragement of our editors at Bergin & Garvey, Sophy Craze and Lynn Flint. This book would not have been possible without the logistical support of the reference staffs at our college libraries, particularly Debra Lamb-Deans of Ithaca College, and the administrative staffs in our departments, especially Donna Freedline of Ithaca College, as well as the financial support of Hobart and William Smith Colleges and of the Office of the Provost at Ithaca College. Special thanks go to Elaine Scott and Sandra Kisner at Cornell University for sharing their word-processing expertise during the preparation of the final manuscript. And, finally, we wish to thank our students for their willingness to explore these questions and to think in new and unconventional ways about world politics, and we wish to thank our families and friends for everything.

WOMEN IN WORLD POLITICS

Introduction

Francine D'Amico and Peter R. Beckman

The central question to be addressed in this book is: How are women *participants* in world politics? Put another way, we are asking, Where are the women?[1] and, once we find them, What effect do they have on world politics?

On first reading this, you might think that the question Where are the women? is rather easily answered. You might say, "Just look at the top leadership positions in a country—the president or prime minister—and see who is making the foreign policy decisions." That is a good answer, and several of the contributors to this book discuss specific women leaders, such as Margaret Thatcher and Violeta Barrios de Chamorro. But what is most interesting at this point about your answer is how you came to it. We would suggest that underneath your answer is a perspective on world politics that tells you to focus on the top leadership positions.

A *perspective* is a point of view based on a particular set of assumptions, in this case, assumptions about what world politics is and how it works, about what "counts" and what doesn't when we talk about world politics. It may help you to understand the idea of "perspective" if you think of a framework or a lens.

A *framework* is a mental structure that we use to help us to sort out complex realities, just as the "pigeonhole" boxes at the post office help postal clerks to sort mail. We construct our mental frameworks based on our experiences and assumptions. Not everything fits the framework that we construct, just as some packages don't fit the post office pigeonholes. Thinking about what fits and what doesn't is important. As we have new experiences, we may alter our frameworks. Indeed, we may want to build a whole new framework if enough doesn't fit!

A *lens* focuses our attention upon certain parts of the whole and brings those parts into sharp relief, like the magnifying glass used by such fictional detectives as Sherlock Holmes. Lenses come in different shades and tints, as in the expression "rose-colored glasses," which suggests that our lens colors our vision in particular ways. Every vision of world politics is seen through some type of lens, but some lenses are not explicitly identified for us (like contact lenses as opposed to eyeglasses!). Different lenses will show us different things or will help us to see the same things in different ways.

You should use whichever term—perspective, framework, or lens—helps you to remember that explanations of world politics and of women's role in world politics are constructed by people with particular points of view. These points of view focus on some things and filter out others. Therefore, much of what we "see" when we look at world politics and when (or whether) we see women's participation in world politics depends on what we're looking for.

Some people see world politics as relations between states and focus on what some call the "high politics" of war and diplomacy. From this perspective, it makes sense to begin our search for women participants in world politics with an examination of female presidents and prime ministers, diplomats and soldiers. But other people see world politics differently. They focus on connections between people across state boundaries. If we think of world politics in this way, then we expand our search for women. We can see that women participate in world politics not only as national leaders but also as grassroots activists, as members of nongovernmental organizations and transnational movements, as opinion leaders, as revolutionaries.

Later on in this introduction we will discuss how some different perspectives on world politics lead us to see (or not to see) women. For the moment, however, we turn to a different question about perspective that also influences how we look for women in world politics.

FROM WOMEN TO GENDER

If the answer to where we might look for women is more complex than a first glance would indicate, the question of how women relate to world politics also has a particular complexity of its own. That complexity rests on how one thinks about "women." Our first thought of women is probably about sex differences. Women are women, and men are men; we are not likely to confuse Margaret Thatcher with John Major, her successor as the British prime minister. But—and here is the crucial point—did it matter for world politics that a woman was prime minister during the 1980s? How did it matter? To simply point to obvious biological differences to answer these questions will not get us very far. We need more effective means to think about the concept of "woman" (and "man"); to do that, we will consider the concept of gender.

Gender can be defined in different ways. We will call one way *gender-as-*

difference. Here, gender refers to characteristics linked to a particular sex by one's culture. For instance, some claim that aggressiveness and a desire to dominate are—at least in Western societies—*masculine* gender traits, and people whom we call "men" (or "real men") are expected to exhibit them. "Women" are expected to show different, *feminine*, traits.

These gender characteristics are *cultural* creations passed on to new members of a society through a process called *socialization.* For example, practices of child rearing and language cause most individuals in a culture to embody assigned gender characteristics. Sandra Harding calls gender "a systematic social construction of masculinity and femininity that is little, if at all, constrained by biology."[2] Thus, we need a concept such as gender to describe what it means to be a "man" or a "woman" in a particular society, to stand apart from biological *sex,* which refers to being male or female physiologically.

This view of gender concentrates on the differences between men and women that culture has created—on the characteristics said to be masculine or feminine, such as aggressiveness. Gender-as-difference becomes one means to answer the question: How do women affect world politics? If a particular culture has shaped women in a way different from men, we might expect that women as policy makers, as citizens demanding a particular policy, or as revolutionaries, might create a world politics different from that created by men, who have been socialized into different characteristics.

In Western cultures, for instance, we often find these paired characteristics that are said to describe gender differences:

Masculine	*Feminine*
rational	emotional
resolute	flexible/fickle
aggressive	passive
competitive	cooperative
assertive	compliant
domination oriented	relationship oriented
calculating	instinctive
restrained	expressive
physical	verbal
detached	caring

If we compare these columns, we see that the traits associated with each gender in Western cultures are opposites, such as aggressive versus passive. They are also exclusive (either/or) constructions. That is, masculine and feminine are defined *in relation to* one another: masculine = not feminine, feminine = not masculine. Conceptions of gender are thus oppositional and relational.[3]

If people whom we call "men" have been socialized to adopt these "masculine" characteristics, they—as leaders, elites, and citizens—may tend to look on the actions of other states as attempts to gain an advantage. The world from this perspective appears to be a zero-sum world, where the gains of other states come at the expense of one's own state. In such a circumstance, one attempts to impose solutions on other states favorable to one's interests through a calculated mixture of threats and promises. Other states led by "men" (i.e., people socialized as masculine) pursue the same strategy. In this world, it presumably pays to be tough and unyielding, making world politics a never-ending cycle of conflict with little cooperation.

Conversely, if we replace those masculine characteristics with the culturally defined feminine ones, world politics might look quite different. Other states' actions might not seem as challenging; indeed, more often such actions would appear to be supportive of the interests of one's own state. Perhaps international issues would be defined as problems to be solved through a creative, flexible discussion, rather than as power contests in which winners impose solutions on losers. World politics would be a positive-sum game, where everyone wins. Or perhaps "women" (i.e., people socialized as feminine) will not see politics as a "game" at all. Perhaps another analogy, such as the family—a group of people living together, sharing work and resources—will be a more comfortable vision of world politics.

If we wanted to create a particular world politics, we might ask, Should women replace men in positions of power? Should we resocialize men to have feminine characteristics? The concept of gender allows us to think about change in creative ways. And it encourages us to ask if there should be gender differences. After all, the social construction of these opposing characteristics denies the commonality of what it means to be "human": Each of us can be both rational *and* emotional, competitive *and* cooperative.

All this assumes that meaningful gender differences exist. Do they? Our own experiences may tell us that there are males who are not aggressive and females who are. The scholarly evidence about gender differences is mixed. It casts doubt on claims of systematic gender differences, although aggressiveness seems to be more common with males.[4] We can imagine, however, that for any characteristic such as aggressiveness or a belief that negotiation produces effective agreement, individuals can be found along a continuum. Some males are not aggressive, and some are very aggressive. Most males' behavior probably falls somewhere between. The same can be said of females.

If we think of gender-as-difference when we think of women as participants in world politics, we can ask two basic questions: (1) How does women's participation differ from that of men? and (2) What significance does that difference have? It has been suggested, for instance, that women leaders are more aggressive than most women. That is, most women leaders appear to think and behave as men leaders do. If this is true, then the cultural construction of people as "women" would seem to have little effect on world politics, if world politics is defined as interstate relations.

A word of caution. Gender differences within a particular culture may differ from gender differences in another culture. Women in a particular society may act differently from men in that society, but they may also act differently from women in other cultures. Indeed, women in one culture may be expected to exhibit behaviors associated with men in a different culture.[5] To the degree in which cultures differ on gender characteristics that are relevant to world politics, generalizations about women and world politics will be limited—and seriously incomplete—unless we are aware of the differences.

GENDER AS POWER

The concept of *gender-as-power* sees gender as a socially constructed relationship of inequality. This view of gender acknowledges that cultures create gender differences, but argues that these differences represent the use of power by one group in the society over the other, and that socializing people into those differences maintains the unequal power relationship. Let's examine this argument.

From this perspective, the very labels "women" and "men" reflect unequal power.[6] To label individuals as "women" or "men" is to exercise power, for the label creates for human beings a set of expectations about who they are, who they are not, and what range of choice is available. The humans carrying one label have more rights or privileges than those carrying the other label. Gender differences thus translates into gender hierarchy.

Imagine that there is a crisis. Which characteristics would you want a person involved in making decisions during that crisis to have? Most of us would likely pick "masculine" characteristics because our culture values them more. The gender-as-power view argues that masculine gender characteristics are more highly valued than feminine gender characteristics. It should come as no surprise, therefore, that "men" (that is, people who are "masculine," whether males or exceptional females or so-called honorary men) are more valued than "women" (that is, people who are "feminine," whether females or males deemed "unmasculine" or "wimps").

Those with the more valued characteristics learn to see themselves as more fitted to govern the nation, the organization, or the home; and those with the less valued characteristics are socialized to accept this arrangement. These attitudes establish and sustain the dominant position of men over women. Men are taught to be dominant and women to be subordinate; the inequality perpetuates itself. Gender hierarchy is institutionalized in the distribution of political power and of economic and community resources, such as social service expenditures and access to education.[7]

If we understand gender-as-power, we can ask three new questions: (1) Where do gender differences come from? (2) How does gender affect our perceptions and interpretations of world politics in general and of women in world politics in particular? (3) How might world politics itself be part of the process of maintaining gender differences and the unequal power relationship? Keep these questions in mind as you read through the chapters in this book.

THEORIES OF WORLD POLITICS

We said earlier that where we look for women in world politics depends not only upon how we see women (and conceptualize gender) but also on how we see world politics. Different perspectives on world politics produce different theories of world politics. In simplest terms, a *theory* is an explanation constructed from a particular perspective. Every theory tries to describe or explain something by simplifying the complex. In doing so, the theorist is selective: What is important to describe? To explain? What matters? What doesn't? Theorists of world politics differ in how they simplify the complex world in which we live in order to build their theories. Our particular concern is how the simplifying and selecting process of any theory treats women as participants or agents in world politics and whether and how the theory conceptualizes gender.

Currently, there are several prominent theories or explanations used by scholars and students of world politics. The predominant theory or paradigm used by Western scholars has been called "Realist" theory. Some alternatives to and critiques of this perspective are Pluralist theories, Critical theories, and, most recently, Feminist theories. (We might just as easily call these the Realist lens, the Pluralist framework, and so on.) We will discuss each of these perspectives here briefly, and we encourage you to have a look at Part 1 of our other book, *Women, Gender, and World Politics: Perspectives, Policies, and Prospects*, for a more thorough discussion than is possible here.[8]

When Realist theorists look at the world, they see world politics as power politics, with *power* defined as the ability to make other states do what you want them to do, using military, political, and economic resources to coerce or persuade other states. For many Realists, military power is the primary means of achieving a nation's goals and defending its interests. Realists focus on issues of what they call "high politics," by which they mean war, diplomacy, and national security issues.

Realists argue that this is a reasonable lens to use because the world is anarchical. Anarchy does not mean chaos; it simply means that there is no government exercising authority over the states of the world.[9] Therefore, states must rely on their own power to protect and promote their interests. In so doing, power creates order in world politics. At some times, there may be a hegemonic system, with one state dominant over all the rest, or there may be a balance of power, with several states possessing comparable power "balancing" one another. Power politics can be quite conflictual, and Realists focus on conflict when they study world politics.

From the Realist perspective, there are not many places to look for women as participants in world politics. Few women have been national leaders—although we learn in chapter 1 that more women have been heads of state or government than most people realize. Few have been diplomats—though there are notable exceptions to this generalization, such as Margaret Anstee and Jeane Kirkpatrick, who discuss the connection between gender and world politics in chapter 7. Few have been soldiers, and fewer still have been officers in the ranks of the militaries of the most powerful states in the world. If world politics is power politics, as the Realists suggest, and power is defined as "power over" others, then few women are involved.

Furthermore, many Realists would argue that looking for women is unnecessary, since *states* and not people are the central actors in world politics. Realists say that states behave pretty much the same, regardless of who their leaders are, because of the context in which each state operates. That context—the anarchy of the international system—requires states to act in certain ways or be either eliminated or damaged in the pursuit of their interests.[10]

The Pluralist perspective provides one alternative to Realist theory. The term "Pluralist" encompasses a broad range of explanations of world politics.[11] While Pluralists differ on many points, their common lens sees a multiplicity of actors (more than just states) in the arena of world politics. Pluralists, for instance, urge us to examine *suprastate actors*—that is, international organizations where states are members, like the United Nations and the European Union. Some Pluralists also recommend that we study *nonstate actors*, such as multinational corporations (MNCs) like IBM and transnational or nongovernmental organizations (NGOs) like Amnesty International. Some Pluralists assert that these institutions and organizations, as well as transnational connections such as migration and tourism, are part of a complex web of international relations.[12]

Furthermore, the Pluralist lens picks out cooperation as well as conflict as an important element of world politics. For example, Pluralists might point to the signing of the North American Free Trade Agreement (NAFTA) by Canada, the United States, and Mexico, as evidence that cooperation is also key in world politics. According to one Pluralist analyst of world politics, most behaviors in world politics are cooperative, but conflict, like disaster on the evening news, gets the headlines.[13]

Conflict remains important to the Pluralist; indeed, conflict avoidance, management, and resolution are the focus of much of the activity of states and of international organizations like the United Nations. The Pluralist lens indicates, however, that there are many situations in which the use of force would accomplish nothing or would not be considered.[14] For example, it is difficult to imagine the United States threatening or using force against Canada or Israel to achieve a policy goal. Pluralists see law and negotiation as well as military power as a means of problem solving and problem avoiding. Conflict, especially in its deadly form, is not the whole story of world politics.

Thus, where Realist theorists see independent states in an anarchical system, Pluralists see *interdependent* states in an international *community. Interdependence* means a situation in which two or more states are mutually or reciprocally dependent upon one another, though not necessarily equally so.[15] *Community* means a set of formal or informal agreements about how to live with each other. This community has rules of the game. These rules can be as important as power and a struggle for power in shaping the behavior of states. Seeing world politics as involving a community of interdependent states expands our vision of world politics in other ways as well. A Pluralist might point to recent international conferences such as the Earth Summit in Rio de Janeiro, Brazil, in June 1992, and the Human Rights conference in Vienna, Austria, in June 1993, as evidence that the agenda of world politics includes important issues that the Realists neglect. Pluralists thus see the issues of so-called low politics, such as the economy, the environment, and human welfare, as significant.

In seeing world politics as more than the actions of states, the Pluralist lens creates more places to look for women's participation. Women are present in international organizations; for example, they are about a third of the personnel at the United Nations, as chapter 6 indicates. Women are active in many transnational nongovernmental organizations, such as the International League for Peace and Freedom discussed in chapter 10. In expanding the agenda of world politics to include issues like the environment and human rights, the Pluralist perspective also reveals more of the ways in which women participate in world politics because of their activism on these issues, illustrated in chapter 11.

A second alternative to the Realist perspective is the Critical perspective. This label encompasses a variety of Marxist and non-Marxist theories, including dependency theory, world-systems theory, and structuralist theory. These theories are called Critical because each stands "apart from the prevailing order and asks how that order came about" and questions "the origins and legitimacy of social and political institutions."[16] That is, Critical theorists want to talk about more than just world politics today. They want to know how today was created yesterday. World politics is not static or "given" or "neutral" but rather always dynamic and always politically significant. Critical theorists also want to evaluate what we have today—to provide a normative critique of existing conditions and to suggest what "should be," rather than to accept what "is" without question.

And finally, Critical theorists explicitly want to understand how we think about our world. They reject the idea of objective knowledge, arguing that all human knowledge is subjective—that is, contingent upon who is doing the observing, describing, and explaining. One's position in life and one's values shape how one understands the world. Theories of world politics, like the meaning of such terms as *world politics* and *women*, depend on who does the describing and explaining. The subjectiveness of knowledge also means that how we think and what we say (and do) promotes some values and demeans others. Critical theorists want to understand the values that a particular claim to knowledge promotes, privileges, or protects, as well as what such a claim eliminates, ignores, or neglects.

Critical theorists provide a different lens through which we can examine world politics. They see the central characteristic of the international system as neither anarchy nor community but *hierarchy* based on each state's position in the global political economy. This "hegemonic order" creates a context for the behavior of states and peoples, and the pattern that emerges is one of dominance and dependency. The people or leader of a Third World state, for instance, might like to pursue a foreign policy independent from, or in opposition to, the dominant states, but they cannot do so without risking severe political and economic repercussions.

Critical theorists often focus on the role of global *social movements* as forces that bring change to the "hegemonic order" of political-economic power. Some examples of social movements are the peace/disarmament movement, the green movement, the civil rights movement, the human rights movement, and the labor movement. Social movements differ from international organizations in that they have a lower level of formal, bureaucratic organization and are made up of people rather than states.

The lens provided by Critical theorists creates new places to look for women in world politics by expanding the definition of world politics. We can now talk about women as members of social movements and as workers in the global economy. Women's organizing and networking in the transnational women's movement is discussed in chapter 9, and women's participation in revolutionary movements in Cuba and Nicaragua is described in chapter 12. Yet Critical theorists have tended to overlook gender as an important category of analysis.

Feminist perspectives put gender at the center of the analysis. Many Feminist theorists have much in common with Critical theorists: they share a focus on historical and contextual analysis as well as on normative questions about what should be. Both seek to explain why we think of world politics as we do. And both promote change in the theory and practice of world politics. Most Feminist theorists also agree that world politics is hierarchical. Critical theorists see a hierarchy grounded in social relations, but most Critical theorists define those relations narrowly in material or economic terms, missing gender. Some Feminist theorists argue that not one but several hierarchies exist, and that these complex, multiple hierarchies are based on gender, race/ethnicity, class/caste, sexuality, ability, and age. They call these intersecting hierarchies *patriarchy* or capitalist patriarchy.

Feminist theoretical perspectives encourage us to look for women everywhere, and they caution us to avoid the trap of assuming that all women think and act similarly and experience the world in the same way or that the differences between men and women are natural rather than socially constructed. This trap is called *essentialism*. When we look for women, say Feminist theorists, we are sure to find gender, and gender is a social creation. Feminist perspectives thus expand our search for women in world politics to an analysis of gender and world politics.

MAPPING THE BOOK: A GUIDE

In the pages that follow, we ask, Where are the women in world politics? And once we have found them, we ask, What effect do women seem to have on world politics? Through Feminist lenses, we can also ask a third question: How does looking for women reveal gender in world politics? The authors of the different chapters have different perspectives on world politics and different ideas about how women participate in world politics. Some see gender as insignificant in world politics; others see gender-as-difference; still others see gender-as-power. As you read, you can now look to see what theory the author might have about world politics and how she or he sees women and defines gender. You can ask yourself what you might see differently if you change lenses or frameworks and, thus, approach the analysis from a different perspective.

In chapters 1 through 6, we consider how women achieve political prominence as national leaders and diplomats and how they use that power, by the policies that they pursue and by their style of decision making and leadership. We also consider how women are perceived and evaluated by their peers and by the public. The authors draw on different perspectives to assess how gender affects the way in which women achieve power as national leaders, how they use their power once in office, and how world politics may be shaped by gender.

In chapter 1, Francine D'Amico offers an overview of women as national leaders since 1945 and looks closely at their paths to power, their governing or leadership style, and their policy agenda. In chapter 2, Harvey Williams describes how Violeta Barrios de Chamorro became president of Nicaragua. He documents her "widow's walk" to power and her transformation from a symbolic surrogate for her husband to an experienced political leader with her own credentials and policy agenda.

In chapter 3, Mary C. Carras analyzes Indira Gandhi's rise to power and policy decisions as prime minister of India. Carras characterizes Gandhi as a political Realist who played the game of power politics shrewdly, for which the media dubbed her the "Iron Lady." In chapter 4, Kenneth Harris turns to Margaret Thatcher, the other leader dubbed an "Iron Lady." Harris examines how gender may have influenced both Thatcher's style of foreign policy leadership and the content of that policy. Did gender give her political advantages? In chapter 5, Vincent Boudreau considers how gender, class, and race/ethnicity converged in the rise to power and administration of Corazon Aquino, former president of the Philippines. Boudreau argues that domestic and international factors, including gender-based expectations and criticisms of her performance, pushed Aquino toward a "routinization of politics," moderating her policy initiatives.

In chapter 6, we move from an examination of national leaders to an analysis of the situation of diplomatic representatives in the United Nations. Here, Kristen Timothy examines the presence of women and the significance of gender in the personnel practices of the United Nations. Timothy finds a "glass ceiling" for women at midprofessional levels and describes efforts to dismantle it.

In chapter 7, women who have been national leaders or who have served in international organizations such as the United Nations offer their insights on their experiences as participants in world politics. Here we hear the voices of Margaret Anstee, undersecretary general of the United Nations; Benazir Bhutto, prime minister of Pakistan; Jeane Kirkpatrick, former U.S. representative to the United Nations; and Golda Meir, former prime minister of Israel. These women see their careers as shaped by gender, but in different ways.

Undersecretary General Anstee recommends that women who seek a career in diplomacy obtain both academic qualifications and firsthand experience, but she argues that women must work harder to be considered qualified and are faced with more difficult choices and greater sacrifices than are men in this profession. Prime Minister Bhutto, on the other hand, argues that because of her parentage and socioeconomic class, she was largely able, in her words, to "transcend gender," moving far beyond the limits that constrain the life choices of most Pakistani women. Yet Bhutto also acknowledges that the political opposition thought of her as "a silly little girl" and that she had to convince people that a woman was capable of governing them.[17]

Former Ambassador Kirkpatrick describes the "process of dequalification" that she experienced as a woman in what is perceived as a "man's world" of diplomacy and security strategy. This process consisted of undermining or underestimating her capabilities and experiences by focusing on gender-based evaluations of her dress and demeanor rather than the substance of her decisions and actions. Former Prime Minister Golda Meir, on the other hand, argued that being a woman in politics never hindered her in any way. Being a working mother without a husband at home, however, made it harder to balance competing demands—harder than any man had to confront.

These first seven chapters examine the participation of women in world politics at a distance. Women heads of state or government or representatives in international organizations seem far removed from our daily lives. Professor Sandra Whitworth has written that we are each engaged in world politics in everyday, ordinary ways.[18] How are ordinary people—and women particularly—engaged as participants in and makers of world politics?

Women as citizens express opinions about world politics that sometimes differ from those of men, for example, with regard to the use of force in foreign policy or the efficacy of international organizations in solving global problems. In nations such as the United States, where decision makers are sensitive to public opinion poll data, this difference of opinion can have consequences for public policy. In chapter 8, Ole Holsti and James Rosenau consider how these differences of opinion can be especially significant when people are opinion leaders. They survey people in positions that affect the formulation of public opinion and of public policies, such as labor, political, and media leaders, government officials, military officers, foreign policy experts outside government, clergy, and educators.

Women also participate in world politics as activists. In chapter 9, Deborah Stienstra explores the ways in which women engage in world politics as organizers and members of international nongovernmental organizations. Stienstra focuses on the groups' strategies for bringing about political change. In chapters 10 and 11, Sybil Oldfield and Petra Kelly describe the work of women for peace and for the environment. Oldfield recounts the work of one woman, Jane Addams, who campaigned against poor working and living conditions in urban areas and advocated international peace and cooperation. Addams' story reveals how one woman saw links between local and global conditions and sought to take action on both. In a montage of her speeches and writings, Petra Kelly speaks to us posthumously about the work of many women around the world engaged in the struggle for human dignity and ecological balance.

As you can see, each of these chapters has expanded the definition of world politics and has brought world politics closer to home. In chapter 12, Margaret Randall discusses women's roles in revolutionary movements in Cuba and Nicaragua. How did we get from women in top political positions, formulating foreign policy and thus seemingly directly involved in world politics (defined from traditional perspectives), to women revolutionaries?

To some, revolutionary movements are matters of domestic politics unconnected to international relations. Others argue that the causes and consequences of revolutionary movements are intimately connected to world politics, pointing out that ideological and material support for and opposition to such movements come from both domestic and foreign sectors. From this perspective, to see women engaged in revolution is to ask how their activities affect world politics and how world politics affects them.

Still others, however, would reject the very attempt to distinguish between domestic and world (or international) politics. That dichotomy, they say, is symptomatic of how women become lost from view when we think about politics. Revolutionary struggles challenge established political, economic, and cultural forms and seek fundamental transformation of those forms. In challenging the established order—the way things are—revolutionary movements provide an opening to examine and confront gender relations.

Connecting women to world politics will be difficult for those who think in traditional—especially Realist—terms. Feminist perspectives help us to see women in world politics—or perhaps more tellingly, how women in what have previously been called "domestic" activities play important roles in world politics broadly conceived—and to see beyond women to gender. Cynthia Enloe says that when we try on our new gender-sensitive lens, we can see a "radical new imagining of what it takes for governments to ally with each other, compete with and wage war against each other":

governments depend upon certain kinds of allegedly private relationships in order to conduct their foreign affairs. Governments need more than secrecy and intelligence agencies; they need wives who are willing to provide their diplomatic husbands with unpaid services so these men can develop trusting relationships with other diplomatic husbands. They need not only military hardware, but a steady supply of women's sexual services to convince their soldiers that they are manly. To operate in the international arena, governments seek other governments' recognition of their sovereignty; but they also depend on ideas about masculinized dignity and feminized sacrifice to sustain that sense of autonomous nationhood.[19]

As you continue reading, think about other ways in which ordinary people in general, and women in particular, participate in world politics. Think about whether and how women's participation makes a difference in world politics. Think about gender-as-difference and gender-as-power. After you consider the analyses provided here, we'll come back to talk about what steps you might take next regarding women in world politics.

NOTES

1. Cynthia Enloe has framed the question this way in her works *The Morning After: Sexual Politics at the End of the Cold War* (Berkeley: University of California Press, 1993) and *Bananas, Beaches, & Bases: Making Feminist Sense of International Politics* (Berkeley: University of California Press, 1990).

2. Sandra Harding, "Introduction," in Sandra Harding, ed., *Feminism and Methodology* (Milton Keynes, England: Open University Press, 1987), 6.

3. V. Spike Peterson and Anne Runyan, *Global Gender Issues* (Boulder, CO: Westview, 1993), chap. 1.

4. See Carol Tavris and Carole Wade, *The Longest War: Sex Differences in Perspective* (San Diego: Harcourt Brace Jovanovich, 1984), 38–78.

5. The pioneering study is Margaret Mead, *Sex and Temperament in Three Primitive Societies* (New York: Morrow, 1963).

6. Elizabeth Weed, *Coming to Terms: Feminism, Theory, Politics* (New York: Routledge, 1989), and Denise Riley, *"Am I That Name?": Feminism and the Category of "Women" in History* (Minneapolis: University of Minnesota Press, 1988).

7. Peterson and Runyan, *Global Gender Issues*, 5–10, 17–44.

8. Peter R. Beckman and Francine D'Amico, eds., *Women, Gender, and World Politics: Perspectives, Policies, and Prospects* (Westport, CT: Bergin & Garvey, 1994).

9. Rebecca Grant, "The Sources of Gender Bias in International Relations Theory," in Rebecca Grant and Kathleen Newland, eds., *Gender and International Relations* (Bloomington: Indiana University Press, 1991), 9.

10. Here we paraphrase J. David Singer, "Accounting for International War: The State of the Discipline," *Journal of Peace Research* 18:1 (1981): 1–18; reprinted in John A. Vasquez, ed., *Classics of International Relations*, 2d ed. (Englewood Cliffs, NJ: Prentice-Hall, 1990), especially 231, 235.

11. See Paul R. Viotti and Mark V. Kauppi, *International Relations Theory: Realism, Pluralism, Globalism*, 2d ed. (New York: Macmillan, 1993).

12. The "web" metaphor is from John Burton, *World Society* (Cambridge, England: Cambridge University Press, 1972).

13. K. J. Holsti, *International Politics: A Framework for Analysis*, 6th ed. (Englewood Cliffs, NJ: Prentice-Hall, 1992), 12.

14. See the classic work by Robert Keohane and Joseph S. Nye, *Power and Interdependence: World Politics in Transition* (Boston: Little, Brown, 1977), 23–29.

15. Ibid., 3–22.

16. Mark Hoffman, "Critical Theory and the Inter-Paradigm Debate," *Millennium: Journal of International Studies* 16:2 (Summer 1987): 231–49, quoted in Sandra Whitworth, "Gender in the Inter-Paradigm Debate," *Millennium* 18:2 (1989): 269.

17. Quoted in Benazir Bhutto, *Daughter of Destiny: An Autobiography* (New York: Simon & Schuster, 1988), 36, 332.

18. Sandra Whitworth, "Feminist Theories: From Women to Gender and World Politics," in Beckman and D'Amico eds., *Women, Gender, and World Politics*, chap. 5.

19. Enloe, *Bananas, Beaches, & Bases*, 196–97.

1

Women National Leaders

Francine D'Amico

To begin thinking about women as participants in world politics, this chapter focuses on women national leaders. We might ask these kinds of questions about women national leaders: (1) What are the "paths to power" for women? (2) Do women govern differently from men? (3) Do women in these positions "make a difference"? Some analysts have argued that women are more apt to use consensus or compromise in decision making or in negotiations than are men. Some people expect women leaders to pursue feminist agendas, to promote women's rights, to be concerned with "women's issues." Some think women are likely to be more pacifist or more liberal than are men policy makers. In this chapter, we will begin to explore these questions and expectations and will discover a whole new set of questions.

NATIONAL LEADERS: POLITICAL CHOICES

National leaders may be heads of state or heads of government or both. For example, in Canada, the governor general is the *head of state* and has formal powers, such as convening the legislature, but has little decision-making power, while the prime minister is the *head of government* who sets the policy agenda. In some countries, the functions of head of state and of government coincide in one office and are carried out by one person. For example, in the United States, the president is both symbolic representative of the nation and chief executive of the government.

National leaders may be elected in general elections by citizens or in parliamentary elections from among the elected representatives, or they may be appointed. Analysts of political leadership have suggested that the kind of selection process and the type of political system affect women's chances for becoming national leaders. In parliamentary systems, the head of government may be elected from among the representatives of the majority party:

This selection is an internal, party affair and favors a party member with experience and seniority. The US president is elected by the public, and party support can be sidestepped by a popular personality backed by political action committee funding. Female stereotypes damage female candidates more in this context than they do in the parliamentary system, where individuals are personally acquainted with candidates and their records.[1]

Some national leaders inherit their position: They come to power by monarchical succession. Hereditary heads of state include currently reigning Queen Elizabeth II of the United Kingdom, Queen Margarethe II of Denmark, and Queen Beatrix of the Netherlands. But these cases do not tell us when and why *women* are chosen as political leaders, except that (in most cases) no male heir was available. Therefore, we exclude hereditary heads of state from our study.

We also exclude women who may exercise power vicariously, through their relationship with the actual head of state or of government.[2] These women are often referred to as "First Ladies," such as Queen Noor-al Hussein of Jordan.[3] Many First Ladies have only an unofficial role in policy formulation or execution, though some, like Hillary Rodham Clinton of the United States, have more formal policy roles. Typically, their ability to influence people is associational or situational; they are part of a "package deal" with their office-holding spouses. We want to think about why women are *chosen* as political leaders. Neither First Ladies nor hereditary monarchs shed light on this.

Selection by election or by appointment is a political choice. What explains that choice? For example, women might be chosen as leaders to symbolize a real or contrived commitment to democracy and egalitarianism. Perhaps they are chosen as agents of reconciliation in a divided society or as compromise candidates in a divided political party. Perhaps they are chosen because of the perception that they are not tainted by the corruption of politics. This and subsequent chapters will examine the dynamics and symbolism of that choice to help us understand how women come to occupy positions of prominence in contemporary world politics.

The time frame for this analysis is the post–World War II era for two reasons. First, women's participation in formal politics, especially in leadership positions, was quite circumscribed before 1945. Only thirty-two nations had permitted women to vote or to hold public office by that date. Since then, women have won these rights in ninety-four other nations, mainly in former colonial states in Africa and Asia as these became independent. Women (and men) are still excluded from political participation in a few nations: "Women do not yet have the vote in Oman, Qatar, Saudi Arabia, United Arab Emirates . . . but neither do men. Kuwait appears at present to be the only hold-out against suffrage for women in particular."[4]

Second, the scope of world politics has changed with the decolonization of Latin America, Asia, and Africa, and with the communications revolution, the globalization of the economy, and the dawn of the nuclear era. Increasing numbers of women are literate, are educated, are wage earners. These changes may affect women's opportunities to be leaders as well as people's perceptions about the ability of women to govern.

For example, two nuclear-capable nations have had women heads of government: the United Kingdom and India.[5] Yet one issue in the 1984 campaign for the U.S. presidency focused on whether or not a woman, vice-presidential candidate Geraldine Ferraro, could "push the button" to launch nuclear weapons during a military emergency. Thus, in this chapter we will consider women who have been elective or appointive national leaders since 1945. We will think about gender as we consider who governs, how women leaders obtain political power, and how they use it.

WHO GOVERNS?

In addition to thinking about women, gender, and positions of power, we also need to think about how our ideas about gender affect how we perceive and evaluate women leaders. To do this, let me begin with Robert Dahl's classic analysis of political leadership in New Haven, Connecticut. Dahl sought to understand "who governs." He identified four "types" of leader backgrounds: patrician, entrepreneur, ex-plebe, and new man.[6] *Patrician* describes someone who comes from "old wealth" or the traditional elite, usually landowners or from "law and the professions." *Entrepreneur* describes someone from "new wealth" or the commercial elite. *Ex-plebe* refers to the European immigrant who rises to power through party politics. *New man* (or "technocrat") refers to the technician or bureaucratic expert, especially in a city management form of government, chosen to counter political corruption and/or urban decay. Dahl constructed these categories to describe "who governed" in local politics in New Haven. His analysis has been applied to U.S. national leaders as well. Perhaps these categories will be useful in describing women's "path to power" in world politics. Let's see "who governs" when women govern.

The category of patrician suggests not only a wealthy socioeconomic background but also a family-based political empire. Here, politics is a family affair. Family members may hold different public offices simultaneously or the same office in succession. Typically, the family dynasty passes from father to son, as with the Somozas in Nicaragua, described in chapter 2 by Harvey Williams. Succession can occur because of violence, as in the Somoza assassination, or because of incapacity, illness, or retirement of the office holder.

The notion of patrician at first appears somewhat useful in describing women's rise to power. If we profile women who have become national policy makers in the second half of the twentieth century, what do we find? Like their male counterparts, most come from wealthy families and are well educated, usually to the university level. Many also come from "political families," that is, they have family members who have been active in politics at the local or national level. Most women (and men) who govern are thus daughters (and sons) of privilege and of politics.[7]

A number of women leaders have come from political families. But many women literally follow in a family member's footsteps; they take what some analysts have called "the widow's walk." That is, they are selected as replacements for their husbands, political leaders who died of natural causes while in office or were killed through political assassination. They are literally "stand-ins," expected to carry on the same policies and to have the same political opinions as those of their husbands. For example, many women in the United States, such as Margaret Chase Smith, have entered the national political arena as widows of prominent politicians.[8]

The "widow's walk" to power has been common in other nations as well. Sirimavo Ratwatte Dias Bandaranaike became prime minister of Sri Lanka after her husband, Prime Minister S. W. R. D. Bandaranaike, was assassinated on September 26, 1959. In Bangladesh, Khalida Zia was elected prime minister on February 27, 1991. Zia, of the Bangladesh National party, is the widow of the former president, Ziaur Rahman. In the election, she defeated Sheik Hasina Wajid of the Awami League, daughter of the deceased former prime minister, Sheik Mujibur.

The patrician category describes families in which members are socialized to political activity and family dynasties in which power is passed along, often from parent to child. Does this tell us how *women* get to power? Daughters sometimes follow their fathers, as Benazir followed Zulfikar Ali Bhutto in Pakistan. But men are the usual (and preferred) heirs. Sons sometimes follow their mothers, as Rajiv did Indira Nehru Gandhi in India. But this is unusual, because so few women have been politically prominent to date. Typically, men do not follow their wives (alive or dead) into politics.[9] Yet wives follow their husbands, whether as First Ladies, widows, or running mates, as in the case of María Estela "Isabelita" Cartas Martínez de Perón of Argentina. This points to the gendered construction of Dahl's categories.

It seems that Dahl looked at "public" but not "private" factors in categorizing political leaders. He considered how leaders made their money and what profession they practiced. While Dahl did examine their family backgrounds, he did so only to identify their socioeconomic status. This is problematic when we try to use his categories to analyze women leaders for several reasons. The "feminine" profession of "homemaker" fits none of

Dahl's categories; this "private" role finds no place with entrepreneurs and technocrats. Yet several women leaders have been homemakers. In addition, social scientists typically consider a woman's socioeconomic status to be included in or derived from that of her husband; therefore, describing a woman leader by her socioeconomic status may tell us more about *him* than it tells us about *her.*

Inadvertently, Dahl's categories may help explain women's *absence* from positions of power in world politics. Most men who have become national leaders come from one of several professions: Law, military service, and business backgrounds are most common, as the patrician and entrepreneur categories suggest. In most nations, women are underrepresented in these professions and in the lower-level political offices that serve as stepping stones to leadership for men. Thus, there are few women in the "apprentice pool" for political leadership.[10]

For example, United States presidents usually come from a state governor's mansion, the Congress, or the military. In 1992, there were 3 women governors of 50, 2 women senators of 100, and 28 women of 435 representatives (6 percent) in the House.[11] After the 1992 elections, the numbers increased to 4 women governors, 6 women in the Senate, and 47 women (10.8 percent) in the House.[12] In June 1993, the number of women senators rose to 7 after a special election to fill a vacant seat; and in November 1993, one more woman became a state governor.[13] Currently, women are approximately 19 percent of practicing attorneys and 11 percent of armed forces personnel in the United States.[14] Only 3 percent of the managers of the 1,000 largest corporations in the United States are women.[15]

Women may thus be at a disadvantage in pursuing positions of political leadership because of this gender-based division of labor. This division is evident in many nations. About one fourth of women national leaders since World War II have practiced law; equal numbers are drawn from education, a profession where women are better represented. Some women leaders have backgrounds in journalism, economics, and medicine, and several have been homemakers (see Table 1.1).

In discussing political leadership, Dahl did not consider other "private" matters to be important, such as whether leaders were married or single, parents or childless. The gender distinction between "public" and "private" is at work here. Leaders' families, their "private" lives, were made invisible, on the assumption that these did not count in talking about politics. Most women national leaders have been married or widowed; most have been mothers; several have been grandmothers. Most men leaders have been husbands, fathers, and grandfathers. These relationships may influence public perceptions of political ability and "gender fitness" for office.

Men with families are seen as responsible, steady, trustworthy; their gender role as "head of household" may even be seen as experience for holding political office. Women with families are reassuring candidates; although

Table 1.1
Women National Leaders since World War II

Country	Executive	Office/Dates	Party*	Profession	Marital/Children
Argentina	María Estela Martínez Cartas de Perón	President 6-29-74 to 3-24-76	Peronist	entertainer	widowed/0
Bangladesh	Khalida Zia	Prime Minister 3-20-91 to current	National	homemaking	widowed/0
Barbados	Ruth Nita Barrow	Governor General 6-6-90 to current	Democratic Labour	medicine	single/0
Belize	Elmira Minita Gordon	Governor General 9-21-81 to current	----	----	----
Bolivia	Lidia Gueiler Tejada	Interim President 11-16-79 to 7-17-80	PRIN	politics/ accounting	married/1
Canada	Kim Campbell	Prime Minister 6-25-93 to 11-4-93	Progressive-Conservative	law/ education	divorced/0
Canada	Jeanne Benôit Sauvé	Governor General 5-14-84 to 1-29-90	Liberal	journalism	married/1
Central Afr. Republic	Elisabeth Domitien	Prime Minister 1-1-75 to 4-7-76	MESAN	politics	married/--
Dominica	M. Eugenia Charles	Prime Minister 7-21-80 to current	Freedom	law	single/2
France	Edith Campión Cresson	Prime Minister 5-15-91 to 4-2-92	Socialist	agr. econ./ politics	married/2
Haiti	Ertha Pascal-Trouillot	Interim President 3-13-90 to 2-7-91	None	law	married/1
Iceland	Vigdís Finnbogadóttir	President 8-1-80 to current	Women's Alliance	education	divorced/1
India	Indira Nehru Gandhi	Prime Minister 1966-1977; 1980-1984	Congress	politics	married/2
Ireland	Mary Bourke Robinson	President 12-3-90 to current	Labor	law	married/3
Israel	Golda Mabovitch Meir	Prime Minister 3-17-69 to 6-2-74	Labor	education	married/2

Country	Name	Office	Party	Background	Marital status/children
Malta	Agatha Barbara	President 2-15-82 to 2-15-87	Labour	education	----
Netherlands Antilles	Maria Liberia-Peters	Prime Minister 9-84 to 11-85; 5-17-88 to current	NVP	education	married/2
New Zealand	Catherine (Anne) Maclean Tizard	Governor General 11-20-90 to current	----	education/politics	divorced/4
Nicaragua	Violeta Barrios Torres de Chamorro	President 4-25-90 to current	UNO	publishing	widowed/4
Norway	Gro Harlem Brundtland	Prime Minister 2-81 to 10-81; 1986 to current	Labor	medicine	married/4
Pakistan	Benazir Bhutto	Prime Minister 12-88 to 8-90; 10-93 to current	PPP	politics	married/3
Philippines	Corazon Cojuangco Aquino	President 2-25-86 to 6-30-92	LABAN	homemaking	widowed/5
Poland	Hanna Suchocka	Prime Minister 7-11-93 to 10-14-93	Democratic Union	law/ economics	single/0
Portugal	Maria de Lourdes Pintasilgo	Prime Minister 7-19-79 to 12-3-79	Socialist	engineering/ diplomacy	single/0
Sri Lanka	Sirimavo Ratwatte Dias Bandaranaike	Prime Minister 1960-1965; 1970-1977	SLFP	homemaking	widowed/3
Turkey	Tansu Ciller	Prime Minister 6-13-93 to current	True Path	economics	married/2
United Kingdom	Margaret Roberts Thatcher	Prime Minister 5-4-79 to 5-15-86	Conservative	law	married/2
Yugoslavia	Milka Planinc	Prime Minister 5-16-82 to 5-15-86	Communist	politics	married/2

Sources: Ruth Leger Sivard, Women...a world survey (Washington, DC: World Priorities, 1985); 28-34; United Nations, The World's Women: Trends and Statistics, 1970-1990 (New York: United Nations, 1991): 31-43; Jennifer S. Uglow, ed. and comp., The Continuum Dictionary of Women's Biography (New York: Continuum, 1989); Guida M. Jackson, Women Who Ruled (Santa Barbara, CA: ABC-CLIO, 1990), and annual editions of International Who's Who, Current Biography, Statesman's [sic] Yearbook, and Europa Yearbook.

Data are current through December 1993.

* PRIN = National Revolutionary Party of the Left, UNO = National Opposition Union, PPP = Pakistan People's Party, SLFP = Sri Lanka Freedom Party, MESAN = Social Evolution Movement of Black Africa, NVP = National People's Party, LABAN = People's Power Movement.

they are entering a "man's" domain in seeking political office, they are doing so in a traditional gender role. They can hardly be perceived as threatening, "man-hating feminists," as some single and/or childless women activists are. However, mothers of young children may find people skeptical of their ability to handle the responsibilities of both their "private" gender role as primary child caretaker and the "public" role of political leader. Many women have waited until their children are grown to enter politics. These "private" aspects of "personal" lives are directly related to how women get, keep, and use power and how they are perceived and evaluated. In subsequent chapters, the significance of these "private" factors is explored.

Dahl's categories do not describe women's paths to power well because they are gender based. Even his category titles tell us that Dahl did not especially have women in mind when making his analysis: Patrician means the male head of the family, and few women in the United States at the time that he wrote or in the era that he studied were entrepreneurs or technocrats/new *men* (!). In order to better understand world politics and women's role therein, we need categories that are gender conscious but not gender exclusive. Three discernible paths to national politics are those taken by (1) "surrogates"; (2) "insiders" or "climbers"; and (3) "outsiders" or "activists."

When someone inherits the mantle of power from an ill or deceased or politically martyred relative, we will call her/him a "political surrogate." This concept of political surrogacy incorporates the patrician category of politics as a family affair identified by Dahl, including parent-child or sibling succession; but it also includes the notion of substitution by the "widow's walk." Surrogates include widows like Corazon Cojuangco Aquino and Violeta Barrios de Chamorro and daughters like Benazir Bhutto and Indira Nehru Gandhi. But "surrogate" also encompasses men, such as sons like Rajiv Gandhi or Luis Somoza as well as brothers like Anastasio Somoza.

A second "path to power" is that of "political insider" or "climber." The candidate rises through party or local political channels as stepping stones to national office. Golda Mabovitch Meir of Israel and Margaret Roberts Thatcher of the United Kingdom appear to have taken this path, since they were neither "surrogates" nor "outsiders" prior to entering the national political arena. The same is true for Canada's recent prime minister, P. Kim Campbell. Some "insiders" have been so-called compromise candidates in a divided political party, as was Golda Meir in the Mapai (Labor) party in Israel. The new prime minister of Turkey, Tansu Ciller, appears to have been chosen to unite factions of the True Path party.

A third "path to power" appears to be that of the "political activist" or "outsider" who enters politics through activity in some grassroots movement or oppositional politics. The candidate asserts her qualifications for office based on her *in*experience and, thus, her innocence or ignorance of dirty, corrupt politics: the "outsider" is the "new broom" that will sweep clean.

This provides a gender-conscious variation on the new man or technocrat category where so-called experts bring the light of specialized knowledge to fix what's wrong with politics. "Outsiders" include leaders such as Marcia Liberia-Peters, who went from kindergarten teacher and school administrator to prime minister of Dominica.

Ideas about gender that see women's primary social role as family nurturer and caretaker make traditional political activity seem unusual for women. Gender-as-difference leads people to see women as "outsiders" even when they have been politically active or are incumbents. For example, Mary Bourke Robinson of Ireland ran for president on a campaign of change, presenting herself as an outsider despite her twenty years as an elected representative in the Seanad, or upper chamber, of the Irish Parliament. And Kenneth Harris points out in chapter 4 that Margaret Thatcher was perceived as a so-called outsider, despite her years of experience and climb through the party ranks.

In the United States, 1992 was said to be the "Year of the Woman" in politics because so many women ran for and won state and national offices. Why were women so successful? Congresswoman Eleanor Holmes Norton argues that voters were fed up with political corruption, such as the congressional bank scandal, and *gridlock*, that is, the inability of political parties and/or executive and legislative leaders to agree and to implement coherent policy. Women, perceived as "outsiders," offered an alternative. Concerns about health care and the economic recession rather than foreign policy dominated the campaign. These are issue areas where gender-as-difference gives women some advantage; women are perceived as compassionate, caring, and accessible.[16] Many women candidates are seen, or project themselves, as homemakers and the state as the household writ large. In an interview in 1982, Margaret Thatcher remarked: "Many women make good organizers. . . . Each woman who runs a house is a manager and an organizer. We thought forward each day, and we did it in a routine way and we were on the job twenty-four hours a day."[17] Thus, when we look at women leaders in world politics, we find notions of gender-as-difference shaping how they present themselves and how they are perceived and evaluated as candidates and as officeholders.

"Surrogate," "outsider"/"activist," "insider"/"climber" may describe the "paths to power" of either women or men. Yet I suspect that the "surrogate" and "outsider" paths may be more common for women than for men, and the "insider" path less so. I think this is in part because of the small "apprentice pool" noted earlier. We know there are fewer women "insiders" below to climb the ladder to political leadership. We can also see from Table 1.2 that a large proportion of women leaders (relative to their total number) have been either surrogates or outsiders to date.

Table 1.2
Paths to Power[a]

Surrogates	Insiders/Climbers	Outsiders/Activists
Aquino	Barbara	Brundtland
Bandaranaike	Campbell	Finnbogadöttir
Bhutto	Ciller	Liberia-Peters
Chamorro	Charles	Pascal-Trouillot
Gandhi	Cresson	Robinson
Martínez de Perón	Pintasilgo	
Zia	Gueiler Tejada	
	Meir	
	Planinc	
	Thatcher	
	Sauvé	

----

[a] Date is missing for Barrow, Gordon, Suchocka, and Tizard.

POLICY CONTENT AND CONDUCT

Once women get into leadership positions, do they govern differently from men? The examples discussed below will illustrate that it is difficult to generalize about women national leaders regarding policy *content* and *conduct*. Their policy agendas and styles of leadership are diverse and challenge gender-based notions of "feminine" values and behavior.

Are women peacemakers? Are they more likely than men to pursue a conciliatory policy, to negotiate during domestic or international conflict? People in states torn by civil strife have sometimes looked to women to heal the wounds of war, particularly women who share their pain of the loss of loved ones in political conflict. Several women leaders have adopted accommodationist strategies with local insurgency forces in the interest of national unity. For example, Violeta Barrios de Chamorro has overseen the demobilization of the Contras and has compromised on personnel matters to maintain peace in Nicaragua. Others have pursued a politics of reconciliation in foreign relations. In her first administration, Benazir Bhutto sought to ease tensions with India over Kashmir, despite the objections of Pakistani military leaders.

But the gendered assumption that women have a special aversion to war and state violence is not borne out by policies enacted by Golda Meir, Margaret Thatcher, and Indira Gandhi. Meir visited the USSR as Israel's envoy in an effort to ease tensions, but as prime minister oversaw the conduct of the October 1973 war and is said to have authorized the assassination of the "Black September" Palestinians. Thatcher resorted to military force in the Falklands/Malvinas conflict with Argentina in 1982 and committed United Kingdom troops to the Gulf operation against Iraq. In one of the most controversial moves in her second administration, Gandhi sent government troops to attack demonstrators at a Sikh temple. She had been prime minister during the civil war between East and West Pakistan (now Bangladesh) in 1971 and sent Indian troops to assist the Bengali rebels, as Mary Carras explains in chapter 3.

These same three leaders—Meir, Thatcher, and Gandhi—have overseen programs of military expansion and nuclear weapons development. Most recently, Benazir Bhutto, in her second term as prime minister, has refused to end Pakistan's nuclear development program. Thus, the record of women leaders on war and peace is mixed. Some have chosen to use force; others have pursued peaceful resolution of conflicts; some have alternated between force and negotiation. Some have overseen demilitarization efforts; others have promoted military buildups.[18] Gender-based expectations are confounded by these examples. Does that mean these leaders are not "real women"? Or that females can't be "women" in the "game of power politics"? Or does it mean that we need to examine our gender-based expectations more closely?

Gender-based expectations suggest that women leaders will enact economic and social welfare policies to "take care of" society's most vulnerable people: the indigent, the elderly, the infirm, and children. Yet Margaret Thatcher adopted a policy of economic privatization that, critics have argued, had the greatest negative influence on precisely these most vulnerable people. She slashed domestic spending on programs that benefited these populations while she increased military spending. On the other hand, Corazon Aquino tried to cut military spending and pledged to increase social expenditures. However, she was pushed by Western creditors to implement austerity programs to control inflation and to meet national debt obligations. The gender-based assumption that women—socially constructed as "nurturers"—will make social welfare issues central is not supported by these examples. That expectation itself neglects factors other than gender that shape policy decisions.

Do women leaders work for women's rights or focus on so-called women's issues? Women leaders' policies span the ideological spectrum from feminist to antifeminist. Women leaders have enacted policies that have greatly affected women's lives—for better and for worse. Many have sought to increase women's political participation and to guarantee their civil rights, such as rights to education and reproductive control. For example, Gro Harlem Brundtland of Norway appointed seven women of seventeen posts in her first cabinet and eight of eighteen in her second and has promoted regulations to balance Labour party representation.[19] Benazir Bhutto of Pakistan challenged the Islamization policy of Zia ul-Haq and recent efforts by conservatives to legalize polygamy, child marriage, and divorce by acclamation.[20]

But in some nations where a woman has been in the top post, women have lost ground politically. Some women leaders reject feminist policies. Thatcher, according to one analyst, displayed "no visible preference for the advancement of her sex" and remarked "What's it ever done for me?" when asked her opinion on the women's liberation movement.[21] Thatcher's cabinet at the end of her tenure as prime minister was composed entirely of men, and the number and proportion of women members of Parliament had actually declined in that ten-year period.

Regarding *conduct*, women's leadership styles vary. Some engage in consensual or people-oriented decision making, while others have a hierarchical task-oriented style. Still others have an androgynous style with both participatory and authoritative elements.[22] In her criticism of the socialist policies of the Labour government, Margaret Thatcher remarked: "I am not a consensus politician, I am a conviction politician."[23] Some argue this characterizes her governing style as well as her legislative position. However, many women leaders do seem to have a consensual style of policy making, for example, as in Golda Meir's "kitchen cabinet." Observers have noted Gro Harlem Brundtland's informality, since she addresses her cabinet ministers and other colleagues by their first names. Ideas about gender difference appear to have little utility for generalizing about the policy agenda or decision-making style of women national leaders.

FROM WOMEN TO GENDER

We have been asking how women leaders get power and whether they use that power differently from men. Should we expect them to? Or are these questions themselves based on the notion that men and women are radically different beings, that is, the concept of gender-as-difference? If we think of gender-as-power, then we begin asking other kinds of questions. We ask how ideas about gender-as-difference affect how we perceive and evaluate women leaders. We can ask how gender and leadership connect not only for women national leaders, but for men national leaders as well. We can also ask how conceptions of gender shape the world political system.

The phrase "national leader" evokes the image of a tall, distinguished, perhaps gray-haired, "states*man*." When we add the qualifier "woman" to the title "national leader," the image becomes divided and contradictory. Either we conjure the "Iron Lady," hard as nails, or the "Little Woman," helpless, incompetent, in need of assistance. Either she is not feminine enough—an exception to the general rule—or she is too much so. The title "states*woman*" is awkward both linguistically and conceptually, given our inherited ideas about gender.[24] Perhaps we can't reconcile our expectations about the "private" role of women in the home/family with the "public" role of national leader: A woman must be either/or, not both?

Gender-as-power affects our perceptions of women national leaders by making us see them as exceptions to the rule that "men govern." Frequently, when I ask students in my world politics classes to identify national leaders, they can name many, both contemporary and historical. But most name only men leaders. When I then explicitly ask them to identify women leaders, they either cannot do so or they can identify only one or two (usually Thatcher and either Aquino or Barrios de Chamorro). Most students are surprised at the number of women leaders shown in the list in Table 1.1. Gender-as-power suggests that we need to think about why so little is known about women's participation in world politics—even at the leadership level. Has it been purposively obscured? If so, for what purpose? how? when? by whom?

A Norwegian research institute study attempted to explain the "exceptional" nature of women's participation and leadership in Norwegian politics by saying that women were entering national politics only because men were abandoning public service for more truly powerful and lucrative positions in the private sector—especially commerce and finance.[25] This hardly seems a generalizable explanation, given the existence of women leaders in nations as diverse as Canada, Nicaragua, and Bangladesh. And even for Norway, the explanation appears infeasible, since many who enter public service come from the private sector and since women are also in high positions there. But the very idea that *women's* political participation must be explained, as though *men's* participation and behavior in office were the norm, tells us that gender-as-power is at work. Seeing men as the norm is called *androcentrism*.

A search for patterns in women's leadership in contemporary world politics has proved frustrating. Generalization is difficult. This tells us that thinking only of *gender-as-difference* offers little guidance in understanding women's participation in world politics. We must move beyond gender-as-difference to conceptualize *gender-as-power*. This conceptualization will help us to understand not only women's participation in world politics but also how that participation—and the participation of men—is shaped by conceptions of gender. Gender-as-power will also help us to understand that world politics itself is gendered.

When we move from thinking about women-as-leaders to thinking about *gender* and leadership, we may now ask how ideas about gender may shape the actions and guide the policy choices of *men* leaders. Through gender-sensitive lenses, we might understand the United States invasion of Panama and military action against Iraq as efforts by then-President (and presidential candidate) George Bush to erase what some called "the wimp factor." Does this mean that to "be presidential," to be a leader, one must be tough, resolute, aggressive—the characteristics that Western cultures associate with masculinity? Could that be why some people asked whether Bill Clinton used a blow-dryer on his hair in the 1992 presidential campaign? Clinton's critics have subsequently accused him of irresoluteness because of his willingness to negotiate and compromise on policy initiatives. Did this mean he is "not presidential" because he is seen as "fickle"—that is, as "feminine"?

Seeing gender-as-power, we can also ask how conceptions of gender have shaped the world political system. The history of colonization suggests that ideas about gender have been used to legitimize the conquest of hitherto free and self-governing peoples. Colonizers depict subject populations as dependent, nonrational, emotional—that is, as feminine. This "feminization" gives apparent justification to the colonizers' dominance: The colonizers are the benevolent, paternal "protectors" who take care of the "uncivilized" (that is, non-Western *and* feminine) colonial people.[26]

In contemporary world politics, Third World peoples remain feminized in media depictions, in popular perceptions, and in First World leaders' policies and pronouncements. The phrase "Third World" conjures the image of starving, helpless, dependent victims—that is, "womenandchildren" (to quote Cynthia Enloe)—who need assistance and guidance.[27] This feminized image also suggests that leaders of nations like North Korea, Pakistan, and Iraq are "irrational" and therefore can't handle the deadly responsibility of owning nuclear weapons—while leaders of nations like the United States, the United Kingdom, and Russia (but not Ukraine?) can. The hierarchy of nations in contemporary world politics is thus built upon Western societies' conceptualization of gender hierarchy. Gender is thus not only a factor in world politics, but world politics itself may be seen as "gendered."

Gender-as-power is evident in the language traditionally used by diplomats, politicians, and scholars of international relations. Masculine pronouns (he/him) refer to the "actors" in world politics: soldiers and states*men*. Feminine pronouns (she/her) have been used to refer to that which is acted upon: States are passive territories that require defending, lest they be attacked, ravaged, pillaged, sacked, looted. (Curious that a masculinized version of the state—the "patria" or "*father*land"—has been used by state leaders pursuing policies of aggression, as in the ancient Greek city-states, ancient Rome, and Nazi Germany). Analyst Carol Cohn has demonstrated how the language of "national security" is gendered. For example, when India developed its nuclear weapons capability, security analysts said that "she" had "lost her virginity."[28] Ideas about gender have thus shaped how we think about, discuss, and understand world politics.

Thinking about women as national leaders has led us to gender-as-difference. Thinking about where ideas about gender difference come from and how gender and leadership intersect has led us to gender-as-power, which in turn suggests that world politics itself is gendered. As you read on, keep thinking about these different conceptions of gender and how different lenses reveal (and obscure) different visions of women and world politics.

NOTES

I am grateful to Peter Beckman, Zillah Eisenstein, and several anonymous reviewers of earlier versions of this chapter for their comments and suggestions. Special thanks also to Debra Lamb-Deans and John Henderson for their research assistance.

1. Jo A. Richardson and Ruth H. Howes, "How Three Female Leaders [Meir, Gandhi, Thatcher] Have Used the Military," in Ruth H. Howes and Michael R. Stevenson, eds., *Women and the Use of Military Force* (Boulder, CO: Rienner, 1993), 150.

2. See Rita Mae Kelly and Mary Boutilier, *The Making of Political Women: A Study of Socialization and Role Conflict* (Chicago: Nelson-Hall, 1978).

3. Elisabeth "Lisa" Najeeb Halaby, an Arab-American and Princeton-educated architect, is Queen of Jordan.

4. Ruth Leger Sivard, *Women . . . a world survey* (Washington, DC: World Priorities, 1985), 28.

5. Nuclear-capable nations are those that have detonated a nuclear device, have a nuclear arsenal, and have the ability to deliver warheads. Israel is believed to be nuclear capable, but the Israeli government will neither confirm nor deny its nuclear-weapons capability. Pakistan has declared itself nuclear capable and is known to be pursuing a program to develop its delivery capability.

6. Robert Dahl, *Who Governs? Democracy and Power in an American City* (New Haven: Yale University Press, 1961).

7. See Michael A. Genovese, "Women as National Leaders: What Do We Know?" in Michael A. Genovese, ed., *Women as National Leaders* (Newbury Park, CA: Sage, 1993), 211–18.

8. Margaret Chase Smith (R-Maine) was elected to the U.S. House of Representatives in 1940 to fill the vacant seat of her deceased husband, Clyde; she served five terms in the House, until 1949, then four terms in the Senate, until 1972.

9. Indeed, the job of "First Husbands" seems to be to stay out of the way rather than to try to help their spouse's career. Even hereditary monarchies make a distinction between the wife of the reigning king (the queen) and the husband of the reigning queen (the "prince consort"). See Antonia Fraser, *Boadicea's Chariot: The Warrior Queens* (London: Weidenfeld & Nicolson, 1988).

10. Vicky Randall, *Women and Politics: An International Perspective*, 2d ed. (Chicago: University of Chicago Press, 1987), 50–94.

11. Women U.S. governors in 1992 were Joan McInroy Finney (D-Kansas), Barbara Roberts (D-Oregon), and D. Ann Willis Richards (D-Texas). Women U.S. senators in 1992 were Barbara Mikulski (D-Maryland) and Nancy Landon Kassebaum (R-Kansas).

12. In January 1993, Barbara Boxer and Dianne Feinstein (D-California), Carol Moseley-Braun (D-Illinois), and Patty Murray (D-Washington) joined Mikulski and Landon Kassebaum in the Senate.

13. Kay Bailey Hutchinson (R) won the Texas Senate seat left vacant when Lloyd

Bentsen became secretary of the treasury in the Clinton administration. Christine Todd Whitman was elected governor of New Jersey.

14. See "Employed Civilians by Occupation, Sex, Race, and Hispanic Origin," *Statistical Abstract of the United States* 113 (1993): 405, Table 644 and *Minerva's Bulletin Board* 6:4 (Winter 1993): 4.

15. Linda Schmittroth, comp. and ed., *Statistical Record of Women Worldwide* (Detroit: Gale, 1991), 27. The *Record* also reports that in 1990, only 2 of 968 CEOs at these 1,000 largest (ranked by market value) companies were women and that only 19 of 3,993 corporate officers at 799 major companies were women.

16. Eleanor Holmes Norton spoke on the "Year of the Woman" at a conference on Race, Gender, and Power in America, Georgetown University Law Center, October 18, 1992. She also argued that redistricting and response to Professor Anita Hill's testimony at the confirmation hearings for Clarence Thomas brought more women into politics.

17. Quoted in Fraser, *Boadicea's Chariot*, 321.

18. Richardson and Howes, "Three Female Leaders," 149–66.

19. Patricia Lee Sykes, "Women as National Leaders: Patterns and Prospects," in Genovese, ed., *Women as National Leaders*, 219–29.

20. Benazir Bhutto, *Daughter of Destiny: An Autobiography* (New York: Simon & Schuster, 1989), 312–18; see also Shahid-ur-Rehman, "Pakistani Women Battle for Rights," *Christian Science Monitor*, July 31, 1990, 3.

21. Fraser, *Boadica's Chariot*, 318–22.

22. Sykes, "Women as National Leaders," 214–15; Nancy E. McGlen and Meredith Reid Sarkees, *Women in Foreign Policy: The Insiders* (New York: Routledge, 1993), 262–97.

23. Speech from February 1975, quoted in *Current Biography* (1989), 567.

24. Sykes, "Women as National Leaders," 219–29. See also Fraser, *Boadica's Chariot*, 297–322.

25. William E. Schmidt, "Who's in Charge Here? Chances Are, It's a Woman," *New York Times*, May 22, 1991, A4.

26. T. Minh-Ha Trinh, *Woman/Native/Other: Writing Post-Coloniality and Feminism* (Bloomington: Indiana University Press, 1989).

27. Cynthia Enloe, "Womenandchildren: Making Feminist Sense of the Persian Gulf Crisis," *Village Voice* 35 (September 25, 1990): 29–32; see also John J. Johnson, *Latin America in Caricature* (Austin: University of Texas Press, 1980).

28. Carol Cohn, " 'Clean Bombs' and Clean Language," in Jean Bethke Elshtain and Sheila Tobias, eds., *Women, Militarism, and War* (Savage, MD: Rowman & Littlefield, 1990), 33–56; see also Carol Cohn, "Sex and Death in the Rational World of Defense Intellectuals," *Signs* 12 (Summer 1987): 687–718, and Carol Cohn, "War, Wimps, and Women: Talking Gender and Thinking War," in Miriam Cooke and Angela Woollacott, eds., *Gendering War Talk* (Princeton: Princeton University Press, 1993), 227–46.

2

Violeta Barrios
de Chamorro

Harvey Williams

On February 25, 1990, Violeta Barrios de Chamorro was elected president of
Nicaragua, becoming the first woman ever to win a national presidential
election in a Latin American country.[1] Chamorro was the candidate for the
National Opposition Union (UNO), a coalition of fourteen parties including
Communists, Socialists, Liberals, and Conservatives. The defeat of the Sandinista Front for National Liberation (FSLN, or *Sandinistas*), who ruled the
country for ten years, came as a surprise to many. In this chapter, I analyze
the role that Violeta Chamorro has played in the politics of Nicaragua, particularly her development from a mere symbolic representation of her martyred husband to an influential political figure respected for her own abilities
and viewpoints.

HISTORICAL BACKGROUND

Through most of its history, Nicaragua has been governed by military dictators or by one of the various groups of elites. As in many of the countries
of Latin America, these elite groups originally aligned themselves into Conservative and Liberal parties. From the time that Nicaragua became an independent nation in 1838, Conservatives and Liberals fought each other for
political control. The reins of government passed back and forth between
these rivals until 1912, when political instability encouraged the United States
to send in the Marines. The occupation forces remained for most of the next
twenty years.

In 1927, nationalist rebels led by Augusto Sandino took up arms against
both the Nicaraguan government and the U.S. Marines. Unable to defeat
Sandino's forces, which had strong popular support, the Marines organized

Violeta Barrios de Chamorro

and equipped a modern National Guard under the command of Anastasio Somoza García. When the Marines withdrew in 1933, Somoza García moved quickly to consolidate his power. He arranged the assassination of Sandino in 1934, and he used the force of the National Guard to take control of the government in 1936. For forty-five years, Nicaraguans lived under the dictatorial rule of the Somoza family: first, Somoza García, until his assassination in 1956; then, his son Luis Somoza Debayle, until his death in 1967; and finally, his son Anastasio, Jr., until 1979.

During their rule, the Somoza dynasty strengthened its power base by extending its influence beyond the military into the political and economic sectors. They took control of the Liberal party and, by coercion and patronage, attained a dominant position in the economy as well. In exchange for unwavering support of U.S. foreign policy, the Somoza government in Nicaragua received generous military and economic aid from the United States, especially the Alliance for Progress and a huge infusion of aid following the earthquake of 1972.

The Somozas used their political control to manipulate government regulations, and they diverted much of the national wealth and foreign aid into their own pockets. They and a few favored associates acquired huge tracts of agricultural, industrial, and commercial properties, ranging from financial institutions and the only cement company to food processing plants and the national air and steamship lines.

Opposition to the Somoza regime was sporadic. The Somozas used force and favors to quell disturbances and to split dissent. The regime was so strong that it allowed limited expression of opposition, such as the formation of small opposition parties. Private enterprise associations, labor organizations, and religious groups were allowed to express themselves as long as they were ineffective. The few instances of violent opposition were labeled "Communist inspired" and, with the support of U.S. advisors, were forcefully suppressed.

Opposition was weak from the traditional elites, who did not consider the Somoza family to be of their class. Most considered themselves powerless and avoided confrontation. Others were content to share in the spoils left to them, prospering in economic activities that did not compete with the Somoza interests. Of the exceptions, the most notable was Pedro Joaquín Chamorro Cardenal, publisher of Nicaragua's principal independent newspaper, *La Prensa*.

THE CHAMORRO FAMILY AND *LA PRENSA*

The Chamorro family had a distinguished history. The first president of Nicaragua was a Chamorro, and three Chamorro men have served as president since. *La Prensa* was founded in 1926 by Conservatives. Pedro Joaquín Chamorro's father became the editor in 1930, and he purchased the paper in 1932. Since then it has been a family enterprise. Pedro Joaquín Chamorro became coeditor in 1948 and took over full editorship upon his father's death in 1952. He was joined later by his younger brothers Jaime and Xavier and other relatives.

From the beginning, the Chamorros used *La Prensa* to promote the views of the Conservatives and to criticize the abuses of the Somoza regime. When the only other daily newspaper became the property of the Somozas, *La Prensa* became the voice of a broad range of opposition. Such audacity had its costs. *La Prensa* was frequently censored, and members of the staff were harassed and jailed on numerous occasions. Pedro Joaquín Chamorro was accused of complicity in the assassination of Somoza García in 1956. After being interrogated and detained for nearly two years, he escaped to Costa Rica, where he was granted asylum. Two years later, in 1959, he led a small armed group in an effort to overthrow Luis Somoza. He was captured and imprisoned but released the following year. For the remaining years of his life, he vigorously opposed the Somoza regime and constantly attacked Somoza and his cronies through *La Prensa*. That he did this at great personal risk was confirmed when, on January 10, 1978, he was shot and killed by gunmen in Managua. He was survived by his widow, Violeta Barrios de Chamorro, and their four children.

VIOLETA BARRIOS DE CHAMORRO

Violeta Barrios Torres was born in 1929 in Rivas, a small city near the Nicaraguan border with Costa Rica. The Barrios and Torres families were traditional elites. They were active in commerce and cattle ranching and were supporters of the Conservatives. Violeta Barrios was educated in private Catholic schools in Granada and Managua, and she attended high school and some college classes in the United States. Her father died when she was eighteen, and she returned to Nicaragua. She met Pedro Joaquín Chamorro in 1949, and they were married in 1950. Over the next several years she gave birth to five children: Pedro Joaquín V (1951), Claudia Lucía (1953), Cristiana (1954), Carlos Fernando (1956), and María Milagros (1958; died at birth).

Violeta Barrios de Chamorro was an excellent wife, by traditional Latin American standards. She was devoted to her husband and children and to the Catholic Church. During her husband's relentless campaign against the Somoza regime, she stood by him, providing moral and material support even in his periods of imprisonment and exile. She was not involved in her husband's political affairs. Rather, she maintained their household and saw to the care and education of the children. Both she and Pedro Joaquín professed great faith in God and trust in God's plan for their lives.

THE OVERTHROW OF SOMOZA

Resistance to the Somoza regime increased markedly in the 1970s. The FSLN recruited rural peasants, students, and intellectuals to their cause. The oppression and corruption of the Somoza regime accelerated following the devastating earthquake of 1972, and both internal and external forces became more vocal in their opposition. Even the traditional elites, including representatives of the Church and the business community, publicly attacked Somoza. Pedro Joaquín Chamorro was one of their most visible and effective protagonists, and he used the editorial resources of *La Prensa* to criticize the regime, attracting considerable international attention.

The murder of Pedro Joaquín Chamorro in 1978, by assassins commonly believed to be agents of Somoza, served as a catalyst for Somoza's eventual downfall. On the one hand, it was "the last straw" for those who had hoped for a peaceful resolution, whereby Somoza would turn power over to the traditional political elites. On the other hand, it dramatically increased the popular support for the FSLN, which was seen as the only force capable of defeating Somoza's National Guard. Most of the traditional elites considered the FSLN to be a guerrilla force of young peasants and students, led by a few radicals. They believed that the FSLN was neither capable of, nor interested in, governing or managing the economy.

Following Chamorro's assassination, the armed struggle against the regime gained strength and Somoza lost both national and international support. After the death of more than 40,000 Nicaraguans, the forces of the FSLN defeated the National Guard and Somoza was forced to flee. On July 19, 1979, the FSLN entered Managua and declared the people's triumph over Somoza.

THE SANDINISTA GOVERNMENT

Some months before the triumph, the Governing Junta of National Reconstruction was formed in Costa Rica. In addition to three FSLN representatives, two representatives of the traditional elites were designated: Alfonso Robelo, a businessman and the head of a new political party, and Violeta Barrios de Chamorro. Although the FSLN dominated the junta, the inclusion of these two popular figures created the image of a broad-based coalition. Robelo was an experienced politician and exercised some influence. Chamorro had taken a more active part in the management of *La Prensa* following her husband's death, but she had virtually no political experience. Although her views were respected, she had little influence. Her role was more symbolic than substantive.

The junta led a working group to formulate a new national policy and design the new governmental structure. After the triumph, the junta became the collective executive and appointed a new judiciary and legislature, called the Council of State, formed of representatives of the groups that had opposed Somoza. Within a year the junta, led by Daniel Ortega, expanded the size of the Council of State by adding representatives of several grassroots organizations that supported the FSLN. Frustrated by their inability to control the direction of the new government, and unwilling to support the fiction of a cooperative relationship between the traditional elites and the FSLN, both Robelo and Chamorro resigned in April 1990. Robelo went into exile in Costa Rica and supported the counterrevolutionary forces (the Contras), and Chamorro dedicated herself to directing *La Prensa*.

During the next several years, the FSLN continued to consolidate its power and to promote the revolutionary agenda: international nonalignment, a mixed economy, a multiparty political system, and social justice, with a preferential option for the poor. Although some of the traditional elites supported these policies, most saw them as a serious threat to their status. Many left the country. Others stayed in Nicaragua and sought accommodation or fought against the revolutionary process within the limits allowed by the FSLN. This opposition was represented most vocally by Cardinal Obando y Bravo and the Catholic Church, by the Superior Council of Private Enterprise (COSEP), and by Violeta Chamorro and *La Prensa*.

Upon leaving the junta, Violeta Chamorro became embroiled in the complications of family and politics that were typical for many Nicaraguans. Her brothers-in-law, Jaime and Xavier Chamorro, had taken over the management of *La Prensa* after her husband's assassination. Two of her children, Pedro and Cristiana, also worked at *La Prensa*, although Pedro left Nicaragua in 1984 to join the Contras. Her other children were active Sandinistas; Claudia was ambassador to Costa Rica, and Carlos became the editor of the FSLN daily newspaper *Barricada*.

The editorial policy of *La Prensa* had been supportive of the new government and the FSLN, but it turned increasingly critical through the first year. At the time of Chamorro's resignation from the junta, there was an editorial crisis. Xavier Chamorro favored a policy of support and positive criticism of the FSLN, while Jaime and Violeta Chamorro insisted on a policy of opposition. The crisis was resolved by splitting *La Prensa*; Xavier Chamorro founded *El Nuevo Diario*, while Violeta and Jaime Chamorro continued with *La Prensa*. Thus the three daily newspapers of Nicaragua, representing a spread of opinion from complete support of the FSLN to uncompromising criticism, were all directed by members of the Chamorro family.

The importance of kinship ties in Nicaragua should not be overlooked. In spite of the conflicting political orientations of her children, Chamorro regularly hosted family dinners during which politics was set aside in the interest of harmony. Violeta Chamorro's kinship network included numerous influential people, many of whom were Sandinistas.[2]

At the time of her appointment to the junta, Chamorro was merely a symbolic representation of her martyred husband and the traditional elites. Even during her year as a member of the junta, she maintained a low public profile, owing in part to the FSLN policy of discouraging the personalization of leadership. She developed her political image more clearly after leaving the junta. Her ability to do so was facilitated when she was relieved of the most constricting of the traditional roles of Latin American women. With her husband dead and her children now adults, she was no longer required to be the attentive and supportive wife or the nurturing and protective mother.[3] She took an active role in the management of *La Prensa* and became the most vocal critic of the FSLN. Both through *La Prensa* and international media, she raged against what she called the totalitarian and godless tendencies of the Sandinistas. The government responded with harassment and censure of *La Prensa*. But this only produced more extreme expressions of outrage from Chamorro and increased her visibility and reputation. As *La Prensa* became more openly supportive of the Contras, the government responded more harshly. When *La Prensa* came out in support of U.S. aid to the Contras in 1986, Violeta Chamorro was accused of treason and *La Prensa* was closed down completely for over a year.

Certainly, Chamorro's initial entry into Nicaraguan politics was due to her position as wife of a hero and martyr. And in the development of her own political persona she continually stressed and built upon that relationship. But she also expanded her image to represent family, motherhood, religion, and patriotism. These themes are seen throughout her writings and public statements. The following quotation from an open letter to President Daniel Ortega in 1988 is typical. She protested the Sandinistas' attacks against her and *La Prensa*, including

exposing through the state media the desecrated body of my husband—a man declared "Martyr of Public Liberties" by your own law—and insulting and slandering his widow, who both as a widow and a woman deserves a minimum of respect. In any country this would be called villainy, infamy, and ignominy: all characteristics of your immoral government—a government that I helped and supported when I was carried away with the strong emotions that characterize a woman, actions that I repent and abhor as I do my sins.

As a Nicaraguan I work for peace. As a woman I unite myself with the widows and mothers of Nicaragua who suffer so much because of your government. And as director of *La Prensa*, I promise you that I will continue denouncing and combating the acts of your government, until you and your government silence me with the brutal club or the assassin's bullet.[4]

Her tone expressed the contempt and lack of respect that elites typically display toward those whom they consider their social inferiors—as if those "inferiors" were someone else's misbehaving children. This was especially true of her remarks addressed toward Ortega and others not of the traditional elite families. Toward Vice President Sergio Ramírez and other Sandinistas from respected families, Chamorro acted more as she did toward her own

Sandinista children—treating them as if they were naïve but civilized people who had merely been led astray.

THE ELECTIONS OF 1984 AND 1990

A national election was scheduled for November 1984 to select a president and vice-president by direct ballot. In the same election, delegates were chosen for a new National Assembly, which would write a new constitution.

Three coalitions of minor parties challenged the FSLN. The conservative group was favored by COSEP, *La Prensa,* some trade unions and professional associations, and by the Reagan administration. It opposed the FSLN on nearly every issue. The liberal-centrist group represented those who, in general, supported the goals of the FSLN but were critical of some of their methods, especially their authoritarian tendencies. The radical left group, consisting of several Marxist parties and their supporters, promoted a more socialist and proletarian agenda.

The election campaign was carried out concurrently with the war against the Contras. There were complaints against FSLN dominance and restrictions of political freedom. Several parties, including the whole conservative coalition, withdrew from the election. In spite of the boycott, the war and other difficulties, there was a large voter turnout. Although there were charges of fraud and coercion, most independent observers judged the electoral process to be exemplary.

The FSLN ticket, headed by Daniel Ortega, won the presidency, as well as sixty-one of the ninety-six seats in the National Assembly. The centrist parties gained twenty-nine assembly seats, while the leftist parties took the remaining six seats. This ensured the continued dominance of the FSLN and gave them overwhelming influence in the drafting of the new constitution, which was completed and promulgated in 1987.

The next election was scheduled for November 1990, but the National Assembly voted to advance it to February 1990. While it was widely believed that the FSLN would win by whatever means necessary, opposition forces were determined to launch a serious challenge. With encouragement from Washington, the fourteen opposition parties agreed to form the National Opposition Union (UNO). Representing political orientations from the far left to the far right, their one common goal was to break the dominance of the FSLN.

The first major task of the UNO was to select its presidential candidate. There was no lack of volunteers. Political party leaders vied with prominent professional and business personalities, and even representatives of the Contras. It became clear that distrust among the traditional politicians was so great that the selection of any one was bound to alienate others. To avoid the divisions that had weakened their campaign in 1984, they sought a candidate who was not identified with any political party. Their attention focused on the one such person who was sufficiently well known and respected and who was unquestionably opposed to the FSLN: Violeta Barrios de Chamorro. Clear signals of support came from the United States. Chamorro was invited to Washington in May 1989 to address the National Endowment for Democracy (NED) and was warmly received by President Bush and representatives of both parties.[5] Chamorro was selected to head the UNO ticket when the delegates met in August with relatively little debate.

The UNO campaign was well financed but not well organized. Perceiving little chance of winning the presidency, most of the parties supported the UNO as a vehicle for promoting their own members' election to the National Assembly. Although most of their campaign consisted of condemning the FSLN, there were many examples of the UNO candidates contradicting or attacking each other, including several instances when UNO's vice presidential candidate, Virgilio Godoy, was critical of Chamorro.

Chamorro's campaign was organized and run by a small group of personal advisors, headed by her daughter Cristiana's husband, Antonio Lacayo. Lacayo, an economist educated in the United States, was a member of a group of young Nicaraguans without political party identification who favored strong structural adjustments as a response to the country's economic problems. The Lacayo group stressed high visibility for the candidate through parades and the media (especially *La Prensa*). Because she was not an effective public speaker, Chamorro rarely made more than a few general statements, and she participated in no debates. She suffered from a debilitating bone disease and was further incapacitated when she broke her knee in January. She went to Texas for surgery and finished the campaign in a wheelchair.

Chamorro's advisors were aware of the many similarities between Violeta Chamorro and Corazon Aquino. In the campaign, they stressed the shared attributes that had contributed to Aquino's successful presidential bid in the Philippines. Both women were seen as symbols of hope for the nation's salvation. They were called upon by God and the people to lead (somewhat reluctantly) the forces of good against the forces of evil. Each was destined to bring about the realization of her martyred husband's dream for freedom and democracy. For example, upon accepting the nomination, Chamorro commented: "I have asked my husband and God if I could serve as a loving link between them and all of you, and they said yes."[6] Indeed, many of the descriptions of Aquino fit Chamorro so closely that, without the names, one can scarcely tell the difference.[7]

Chamorro presented a very difficult target for the FSLN. Their presidential candidate, Daniel Ortega, was portrayed as a fighting rooster: ready to take on the Contras and the United States in defense of the revolution. But it was awkward to direct this attack against Chamorro who, dressed in white and with her arms outstretched, was carried about like a statue of the Virgin Mary in a religious procession. With frequent references to her martyred husband

and to God, she stressed faith and good will. She urged reconciliation, reminding the voters of her own suffering as a widow and as a mother with children on both sides of the conflict.

Her promise of renewed good relations with the United States, including substantial aid and an end to the economic boycott, was backed by President Bush. Most significantly, she pledged an end to the Contra war, including the abolition of Patriotic Military Service (SMP, or the draft) and the demobilization of all military forces. Even among those who opposed the Contras, the SMP was the most objectionable of the FSLN policies. Having to defend the SMP as a necessary policy of the war, and unable to deny the terrible social and economic conditions that prevailed, the FSLN could only promise that "everything will be better" (their campaign slogan) under continued FSLN rule.

The most carefully observed election in Latin American history was held in Nicaragua on February 25, 1990. To the surprise of nearly everyone, the UNO won the presidency for Chamorro, with 55 percent of the popular vote, and an overwhelming number of the mayoral contests. In spite of the losses, the FSLN made a decent showing with over 40 percent of the vote. Because of proportional representation, the FSLN won thirty-nine of the ninety-two seats in the National Assembly. This gave them by far the largest number of delegates for a single party, and also deprived the UNO of the 60 percent necessary to change the constitution or to override a presidential veto. Daniel Ortega conceded gracefully, embracing the president-elect and promising Chamorro his cooperation in effecting a smooth transition. To the nation, and especially to its supporters, the FSLN promised that it would "govern from below" and defend the gains of the revolution.

THE GOVERNMENT OF VIOLETA CHAMORRO

The UNO victory wasn't the only surprise that year. In the UNO, the same groups (and in some cases the very same persons) who had believed that the FSLN would turn the government over to them after the defeat of the Somoza regime, also believed that Chamorro would turn the government over to them after the defeat of the FSLN. The politicians, especially those of the conservative and liberal factions, and most especially Vice President Godoy, thought it right (both morally and pragmatically) that they should be in charge. They imagined that Chamorro, whom they credited with neither the experience nor the skill necessary to govern, would continue to serve only as a symbol. She would be a kind of Queen Mother for Nicaragua, while they would put the nation in order. They would restore themselves to their rightful prominence, both socially and economically, and would eliminate the FSLN as a political force.

President Chamorro had other ideas. Between the election and her inauguration in April, she and her personal advisors put together a new administration with little help from the UNO. Her son-in-law Lacayo was named Minister of the Presidency. By the end of March the teams of Ortega and Chamorro signed an accord detailing the terms of transition. As expected, it included the immediate demobilization of the Contras. It also clearly placed the military and police forces under the authority of the president. But, much to the dismay and annoyance of many UNO politicians and the U.S. government, it was announced that General Humberto Ortega, Daniel Ortega's brother and a Director of the FSLN, would remain as her senior military officer. In return, General Ortega pledged his allegiance to the president and resigned from his leadership role in the FSLN. Finally, the new government agreed to honor transfers of property made under the FSLN. Most of these titles were for agricultural land formerly owned by Somoza and his associates and given to peasant farmers as part of agrarian reform. However, included in such transfers were grants to members of the FSLN and their supporters, more in the interest of patronage than social justice.

Following her inauguration, President Chamorro further offended the UNO by appointing as ministers of state men personally loyal to her rather than to the UNO political parties. Even more of an affront, she virtually ignored Vice-President Godoy and went so far as to deny him office space within the executive building. Many UNO supporters, particularly politicians of the right and center factions of the UNO, complained that President Chamorro had abandoned the UNO and was "cogoverning" with the FSLN. Some of the more outspoken, including Godoy, even accused her of treason and urged her ouster. But with widespread popular support and the aid of the FSLN and the less extreme UNO politicians, Chamorro repeatedly rebuffed the challenges of her detractors.

During the first three years of the six-year term, the Chamorro administration accomplished several of its major objectives. The end of the Contra war was declared, the SMP was abolished, and there was a general demobilization. While General Ortega continued as head of the military, its size was reduced to less than 25 percent of the 1989 level. The police force was reduced in size, and many ex-Contra soldiers were integrated into it.

Regarding women's issues and social programs, Chamorro's approach has been traditional and conservative. Unlike the FSLN, which had a fairly good record of appointing women to high positions, Chamorro has appointed few women. Discounting her self-designation as Minister of Defense, there was not a woman among the ministers of state until 1993. Governmental support for feminist organizations, which had generally opposed her candidacy, has been suspended. State-funded welfare programs that had been initiated by the FSLN to address women's needs have been drastically reduced. The programs for the rehabilitation of street children and of prostitutes, and most of the child-care and nutrition centers, have been eliminated.[8]

After some early problems, Lacayo's structural adjustment and austerity program has brought the inflation rate (estimated at over 40,000 percent at its high point during the FSLN administration) under control. There have been heavy costs. Between the mass demobilization and reductions in government employment, particularly in social programs, unemployment has risen to over 50 percent. Whereas under the Sandinistas people complained of scarcity, under the Chamorro administration there was much available but few who could afford it. Health care and education, which were of marginal quality but free under the FSLN, have greatly deteriorated. Added fees for services and for tuition have given access only to the few who can pay.

As the fourth year of her administration began, Chamorro and Nicaragua still faced serious obstacles. With the election of Clinton, it appeared the relations between the United States and Nicaragua might improve. Aid withheld by the Bush administration was released, but State Department officials and members of Congress expressed concern over Chamorro's attitude of compromise and accommodation with the FSLN. This was increased when the FSLN and the UNO moderates joined forces to defeat the UNO hardliners by electing a new slate of officers for the National Assembly in early 1993. The action of this new coalition, which supported Chamorro, so incensed the UNO hard-liners that they declared themselves out of the UNO and in open opposition to the government. Together with little support from the United States, this opposition and unrest within Nicaragua discouraged much needed aid and investment.

SUMMARY

Violeta Barrios de Chamorro's initial entry into political office, as one of the five members of the junta that followed Somoza's overthrow, was undoubtedly due to her symbolic value as a "political surrogate." As the widow of a national hero and prominent political figure, and as a woman with deep traditional roots, Chamorro gave much needed legitimacy to the revolutionary government.

In the ten years following her resignation from the junta, Chamorro developed her political skills, taking an active role in the direction of *La Prensa* and becoming a leading critic of the FSLN. Still, when she was chosen to head the UNO ticket, it was more for the image that she represented than for her political skills. But in choosing her advisors and in leading the government since her election, she has shown a tenacity, spirit, and political skill that has surprised and perplexed her opponents.

President Chamorro consistently advocated consensus and reconciliation over confrontation and vengeance. That these attitudes were frequently seen as "feminine" probably helped her to communicate her beliefs, thus gaining the support of voters who wished to see those qualities realized in government policy. Her lack of political affiliation and her social position as a descendant of traditional conservative families engendered trust in many. She was able to keep open lines of communication and reinforce bonds that facilitated building political support, even among the Sandinistas. But as her political power has increased, so have the attacks against her. Her political skills, her faith, and her health will be put to the test as she strives to hold her administration and her country together.

NOTES

1. María Estela Martínez de Perón became president of Argentina in 1976 and Lidia Gueiler Tejada became president of Bolivia in 1979, but both of these political accessions were through constitutional succession rather than by popular election.

2. Carlos M. Vilas, "Family Affairs: Class, Lineage and Politics in Contemporary Nicaragua," *Journal of Latin American Studies* 24:2 (1992): 309–41.

3. I am grateful to the Dutch anthropologist Anton Bloc for calling this point to my attention.

4. Jaime Chamorro Cardenal, "*La Prensa*": *The Republic of Paper* (New York: Freedom House, 1988), 181.

5. The role of NED and the United States in the 1990 election has been extensively documented; see, for example, William I. Robinson, *A Faustian Bargain: U.S. Intervention in the Nicaraguan Elections and American Foreign Policy in the Post-Cold War* (Boulder, CO: Westview, 1992).

6. "Getting to Know UNO," *The Economist*, 312, September 9, 1989, 49.

7. See, for example, Ian Buruma, "St. Cory and the Evil Rose," *New York Review of Books* 34:10 (1987): 10–14.

8. For a comparison of the situation of women before and after the overthrow of Somoza, see Harvey Williams, *Women and Revolution: Women's Changing Role in Nicaragua*, Women in International Development, Working Paper no. 133 (East Lansing: Michigan State University, 1986). See also Margaret Randall, "Women in Revolutionary Movements: Cuba and Nicaragua," chap. 12 in this volume.

3

Indira Gandhi: Gender and Foreign Policy

Mary C. Carras

As more women throughout the world assume positions of power, challenging a long-held monopoly enjoyed by men, questions arise about the effect that women's accession to political power may have on international relations. Will the conduct of the affairs of state vary significantly, reflecting a so-called woman's touch? Do the social and economic backgrounds of female leaders differ from those of male leaders, and if so, would these differences be reflected in the style and policies of women who hold the reins of state? How might they handle matters of national security, war and peace, and other issues of "high politics?" How might they handle the "low politics" of human rights and development? In this chapter, we will look for answers to these questions by examining the rise to power and rule of the late Indira Gandhi, India's prime minister for more than a decade, until she was assassinated on October 31, 1984.

FAMILY BACKGROUND AND PATH TO POWER

Gandhi came from an upper-class, well-educated family, active in politics. Her father, Jawaharlal Nehru, was the son of Motilal Nehru, a successful and respected barrister under the British, whose wealth allowed him to support a privileged lifestyle. He was a major influence on Indira in her early years. Jawaharlal, on the other hand, came under the powerful influence of the revered Mahatma Gandhi, who, while not a cleric, was deeply religious, *mahatma* meaning "Great Soul."[1] With Nehru as his political lieutenant, Gandhi led India to independence. He anointed the young Nehru as head of the Indian National Congress, the political movement seeking total independence from Britain. Nearly twenty years later, the mahatma declared his desire

Indira Gandhi

to see Nehru become head of the government-to-be. And so it was that, on August 15, 1947, Indira Gandhi's father became independent India's first prime minister.

In 1966, two years following the death of her father Nehru, Indira Gandhi became prime minister of India. In 1977, she suffered an electoral defeat but was returned to office in 1980. She served until her assassination in 1984 and was succeeded by her eldest (and only remaining) son, Rajiv Gandhi, until his assassination in 1991.

In chapter 1, Francine D'Amico introduced a model of common paths to politics. Her paradigm encompasses three categories of leaders: (1) "political surrogates," (2) "political insiders" or "climbers," and (3) "political outsiders" or "activists." Of the three paths, the first two, says D'Amico, are most characteristic of women leaders. The first of these, surrogacy, goes beyond family origins to include the dynamics of choice by political king or queen makers and the image projected by the surrogate, all of which combine to produce the preferred leader. Although D'Amico does not distinguish between Western and non-Western cultures, her model seems particularly well suited for an analysis of women's rise to political power in the Third World.

Was Indira Gandhi simply her father's political surrogate, reaching office through a figurative "widow's walk"? She came to power in 1966, succeeding Lal Bahadur Shastri, who had become prime minister upon Nehru's death in 1964. Had Shastri not died on January 10, 1966, little more might have been heard about Gandhi and the Nehru-Gandhi dynasty. This time gap somewhat weakens the "widow's walk" explanation of Gandhi's rise to power.

The Old Guard of the Congress, whose legitimacy within the party was declining, sought to refurbish their image and restore some of their power by picking Gandhi as party leader and, thus, head of government in India's parliamentary system. She had important assets that the party elders could use to their advantage, or so they thought. She still enjoyed the aura of her legendary political family and its connection with Mahatma Gandhi. And the Old Guard thought she could be more easily controlled and manipulated than the usual pool of ambitious and often ruthless male politicians. Indira, a "chit of a girl" (as the Old Guard scornfully called her after their falling out), appeared at the time to be the least ambitious and, therefore, the least dangerous. They knew her from childhood to be shy and in adulthood to be a quiet, frail, and self-effacing young woman who, despite years of serving as her father's companion and hostess, shied away from the political limelight. Had she projected an assertive, aggressive, shrewd image at that time (as she later did), the "old boys" would surely have passed her by with not a thought to her lofty paternal origin. When their expectations were dashed after two to three years, the Old Guard proved helpless to dislodge her.

Gandhi's path to power had elements not only of the "political surrogate" category but also of the "outsider"/"activist," one who, as D'Amico says, "asserts her qualifications for office based on her *in*experience." Gandhi had done little to disabuse the party leaders of the notion that she was a babe in the woods, while her supporters, the so-called Young Turks, idealized her and looked to her to clean up the game of dirty, corrupt politics.

While friend and foe alike perceived her as someone innocent of the rough-and-tumble of the political game, she had given signs years earlier (speaking in a small circle of friends) of possessing considerable shrewdness. She told a friend that her father was too gentle with those who were corrupt, who had crossed him in some way, or who were simply deadwood.[2] She said that if it were within her power, she would summarily dismiss such people. And indeed, when she later came to occupy the *gaddi* ("throne"), she exercised that option frequently.

Gandhi was also her father's confidante and a "political insider" or "climber" who rose through the party hierarchy. She became a member of the Congress party in 1948, was elected to the party's Working Committee in 1955 and to its presidency in 1959. In 1964, she was elected to the upper house of Parliament and appointed by Shastri to be Minister of Information and Broadcasting.

Gandhi's rise to power had elements of all three categories that D'Amico describes: She was a "surrogate" *and* an "insider"/"climber" *and* an "outsider"/"activist." But she would have been none of these were it not for her patrician origin; for, as Benazir Bhutto of Pakistan put it, her class enabled her to "transcend gender."[3] Such a blend is more commonly found in the Third World than in the West. Americans take it for granted that politicians of any class will have at least a college education. In India, even a good high school education is expensive. Hence, college and university education, and the status thus conferred, are more typical of the higher castes and classes, especially in the urban areas.

Membership in a high caste and a wealthy upper-class family at times creates equality, not only among men but among women, too—and, sometimes, even across genders. This helps explain phenomena like Indira Gandhi and her aunt, Vijaya Lakshmi Pandit. Pandit served as ambassador to the Soviet Union, the United States, the United Kingdom, and the United Nations. In 1953–1954, she became the first woman President of the United Nations General Assembly. True, Vijaya Pandit was Nehru's sister and Indira his daughter. Still, one could never imagine a woman of the Royal Saudi family holding such positions. In India, politically ambitious women have a good chance of entering a so-called man's field if they are supported by a liberal, progressive family. So, the family variable, especially the patrician family, is important, if not crucial, for women who have political ambitions. And in South Asia especially, it has become fairly common (and indeed acceptable) for women of patrician origin to become political surrogates, replacing deceased husbands, fathers, or other male officeholders. This is shown by the experiences of Sirimavo Bandaranaike in Sri Lanka, Benazir Bhutto in Pakistan, and Khaleda Zia in Bangladesh, as D'Amico describes in chapter 1.

FAMILY BACKGROUND AND ITS EFFECT
ON FOREIGN POLICY

Growing up in a partly traditional, partly modern Indian household provided Indira Gandhi with models of behavior and patterns of thought and values that stayed with her in later years. Many of the important leaders in India's movement for national liberation from British rule came from her family. In 1917, the year of her birth, India itself was stirring into life and was to achieve independence in the same year that Indira reached her thirtieth birthday. Her early years, therefore, were a time of great instability and change in the country, which inevitably touched her family life. Her childhood was spent in an insecure environment: Her father was in and out of jail, as was her mother, although less frequently.

On such occasions, she was left alone (except for servants) or was sent off to a boarding school. As the oldest child, she looked after the younger children and was often called upon to shoulder relatively heavy responsibilities at a tender age; but there was no one in whom to confide what must have been feelings of fear, insecurity, and anger. She suppressed these emotions, but they found an outlet in expressions of aggressiveness that took various forms: playacting as Joan of Arc or heading the Monkey Brigade, a group of children organized to transmit secret messages among the nationalists.

The Nehru household was probably one of the most important sources of the aggressiveness that was to mark her style of leadership as prime minister (and the isolated setting in which she often made her final decisions). It was also the genesis of Indira's ambivalent feelings toward her father, which I believe continued (probably subconsciously) even after his death. Her ambivalence stemmed in part from her father's insensitivity to his wife's complaints about her ill treatment at the hands of his sister. The young Indira was deeply touched by her mother's tears and anguish, and she tried to comfort her. It was a colossal blow to the seventeen-year-old Indira when her mother died of tuberculosis at age thirty-six. One can only speculate about the mixed feelings toward her father that must have welled up in an already badly traumatized young girl.

Later on, Indira Gandhi was often wounded during the nearly fifteen years when she served as her father's official hostess after he became prime minister. Nehru at times took out some of his frustrations on his daughter. And she, again conscious of the great burden of leadership borne by her father, felt compelled to swallow such hurts. But this must have left a bitter aftertaste, considering that she had sacrificed her family life and her marriage to be with her father.

As prime minister, faced with intractable problems at home and a geopolitical environment alive with minefields, Gandhi brought to these tasks all the inner conflicts and insecurities that she had carried into her adulthood.

Just as she had relied on herself to deal with problems during her childhood and teen years, she continued to play the political game "close to her vest," as many of her associates and rivals often said to me. Except for her children (especially the youngest, Sanjay, until his death in 1980), she did not take people into her confidence easily, particularly in important political matters. Her personal friends were few and were not from the political field. This mistrust of the outside world carried into her international dealings as well. There were few foreign leaders with whom she developed even a modicum of friendship or cordiality—except possibly the other "Iron Lady," Margaret Thatcher, whose story is told by Kenneth Harris in chapter 4.

Gandhi's involvement in the national struggle for independence also contributed to her mistrust of others. It was a struggle deeply etched in her consciousness, so much so that it must have been difficult at times for her to distinguish between challenges to India's independence and threats to her own autonomy. The nationalist movement had identified as the enemies those who sought to impose their will on India. And Gandhi responded as an Indian *and* as Indira. Whether as a child, an adolescent, a young adult, or a prime minister, whenever she was challenged, she became more obstinate.

President Johnson had that effect on her during the second half of the 1960s when he tried to impose on India a policy of economic liberalization and when he tried to punish her for criticizing his Vietnam policy. President Nixon and Secretary of State Kissinger had that effect on her in 1971 when they threatened to have China open a second front of battle if she entered the Bengali struggle for independence from Pakistan. They backed up this threat by sending a Naval Task Force to intimidate her into submission, a tactic that failed miserably.

I have noted here some of the ways in which Gandhi's family background shaped her characteristic responses to politics. Principal among those that carried over into her foreign-policy style were aggressiveness, obstinacy when challenged, and mistrust. Her gender seems of little consequence in the formation of those responses; indeed, she seems indistinguishable from typical male leaders. Would an analysis of specific foreign policies show some greater influence of gender?

NONALIGNMENT AND RELATIONS WITH THE UNITED STATES

While Gandhi's interpretation of nonalignment deviated sharply from the Nehru original, Indira and her father shared a perception that India was threatened by Western efforts to enroll it and other Asian nations in an anti-Communist alliance. And to both, nonalignment embodied India's passionate commitment to the preservation of its hard-won independence. Their shared determination to stay clear of the cold war conflict lest India be drawn into it was largely prompted by a domestic economic imperative: economic development. This goal could be advanced by staying out of East-West quarrels that might divert Indian resources from economic needs and also allow access to the resources of both camps.

But Nehru was part pragmatist, part idealist. He based his policy on a realistic understanding of India's limited military capabilities and urgent economic needs and was content to exercise India's "moral influence."[4] With respect to China, for example, Nehru had thought that, if befriended, China would be less bellicose, and so he neglected the development of India's military capabilities. This resulted in the humiliating military and diplomatic defeat for India in the 1962 war with China over a border conflict. Gandhi, on the other hand, was primarily a political Realist and was far more cautious in her dealings with the Chinese, whose hand she sought to counter by befriending the Soviet Union—far more than her father had. The time was right for this step; by the early 1960s, the Soviets had a falling out with China and were anxious to maintain friendly relations with India.

The Bangladesh crisis (discussed below) provided both India and the USSR with the incentive for a closer relationship. In August 1971, a joint statement was issued by the Soviet foreign minister and the Indian prime minister, announcing the conclusion of a treaty of friendship between their two countries. This was viewed with dismay in Washington—not the first time that India had displeased the Americans. But others also saw this as a virtual abandonment of India's traditional nonaligned policy.

India's relations with the United States were strained almost from the start, barring a few good moments. But Gandhi's style and her policies became a major irritant in Indo-American relations early on, and remained so. After a very short honeymoon period when Gandhi first came to power in 1966, relations deteriorated. In her first trip abroad as prime minister, Gandhi met with President Johnson in Washington, who was at first quite taken with the "little lady" and promised to help India meet its agricultural crisis. Loan agreements and emergency food aid did follow Gandhi's visit, but only after Indian assurances to move toward further economic liberalization. India's strained circumstances had followed a bad drought, the 1965 Indo-Pakistan war, and the leadership crisis occasioned by the emergence of a new and somewhat inexperienced leader, Indira Gandhi. Recognizing India's vulnerability, Johnson thought he could achieve the long-sought objective of liberalizing Indian economic policies by withholding food shipments in conditions of near famine.

After three to four years of this diet, Gandhi's response was to ensure that India would not again endure this humiliation; economic self-reliance became an imperative of India's Fourth Plan, launched in 1969. America's goal of economic liberalization was in the end thwarted by a deepening mood of anger pervading the country and moving Indian economic policy leftward.

THE SEARCH FOR REGIONAL HEGEMONY

Like her father Nehru, Indira Gandhi was committed to the goal of economic development. She was equally dedicated to her version of nonalignment, both as a diplomatic strategy and as a strategy for development. But unlike Nehru, she also pursued regional hegemony, though no one in her government would admit it. And her way of achieving foreign policy goals also differed markedly from her father's. Nehru was ambivalent about acquiring, maintaining, and using political and military power. Having avoided military involvement with China in the 1950s despite several provocations, Nehru was finally drawn to war across the Himalayas in 1962. India's defeat illustrated the sad state of the nation's military readiness. Gandhi, by contrast, having consolidated her power at home, proceeded in 1969 to develop rapidly India's military capabilities.

Nehru dreamed of achieving *Asian* solidarity, and he projected India as a *moral* force in world affairs, whereas Gandhi sought to increase India's tangible power in order to attain *regional dominance* in the Indian subcontinent and beyond. Her policy goals were also more sharply defined: not just regional hegemony but recognition of that status by India's neighbors, especially Pakistan, and by the Americans. Like the better-educated Indian public, Gandhi believed that America sought to diminish India's regional standing by arming Pakistan—with which India had fought three wars since independence in 1947—and by supporting its military dictators.

Her policy of regional hegemony was tested in the Bangladesh crisis of 1971. When the majority Bengali population of East Pakistan pressed for more autonomy from West Pakistan, the central government tried forcibly to repress the agitation in March 1971, initiating a civil war. The Bengali rebels received military, financial, and diplomatic support from India; they were allowed to set up bases of operation along the Indian border where they could retreat if necessary. And Gandhi opened India's doors to a flood of Bengali refugees.

In December 1971, after nine months of diplomatic moves, Gandhi opted for war. But from the beginning of the crisis in March, her wait-and-see approach was sharply criticized by the Indian press and opposition leaders (and quietly by many in her own party) as too hesitant and too drawn out. In the month before hostilities began, she had undertaken a tour of various Western capitals, including Washington, to present India's position and to seek a diplomatic solution to the crisis. Having failed, especially in Washington where Nixon and Kissinger were suspicious of her aims and decidedly hostile to her, she returned to Delhi empty-handed.

The use of Indian military power brought the war to a swift and victorious end. The new, weak state of Bangladesh emerged where East Pakistan had stood, and the remaining Pakistani state in the west had been weakened. For

Gandhi, an important war objective was realized: the return of more than a million Bengali refugees to their homeland.

With the exception of the 1971 war, no major military engagements were undertaken by India during Gandhi's term of office. But one other noteworthy development of the 1970s was the most ambitious program of military buildup and modernization of military power ever pursued by India. One component of this was a commitment to create a more powerful navy, capable not only of a coastal defense but also the projection of India's military power abroad in the Indian Ocean area. By 1980, India had become the principal naval power in the region.

An even more dramatic demonstration by Gandhi of India's potential military might came in 1974 when she announced to the world that India had conducted its first (and thus far the only) peaceful nuclear underground explosion. India thus entered, uninvited, the exclusive so-called nuclear club. Under Gandhi's leadership, the scientific establishment acquired substantial delivery capabilities through its rocket-development program. Despite American efforts for over two decades to persuade New Delhi to sign the Nuclear Non-Proliferation Treaty, Nehru, Shastri, Gandhi, and successor governments have refused to do so. These military initiatives indicate that Gandhi's approach to military power was far more ambitious than her father's. The question is whether, apart from broad historical and cultural factors, Gandhi's policies and conduct in foreign affairs can be explained by her patrician family background and her "surrogate" path to power *as a woman* in a traditional society and semimodern family. Specifically, did gender make a difference in the defense policies adopted by the Indian government under Gandhi's leadership?

The answer is a *qualified* no. Her style and policies might have been predicted by anyone using a Realist model to analyze her conduct, if by this we mean that she was aggressive, assertive, shrewd, and ruthless in her pursuit and exercise of power in the service of India's interest—or indeed in her own—both of which were often viewed interchangeably by her and many supporters. But the *realpolitik* model has a significant weakness: It does not allow for a clearcut distinction between national interest and the personal or special interests of the policy makers. Similarly, anyone trying to predict her actions based on traditional assumptions about "feminine" behavior would be surprised by Gandhi's "masculine" views and conduct. She did not urge the types of policies suggested by traditional assumptions about women leaders, such as increased spending for social welfare relative to military expenditures.

Gandhi's conduct in the Bangladesh crisis supports the traditionalist's perspective that the conduct of foreign policy, especially in a time of crisis, is affected not by the leader's individual traits but by the character of the international system.[5] Where the national interest is seriously threatened by another state, any leader—man or woman—is inclined to seek a military solution to the crisis. Many analysts, eager to point out that women are no different than men in their disposition to war, will invariably mention Indira Gandhi in 1971, Golda Meir in 1967, and Margaret Thatcher in 1982.

Their point is well taken. But another plausible explanation may account for the tendency of women leaders to "act like men," especially during military crises. Women players are few, and new at an international game whose rules of war and diplomacy have long been formulated by men. Gandhi and other such notable women leaders have been tentatively allowed to enter the power club. Whether consciously or not, they know their conduct is being monitored. Caught up in diplomatic skirmishes and war games, they have felt compelled to play by the established rules. When they succeed, they are roundly applauded by men and women alike. Thus is the traditional power play reinforced. It is difficult to succeed in a game by observing rules that are different from those used by the rest of the players. Above all, Gandhi was a pragmatist.

Such behavior is not unusual. As new entrants in the political arena, women have been anxious to show that they are as good at the game as men are. This has led some feminists to argue that, in trying to win at the men's game, women often sacrifice those talents and traits that distinguish them as women, and through which more innovative approaches could be devised to tackle the unique problems facing the world as we approach the twenty-first century.[6] I will return to this point at the end of the chapter.

WOMEN IN DEVELOPMENT

If Gandhi's gender had such a minimal effect on the "high politics" of national security, are there areas of "low politics," like development and welfare, where she or other women leaders might act differently than men, pursuing gender-conscious policies? As noted, Gandhi strongly emphasized economic development, but when she became prime minister in the mid-1960s, the question of women's contribution to the nation's economic and social development process was not a burning issue. The Fourth and Fifth "Five-Year" Plans, prepared by Gandhi when she was both prime minister and head of the Planning Commission, gave little notice to women. Nor did international policy planners or foreign aid–granting nations and agencies recognize the development potential of women in those years.[7]

Gandhi was not alone in the Third World where mostly male leaders also neglected this issue. Moreover, her views of women tended toward the stereotypical. She was inclined to place Indian women on the proverbial pedestal. In 1973, for example, while addressing young college women of middle- and upper-class backgrounds, she praised "the beauty and elegance of Indian women."[8] In her speeches, she often returned to themes like the richness of Indian culture and cautioned against imitating Western women.

By the middle of the 1970s, however, the much publicized global women's movement inevitably drew Gandhi's attention to this issue. She had accepted an invitation to attend the International Women's Conference in Mexico City during the summer of 1975, which launched the first United Nations Decade for Women and Development. But domestic concerns with growing signs of instability forced her to stay at home. Her references to women's problems remained peripheral. Indeed, when commenting on a forthcoming conference on women's issues, she said she was "allergic" to such meetings.[9] When she did talk about women, she emphasized themes painfully familiar to her own childhood: parental influence on children's attitudes, especially that of the mother, "*because she is there more of the time than the father is* [emphasis added]."[10]

The Sixth Five-Year Plan (1980–1985), however, acknowledged for the first time that a "woman's status" was more than an appendage of her husband's status; that she had an existence of her own; and, moreover, that she had a significant effect on the nation's economic welfare and development.[11] The plan called for improving and extending programs involving the education, health, and social welfare of women. Even more encouraging was a segment on the employment of women—including promoting the development of marketable skills, the modernization of women's traditional occupations, mechanization in certain areas, and, most important, "support to self-employed women," in the form of loans and training.

On balance, Gandhi's contribution to programs aimed at raising women's economic and social status was modest and most often followed others' initiatives. Her disinterest did not encourage planners to be sensitive to the needs and potential of Indian women. More could have been done if she had not been so committed to the liberal democratic tenet that great accomplishments are the result of individual effort only.

In her favor, however, it must be acknowledged that in 1971 she appointed a Committee on the Status of Women in India, which issued a damning report on January 1, 1975. (It is perhaps revealing of Gandhi's view on this subject that in collections of her speeches covering the period 1971–1975, there was only a single laconic reference to this committee and its report.) In its wake, however, some of the legislative measures adopted dealt with equal pay, maternity benefits, and the improvement of women's legal status with respect to marriage, divorce, and dowry.[12] But these helped mainly urban middle-class women, a tiny minority of the female population. And even there, implementation was poor. The most vociferous criticism of Gandhi on this score was leveled by her critics during an emergency period, June 1975 to March 1977, when, among other things, she suspended due process of law, opted for press censorship and, under her son Sanjay's direction, forcibly sterilized some women.[13]

CONCLUSION

Traditional theoretical assumptions denying the influence of gender on foreign policy and defense matters are borne out not only by the policies and conduct of Indira Gandhi in these fields, but also, as noted, by her approach to social welfare at home. She herself had insisted (to me and others who interviewed her) that her gender did not in any way influence her policies or her political conduct. Gandhi did not pursue a feminist agenda and took every opportunity to disown the feminist label. "I am not a feminist," she said once in an address to a women's college, "and I do not believe that anybody should get a preferential treatment merely because she happens to be a woman."[14] And at a press conference on the day that she became prime minister, she said: "I do not regard myself as a woman. I am a person with a job."[15]

Statements such as this are in accord with findings of a British study that the typical woman member of Parliament sees "herself as an MP first and a woman second"[16] and that women "are not exclusively, even mainly, concerned with women's affairs."[17] This is not to say that Gandhi was not a nurturing woman but rather that individual traits do not always carry over to a public role, especially one with so great a responsibility for the safety and welfare of a nation. Her self-characterization seems apt when her conduct is held up to scrutiny. In her political demeanor, Gandhi rarely revealed any of the "feminine" traits ascribed to women in most cultures. In her public persona, she did not fit the gender model as either "nurturer" or "peacemaker." But in her dress and in her bearing, she was very "feminine." And in the privacy of her home, with her children and especially her grandchildren, she was decidedly a "nurturer."

In domestic policies, she was not inclined to seek amicable, nonaggressive solutions to quarrels. If a crisis could not be defused, she would not hesitate to take drastic measures. She suspended certain constitutional rights in June 1975 in the face of what seemed to her as destabilizing conduct by some of her opponents. In June 1984, she sent troops into a Sikh temple to flush out a militant group of armed Sikhs who had taken refuge there. For this action, she would lose her life. Her leadership style was often contrasted with Nehru's consensual style; hers was almost universally described as confrontational.

When female leaders do not fit the usual stereotypes, they are viewed (both in the West and in India) as deviant versions of their gender and are derisively labeled "Iron Ladies," as both Gandhi and Thatcher were. Gandhi was given a backhanded compliment by her supporters and even by some of her critics who would say, with grudging respect, that she "wore the pants" in the Cabinet. The implication was that strong women were simply improved versions of men! Whether as an "Iron Lady" or as a woman "wearing the pants," she was perceived by both supporters and critics as atypical or abnormal.

Indira Gandhi's conduct as a national leader did not yield to traditional assumptions about the pacifist or nurturing nature of women. But as one analyst observed, it is common for women in positions of power to deny holding views that might be interpreted as feminist—lest they endanger their ability to acquire and retain power.[18] This assertion correctly applies to Gandhi who, as we saw, rejected—sometimes heatedly—any linkage between gender and leadership. She saw world politics as a traditional leader would, and she was moved to action by considerations similar to those that might move men who were heads of government.

Does this mean that gender makes no difference in the way in which affairs of the world are conducted? In the present political climate, this appears to be so for most women leaders (including Gandhi) who have reached the highest political office. In time, this may change. Many women in the West and the United States in particular believe that, as the women's struggle continues, the number of women in positions of leadership will increase to the point where they would not be bound by male rules of a power game, since material-based power would not be the only coin in global politics. One could then argue, as Carol Gilligan does, that the more nurturing, co-operative, community-oriented nature of women leaders could move international relations away from military approaches to world problems, away from such power-oriented solutions and power-defined relations, all of which invariably lead to conflict and violence.[19] Indira Gandhi, as leader of India, would be uncomfortable in such a world, as would men leaders weaned on the power game.

One other trend may make the traditional leadership model irrelevant. In nations and other types of organizations, the engine of political and economic power is fueled increasingly by knowledge—technical, professional, and scientific. Eventually, the power hierarchy will be shaped by those who can generate and transmit such knowledge or impede its communication. Material wealth will still be important, especially for Third World nations who want to buy the technological hardware (and software) that will make valuable information accessible. But the key gap among nations will increasingly be less between the rich and the poor in material terms and more between the rich in knowledge and the poor in knowledge.[20] Such differentiations are already being made, and a new elite is gradually emerging.

In an information-based society, accessibility to knowledge will not be denied because of gender. Those who are computer literate, regardless of gender, will be able to tap into databases in all fields of knowledge and into the services provided therein. The economic and social benefits that accrue to the haves of *knowledge* will be denied to the have-nots. A new ruling class may emerge, with secular "Brahmins" atop the pinnacle of power. Indira Gandhi would not number among them.

NOTES

1. Mohandas Karamchand Gandhi was not related to the Nehru family. When Indira Nehru married Feroze Gandhi, she took her husband's last name.

2. See Marie Seton, *Panditji: A Portrait of Jawaharlal Nehru* (New York: Taplinger, 1967), 265.

3. Benazir Bhutto, *Daughter of Destiny* (New York: Simon & Schuster, 1989), 169.

4. Surjit Mansingh, *India's Search for Power: Indira Gandhi's Foreign Policy, 1966–1982* (New Delhi: Sage, 1984), 2.

5. J. David Singer, "Accounting for International War: The State of the Discipline," *Journal of Social Research* 18:1 (1981): 1–3, 6–18, reprinted in John Vasquez, ed., *Classics of International Relations*, 2d ed. (Englewood Cliffs, NJ: Prentice-Hall, 1990), 231, 235.

6. Carol Gilligan, *In a Different Voice* (Cambridge: Harvard University Press, 1982).

7. What *was* being considered, globally, was women's political and civil rights. In 1979, the General Assembly of the United Nations adopted the "Convention on the Elimination of All Forms of Discrimination Against Women," and this entered into force in 1981. For the text of this document, see Barry E. Carter and Phillip R. Trimble, eds., *International Law: Selected Documents* (Boston: Little, Brown, 1991), 399–409.

8. See Indira Gandhi, "The Challenge Before Women," Address to Miranda House College for Women, Delhi, March 7, 1973, in Government of India, Ministry of Information and Broadcasting, *Indira Gandhi: Selected Speeches and Writings, 1972–1977* (New Delhi: Publications Division, n.d.), 3:481.

9. Ibid., 523.

10. Ibid., 526.

11. See Government of India, Planning Commission, *Sixth Five-Year Plan, 1980–1985* (New Delhi: Government of India, 1985), chap. 27.

12. See Research and Reference Division, Ministry of Information and Broadcasting, Government of India, comp. and ed., *India 1987: A Reference Manual* (New Delhi: Government of India, 1988).

13. Numerous articles criticizing Gandhi's actions at this time were published. A collection of these was published by The Friends of India Society International, in Makarand Desai, ed., *The Smugglers of Truth* (New Delhi: Government of India, 1978).

14. Government of India, *Gandhi: Speeches and Writings*, 3:481.

15. See Khwaja A. Abbas, *Indira Gandhi: Return of the Red Rose* (Delhi: Hind Pocket Books, 1966), v.

16. Melville Currell, "The Recruitment of Women to the House of Commons" (Paper presented to the United Kingdom Political Studies Association Conference, March 20–22, 1978, quoted in Vicky Randall, *Women and Politics: An International Perspective*, 2d ed. (Chicago: University of Chicago Press, 1987), 154.

17. Elizabeth Vallance, *Women in the House* (London: Athlone, 1979), 197, quoted in Randall, *Women and Politics*, 154.

18. Randall, *Women and Politics*, 154–55.

19. Gilligan, *Different Voice*, chap. 6.

20. See, for example, Chakravarthi Raghavan, *Recolonization: GATT, The Uruguay Round, and the Third World* (London: Zed, 1990), 95–98.

4

Prime Minister Margaret Thatcher: The Influence of Her Gender on Her Foreign Policy

Kenneth Harris

Margaret Roberts was born in 1925, the younger daughter of Alfred and Beatrice Roberts, who owned a small grocery store in Grantham, a market town in the mainly agricultural county of Lincolnshire. By her own account, her mother, a quiet, colorless woman, seems to have figured little in her development. Her father, on the other hand, dominated her childhood and youth. He was her guide, teacher, and friend. She idolized him.

Margaret Roberts attended the local school, then won a place at Oxford University. There she studied chemistry, but planned later to study for the law as a stepping-stone to a career in national politics, in which as a child she had taken a precocious interest. Her father was involved in local government; he spent many years on the town council and had a spell as mayor.

From an early age Margaret Roberts had been a member of the Conservative party. She has said that the main formative influence on her as a girl and a young woman, before and during World War II, was her hero, Winston Churchill. Her passionate belief in free enterprise, reinforced in retrospect by her experience working in her father's shop, then influenced by the writings of conservative economists Friedrich Hayek and Milton Friedman, was to come later.

After leaving Oxford, she showed herself able and energetic enough to combine earning a good living as a chemical research worker with voluntary work for the Conservative party. At twenty-six she married Denis Thatcher. Twelve years older than she was, divorced many years previously, and managing director of his family-owned paint and chemicals business, Denis Thatcher was rich enough to support her. An active worker for the Conservative party and enthusiastic about her political career, he made it possible for her to give up her job, pursue her legal studies, and spend as much time

Margaret Thatcher

as she could raising their boy and girl twins—her only children, born two years after their marriage.

Margaret Thatcher (from now on referred to as "Thatcher") continued her work for the Conservatives. After two unsuccessful previous attempts, she was elected to the House of Commons at the general election of 1959 as Member of Parliament (MP) for Finchley, a northern suburb of London.

The Conservatives, led by Harold Macmillan, were in government. Thatcher's good looks, her expertise in tax law, and her outstanding skill as a debater marked her for promotion. In 1961 she became Parliamentary Secretary to the Ministry of Pensions and National Security. When the Conservatives lost the election of 1964 and went into Opposition, she spoke impressively for them on a variety of subjects. When the Conservatives won the election of 1970, the new prime minister, Edward Heath, invited her to become Secretary of State for Education. She was the only woman in the Cabinet.

Over the next four years her reputation grew. After the Conservatives were defeated in the two elections of 1974, Conservative MPs decided to choose a new leader. Thatcher's election to that post in early 1975 was almost a bombshell of surprise and certainly an extraordinary achievement. The shortage of qualified competitors paved the way to her success, and it was cleared for her by the refusal of the deputy leader, William Whitelaw, to run against Heath, his former leader. But her readiness and ability to seize her chance reflected the strength of her character and the quality of her political instincts.

Four years later the Labour government under James Callaghan was defeated in the general election of 1979, and Margaret Thatcher became prime minister. She led the Conservatives to victory again, with an increased majority, in 1983, and again, though not so spectacularly, in 1987. In November 1990 she was removed from her positions as party leader and prime minister by what was virtually a party revolt, brought on mainly by the fears of Conservative MPs that her stubborn resolve to substitute the poll tax for the existing system of local taxation would cost them their seats in the next election.[1]

There is much to be said about Thatcher in the context of the themes examined in this volume, but the purpose of this essay is to consider her as a maker of foreign policy and to attempt an assessment of the effect of gender on her policy and on the process of creating that policy. That Thatcher's gender had an influence on the *making* of her foreign policy is, in my view, true and demonstrable, but students should beware of claiming too much influence for it. If this or that feature of her foreign policy were attributed exclusively to her gender, the attribution would have to be justified by showing that such a feature would not have existed had she been a man.

Two important features of her foreign policy have been much discussed in relation to her personality: her cultivation of the "special relationship" between Britain and the United States and her opposition to a closer relationship between Britain and the European Community. There is nothing in the *content*, in the narrow sense, of these policies that is the result of Thatcher's gender. It could have been produced by several of the men who might have been prime minister had Thatcher not happened to occupy that post.

However, if the *conduct* of foreign policy as well as content is taken into account, it can be observed that in some respects Thatcher, a woman, did things that a man would not or could not have done. Furthermore, there can be an area in which *conduct* so influences *content* that conduct *becomes* content.

This distinction between content and conduct is important because Thatcher's foreign policy had a distinctively negative character. Although she restored Britain's reputation in the world and enhanced her own in doing this, her foreign policy—with the exception of her relations with the United States—was largely negative. She was the "Iron Lady,"[2] who so often said, "No," or "Not now," or "Never."

To be negative is not characteristic exclusively of women, and millions of men would have said "No" as often as Thatcher did. It is not *that* Thatcher said "No" so often that is relevant to the proposition, but *how* she said "No." For how she said "No" introduced another factor—however desirable or undesirable—into British foreign policy as real as a new initiative or a change of stance might have been.

THATCHER AS A MAKER OF FOREIGN POLICY

Some of the women who have had an influence on the history of their times have shown such qualities associated traditionally with masculinity that it has been said of them that essentially they were more "male" than "female," even in their sexual orientation, their recreations, and the way in which they dressed. Thatcher is, by contrast, attractive in a traditionally feminine way, conventionally dressed, conscious of being a woman in the traditional sense, and fully aware of the attractions of the opposite sex. She appreciated the presence of good-looking men who responded to her femininity. Some of these were granted preferment that they may not have won from a male prime minister.

Thatcher as a leader of her political party and then as prime minister at no time ceased to be aware of her femininity and of its effect on the powerful men around her. When she could get the agreement and support from her colleagues in her Cabinet by cajoling, she cajoled. If it was necessary to hector, she hectored. Sometimes she shed tears. Here she was at a great advantage. The men who surrounded her in Cabinet were not used to being led by a woman, and tolerated from her, since they had no alternative response, a manipulation that they would not have accepted from a male colleague. One member of her first Cabinet put it to me in this way: "If any male prime minister had said things to me in Cabinet in the terms and tone she often adopted, I would have gone to him privately afterwards, given him a blasting, and told him that if he did that again I'd resign. But you can't treat a woman like that."

Her peers in the Conservative party had no previous experience of being commanded by a woman in politics and did not know how to cope with it. This phenomenon has been well described by Professor Anthony King, who as a Canadian brings a valuable objectivity to the subject:

Mrs. Thatcher long ago observed that most well-brought up Englishmen . . . have no idea what to do with a strong assertive woman. Not only are they brought up not to deal with women in the same matter-of-fact, direct way that they deal with men. Women to them are mothers or nannies to be feared or sisters to be bullied (or, alternatively, adored); they are not colleagues or fellow politicians, to be stood up to and shouted at when necessary. The average Englishman of the middle and upper classes simply quails in the presence of a formidable female personality, torn between the desire to strike and the desire to sulk, not knowing what an appropriate response would be. Mrs. Thatcher long ago noticed that such Englishmen found it hard to stand up to her—and conceived contempt for the whole tribe. As one of her former ministers, Sir John Knott, said . . . "She thinks all men are wimps."[3]

THE THATCHER STYLE IN THE CONDUCT
OF FOREIGN POLICY

The pattern of behavior by which she succeeded in dominating the British Cabinet became a habit with her, and she took it to conferences with European political leaders. Just as her gender enabled her to dominate her colleagues in the British government, for a different purpose and with different results and in a much less aggressive mode, she displayed self-confidence and strength on occasion in her dealings with President George Bush, notably at the time of Saddam Hussein's invasion of Kuwait, when she vigorously urged the president to take immediate military action against Iraq.

The history of the European and international summits highlights one very important aspect of her gender that had a bearing on her influence in world affairs: her appearance. Her ability to orchestrate photo sessions was based on the unnegotiable difference between her and the rest of the world leaders that came from the fact that she was a woman. She was not wearing a gray suit, she was not a middle-aged or elderly man with an expanding waist and retreating hair; she was a woman, eye-catching, with a pronounced personal style of dress and speech. These photo sessions may be marginal to the nitty-gritty of power brokering behind closed doors, but they contribute greatly to the world's perceptions of the relative standing of its leaders. Thatcher was always shown at center stage, or next to President Ronald Reagan.

Her style did translate into power. The more the public in Britain perceived the effect she was having abroad, the more strength Thatcher acquired at home. The more strength she was seen to acquire at home, the stronger she became abroad. This reciprocal, mutually reinforcing process must be re-garded as a constituent part of her foreign policy, and as due initially to her gender.

THE DOMESTIC BASIS FOR THATCHER'S FOREIGN POLICY

Professor David Marquand has drawn a striking analogy between Thatcher and a nationalistically inspired European leader, Charles de Gaulle. While acknowledging the important difference between Gaullism and Thatcherism (namely, that de Gaulle believed in an active state to support nationalist aspirations, whereas Thatcher believed in the minimalist state), Marquand wrote:

Thatcherism is a sort of British Gaullism . . . borne out of a growing sense of despair, reflecting the experience of a generation of apparent national decline. That sense of despair was often focused on the economic sphere, because relative economic decline was the most obvious aspect of national decline. It was not, however, the only aspect. Political decline, though less obvious, was in some ways even more important. As in Fourth Republic France, moreover, a generation of political decline seemed to many to have led to a crisis of governability and of legitimacy—not of course anything like as severe as that which brought President de Gaulle to the Elysée but nevertheless a crisis of governability more severe than anything experienced by the British political class since before the First World War.[4]

Marquand finds it impossible to separate the foreign policy agenda that Thatcher set for her government from her domestic economic agenda. With-out the supposed renaissance in the British economy, there could have been no renaissance in Britain's world role. He quotes Thatcher as saying: "I be-lieve that Britain's role and standing in the world have increased immea-surably as we have succeeded in overcoming our problems at home, getting our economy right, and proving ourselves as a staunch ally. We are now able once again to exercise the leadership which we have historically shown."[5] Getting the economy right meant breaking with the "corporatist political consensus" that had existed in Britain under both Conservative and Labour administrations for several decades. She could, and did, present her philosophy of monetarism as "good housekeeping." But the idea that "housekeeping" was the basis of her conversion to monetarism is simplistic and vaguely patronizing. She is an intelligent, rational woman who came to a conclusion for intelligent, rational reasons and then dressed them up in homespun wisdom for the consumption of the media and the general public.

CONDUCT AND CONTENT OF FOREIGN POLICY

To the question of gender and the conduct that emerged from her dealings with men, we need now to consider the content of Thatcher's foreign policy.

To begin with, it should be said that Thatcher's foreign policy was a policy of assertions, even if some of these assertions were negations. She asserted Britain's interests in the European Economic Community, British and European interests with the superpowers, and her claim that Britain was no longer a nation in decline. It was a policy against compromising with dictatorship, communism, or terrorism.

This uncompromising assertiveness was sometimes resented by the international community:

Reagan used to retell with relish a joke that he had heard from Eduard Shevardnadze at a meeting in the White House after the Soviet foreign minister had just visited Thatcher. Gorbachev, Reagan, and Thatcher all went to heaven and the Lord said to Gorbachev: "My son, you have done well. You are here in this place. God bless you." Reagan came and the Lord said the same to him. Margaret Thatcher arrived and the Lord began: "My son, you are here in this place . . . ," and she interrupted him: "I am not your son, and this is not your place. This is my place.[6]

Part of the cause of the resentment shown in Shevardnadze's joke was the extent to which Thatcher was different; part of that difference was that she was a woman. The resentment felt toward Thatcher was matched by qualified admiration, best summed up by François Mitterrand's quip that she had "the eyes of Caligula and the mouth of Marilyn Monroe."[7] Other European leaders had asserted their countries' interest with equal vigor, but in a sense that was expected of them. That Thatcher did so with such vigor was something of a surprise.

Thatcher did not become as powerful as she did because she was a more ruthless politician, a more articulate advocate of the things she believed in, or a more political prince.[8] She succeeded because upper- and middle-class men could not deal with her because of their perceptions of gender. If one combines the Shevardnadze joke, the Mitterrand quip, and the sort of excuses highlighted by King, one has a critique of Thatcher that is clearly gendered. The critique deals with her success by using the fact that she is a woman to detract from her performance owing to her innate ability. Her mouth does not particularly resemble Marilyn Monroe's, but by identifying her with a sex symbol, Mitterrand was trying to undermine her credibility, to undermine her status as a serious and important political figure by trivializing her. The joke is not particularly funny, and Thatcher is most unlikely to have corrected the Almighty about her being his son; but the joke does illustrate the resentment that her forthright style evoked.

There could be no better witness than Sir Nicholas Henderson to the transformation in Britain's reputation abroad brought about by Thatcher as prime minister. When he retired in 1979, Sir Nicholas was Britain's senior diplomat. In the valedictory dispatch that retiring ambassadors are required to write for the Foreign Office, he gave a disturbing account of Britain's place in the world at the time and a pessimistic forecast of what it was likely to be in the future. In 1988, however, he wrote to me as follows:

> It is impossible for any unbiased witness not to be struck by the profound changes, whether measured by objective statistics or subjective scrutiny. . . . Mrs. Thatcher herself is probably better known to the public from Lima to Beijing than any British political figure since Winston Churchill. What she stands for is unblurred. Her determination is seen as positively de Gaullean. . . . I am in no doubt of the clear ring it gives to Britain's voice in the world.

Thatcher presented and differentiated herself as the outsider, challenging the liberal establishment and representing "ordinary" people and "decent" values—a populist approach in which her gender played an important part. She was different anyway, and part of this difference was that she was a woman.

It is essential to note that, as Hugo Young and others have pointed out, Thatcher showed only a limited interest in the fate of other women. "The battle for women's rights has largely been won," she said. "The days when they were demanded and discussed in strident tones should be gone for ever. I hate those strident tones we hear from some women's libbers."[9]

Just as gender enabled her to dominate her colleagues in the British government because they were unused to being bossed by a woman and did not know how to respond, it gave her an advantage with the European leaders. She was the first woman to have a place at the highest level of European Community diplomacy. One major reason for the way in which the influence (however resented) of the British prime minister advanced within the European Community between 1980 and 1990 is that the British prime minister in those years was a woman.

RELATIONS WITH THE UNITED STATES, USSR, AND EUROPE

As early as 1976, Thatcher made plain her "bottom line" on foreign policy: "The priority of any government should be to defend its citizens from external threat or actual aggression."[10] Underpinning her general foreign policy was her dedicated anticommunism. This manifested itself in her desire to see defense spending escape the general cuts she was making in public expenditure: "Good housekeeping" did not apply to defense. Thatcher's gender may have made her more conscious of potential charges of weakness in the conduct of defense and foreign policy, and this may explain her hard-line approach that gave her the sobriquet of "The Iron Maiden": She was compensating for the gendered evaluations of her political performance.

In tandem with her "Cold Warrior" stance was her initial understanding of Mikhail Gorbachev: "At crucial moments in the later 1980s her influence was considerable in shifting perceptions in President Reagan's Washington about the credibility of Mr. Gorbachev when he repeatedly asserted his intention to end the Cold War."[11] She was able to play this role with Reagan because of her unquestionable cold war credentials.

The relationship between Thatcher and Reagan was of recurring importance in the development of her foreign policy. At critical times the Atlantic Special Relationship made the vital difference between success or failure, most notably in the Falklands War. Reagan responded to the clear ideological sympathy that existed between them, but their personal relationship was based in part on gender. As Geoffrey Smith argued in *Reagan and Thatcher*, there were times when her "considerate nature" helped score points in Washington.[12] Moreover, Reagan responded to her femininity:

"Ronald Reagan has a very soft spot for a lady," Michael Deaver, one of his closest aides throughout the first Reagan term, remarked. Charles Price, the American Ambassador in London from 1983 until the end of the Reagan Administration, made much the same point: "Reagan is very deferential to ladies in general." One of the reasons why Reagan liked Thatcher, according to Deaver, is that "she carried a purse, and wore funny hats, and was a lady."[13]

The great leap in Thatcher's reputation and influence—and, therefore, in her ability to impose her policies at home and abroad—came with the Falklands War in 1982.[14] She was presented to the world as a warrior and a mother. She could display emotion in public and weep in private, in marked contrast to the demeanor of the men associated with the war, from the members of the War Cabinet to the Defence Department spokesperson. She was presented as Britannia or even Boadicea, the Warrior Queen of a British tribe who in A.D. 60 led a revolt against the occupying Romans.[15] Thatcher's gender made a difference in the way in which the policy was presented, in the way in which her influence after the victory was presented, and, therefore, in her ability to make foreign policy different from what it might otherwise have been.

This enabled her to take her own line to a large extent in such matters as the future of the European Economic Community. On the particular issue of the level of contributions that the United Kingdom was to make to the European Community budget—the negotiations that established her reputation in Europe and defined many of her subsequent relationships with European leaders—she was arguing a strong case. Even keen advocates of the European Community like Roy Jenkins, President of the European Commission from 1977 to 1981, acknowledged that the level of contributions needed revision. The characteristics that Thatcher brought to these negotiations were aggression, rationality, and stubbornness. These characteristics are not defined or determined by gender. But Thatcher displayed and exploited these characteristics in pursuit of her foreign policy in a manner and to a degree made possible only by her gender.

At times, taking her own line meant going against the advice of the Foreign Office. This practice reinforced the ability that she already had to take a different line as a result of being an "outsider." Her effectiveness as an "outsider" in turn was strengthened by the fact that she was a woman. She had driven away the myths and broken through the taboos, and she had been able to do so because of her gender.

Her readiness and ability to "be her own woman" was exemplified by her most famous speech on Europe, delivered at Bruges in September 1989. The Foreign Office prepared a draft of the speech, but Thatcher then modified it. She attacked all attempts to persuade Britain to accept a reduction in national sovereignty and warned the countries of Europe against the drift to socialism. Her punch line, which reverberated around the capitals of Europe, was: "We have not successfully rolled back the frontiers of the state in Britain only to see them re-imposed at a European level, with a European superstate exercising a new dominance from Brussels." The result of this speech was to leave Britain a semidetached member of the European Community in the slow track of European progress toward cooperation and unity. This was certainly not the intention of the Foreign Office when they prepared the draft for her.

Whether the effects that Thatcher had on foreign policy will last, and whether they will prove to be good or bad for Britain, cannot be answered here. But there is no doubt that there were effects and that some of them must be attributed to gender.

It is too soon to assess the successes and failures of Thatcher's long period in power, which of her policies will in time disappear, and which will endure. However, there can be no doubt that her record has made the idea of leadership by women in politics in Britain more, and not less, credible. In early 1975, when Thatcher announced that she would run for the leadership of the Conservative party, many, if not most, students of politics would have said that the Conservatives would not elect a woman to lead them—at any rate, for many years to come—and that if they did, the British people would not vote to make her prime minister. This, obviously, could not be said today. For most of her ten years at the head of affairs, Thatcher showed herself to be one of the most powerful British prime ministers of the century. Much of this power came from the fact that she was a woman.

NOTES

1. See her own account of the election in her recent autobiography, Margaret Thatcher, *The Downing Street Years* (New York: Harper-Collins, 1993).

2. See Hugo Young, *The Iron Lady: A Biography of Margaret Thatcher* (New York: Farrar, Straus, Giroux, 1989).

3. Anthony King, "Margaret Thatcher as a Political Leader," in Robert Skidelsky, ed., *Thatcherism* (London: Chatto & Windus, 1988), 58.

4. David Marquand, "Paradoxes of Thatcherism," in Skidelsky, ed., *Thatcherism*, 160.

5. Marquand, quoting from Peter Ridell, *The Thatcher Decade* (Oxford: Basil Blackwell, 1989), 184.

6. Quoted in Geoffrey Smith, *Reagan and Thatcher* (London: Bodley Head, 1990), 253.

7. Quoted in Riddell, *Thatcher Decade*, 185.

8. The reference is to *The Prince*, by Niccolò Machiavelli.

9. Quoted in Hugo Young, *One of Us* (London: Harper Collins, 1991), 306.

10. Quoted in Diana Elles, "Foreign Policy of the Thatcher Government," in Kenneth Minogue and Michael Biddis, eds., *Thatcherism, Personality and Politics* (London: Macmillan, 1987), 97.

11. Peter Hennessy, "The Last Retreat from Fame: Mrs. Thatcher as History," *The Modern Law Review* 54 (July 1991): 492.

12. Smith, *Reagan and Thatcher*, 49–50.

13. Ibid., 1.

14. Bernard Ingham, *Kill the Messenger* (London: Harper Collins, 1991), 304.

15. See Antonia Fraser, *Boadicea's Chariot: The Warrior Queens* (London: Weidenfeld & Nicolson, 1988).

5

Corazon Aquino: Gender, Class, and the People Power President

Vincent G. Boudreau

Corazon Cojuangco Aquino rose from the turmoil of an unprecedented crisis of governmental authority to lead the opposition to strongman Ferdinand Marcos and eventually to become president of the Philippines from February 1986 to May 1992. The rarefied atmosphere of that crisis temporarily suspended some basic aspects of Philippine politics, especially the unwritten rule relegating women to marginal roles in national politics. That she is a woman, and particularly the widow of political martyr Benigno "Ninoy" Aquino, was in fact central to both her rise to power and her early presidency. Yet, as President Aquino shifted from protest and campaign work to the more routine administration of the newly created political system, she evolved. Her explicitly feminine, nominally classless, activist persona faded into the background, while class and family interests became increasingly salient aspects of her presidency.

Were she a man, one might begin the account of Aquino's rise to power by recalling her birth into the Cojuangco family, one of the Philippines' mightiest political and landed dynasties. Had she been born male, that is, her formal and informal education would almost certainly have directed her in a more or less single-minded fashion toward public office, in which direction, for years, the men of the Cojuangco family had been directed. As a woman born into a tradition-bound oligarchy, however, Corazon Cojuangco's political career began more privately, with her marriage to Senator Benigno Aquino, the favorite son of another large and important political clan. The marriage connected the two powerful political families into an alliance and cast Corazon Aquino in the supporting role of wife to the rising politician. In this light, Aquino's presidency can be viewed as the interaction of her two lineages—one stretching along Cojuangco blood lines into the

Corazon Aquino
Photograph from the private collection of Corazon Cojuangco Aquino.

landed elite, the other of more recent origin, rooted in her leadership of a mass movement.

THE PHILIPPINES BEFORE AQUINO

The Aquino presidency's dual lineages converged against the backdrop of the rapid decline of the Marcos dictatorship after 1983. By then, President Ferdinand E. Marcos had ruled for some nineteen years, almost twelve of which as a dictator who, under martial law, suspended democratic institutions and promoted individuals (mainly from his own Ilocano ethnolinguistic group) who rendered him personal loyalty. This political cronyism engendered an economic counterpart: powerful monopolies, under the direction of Marcos supporters, that stifled market competition. As early as 1980, Marcos had concentrated such wealth and power into the hands of a small subsection of the political and economic elite that he drove segments of the disenfranchised upper and middle classes to oppose his regime. In addition to this mainly parliamentary and moderate opposition, the Communist party of the Philippines (CPP) thrived and rapidly expanded insurgent activity in response to Marcos' overt and widespread oppression.

Marcos had long been a staunch Western ally, a particularly valuable U.S. asset in the volatile Pacific Rim region. He consistently defended the presence of the Clark Air Force Base and Subic Naval Facility, the two largest U.S. extraterritorial military bases. However, as internal opposition to Marcos grew, many international supporters, especially U.S. policy makers, questioned his regime's stability. Doubts over who would succeed the clearly ailing president troubled many, especially when signs indicated that the unpredictable and much discredited Imelda Romualdez Marcos stood to replace her husband. As early as 1981, some U.S. policy makers searched the horizon for a successor midway between Marcos' iron fist and the anti–U.S. radical opposition.

On August 21, 1983, the man whom most viewed as Marcos' chief moderate political rival, Ninoy Aquino, returned to Manila from U.S. exile. As he disembarked from his plane, he was shot by Marcos security forces and fell dead on the airport tarmac. National turmoil immediately erupted; the murder, dramatizing the regime's worsening human rights record, stirred the opposition to life. A broad human rights coalition called Justice for Aquino, Justice for All (JAJA) united for the first time an antidictatorship constituency that stretched from conservative parliamentary oppositionists to legal left protest organizations. Aquino became a martyr whom Marcos could not explain away as a Communist or an escaping felon. Moreover, Aquino himself had gathered considerable U.S. support during his American exile and was widely considered to have CIA backing. If Marcos' long-term viability was questioned by U.S. supporters before 1983, the Aquino assassination deepened these doubts by both eliminating an acceptable successor and triggering serious unrest.

The political instability soon acquired economic dimensions. From August to October 1983, investors withdrew an estimated $1 billion from the country. In October, the Philippines defaulted on its foreign debt payments, causing international lending institutions like the International Monetary Fund (IMF) to suspend import credits essential to manufacturing. The economy ground to a virtual halt. In response, the Philippine government printed more pesos and overstated its foreign currency reserves by some 600 million pesos; in combination, these two factors raised inflation to 40 percent by 1984.[1]

Marcos faced a deepening crisis throughout 1984 until, in a move indicative of the regime's sensitivity to international opinion, he announced the 1986 presidential elections on the U.S. television program "This Week with David Brinkley." In the Philippines, the news triggered a scramble to construct an electoral campaign from the broad and diverse antidictatorship movement, a difficult problem at best. Leaders from the anti-Marcos coalition individually attracted support from only narrow segments of the entire popular movement. Virtually every section of the antidictatorship movement had, however, in some way appropriated the person of Ninoy Aquino, thus making his widow Corazon the ideal coalition candidate: a woman with no specific organizational interest, nor any political debts, who could represent an overarching national interest.

The opposition slate enjoyed substantial international sympathy and support. The main U.S. foreign policy concern was for credible elections, since these were viewed as a prerequisite to stability. The National Movement for Free Elections (NAMFREL), originally organized by the CIA to promote Ramon Magsaysay's presidential bid in the 1950s, was revived as a poll watchdog. In 1985 and 1986, NAMFREL was said to once more enjoy political and material support from the Pentagon and included leading figures in the Philippines business community.

Although Marcos quickly proclaimed himself the winner of the 1986 elections, evidence of widespread cheating undermined that declaration. Aquino announced a sweeping civil disobedience campaign and set a wave of post-election protest into motion. Even Ronald Reagan's initial remarks that "both sides" had cheated met such strong criticism that on February 15, the White House publicly condemned Marcos' Kilusan ng Bagong Lipunan (Movement for a New Society) for fraud and violence.[2] Resistance to Marcos peaked in February, involving more than a million Filipinos in what came to be called the EDSA uprising, named for the Epifanio de los Santos Avenue where the decisive confrontation between government forces and protesters occurred.

The uprising was triggered by an attempted coup d'état by a faction of the military elite, the Reform and Armed Forces Movement (RAM). The RAM, a small group of young officers, opposed the personalistic character of the military under General Fabian Ver's command. Like NAMFREL, the RAM had

U.S. ties and had reportedly been in contact with the U.S. embassy in Manila for over two years. On February 21, RAM officers, along with General Fidel V. Ramos and Defense Minister Juan Ponce Enrile, seized control of Camp Aguinaldo along EDSA in Metro Manila. At the request of the rebels, at the time besieged by government troops, Archbishop Jaime Cardinal Sin and Aquino appealed for public support for the rebels over the Catholic-run Radio Veritas. Within hours, tens of thousands began to converge at EDSA. From that point on, defections to the rebel side accelerated; and on the fourth day, the Marcos family fled the country with a coterie of followers. Aquino was inaugurated on February 25, 1986.

AFTER EDSA

The EDSA uprising became the founding myth of the new Philippine government, constructed on the image of a militant yet peaceful population expelling the dictator through "people power." Yet within that central image of the uprising exists another animating vision: prominent among EDSA's yellow banners and the thumb-and-forefinger salutes raised to signal the "L" of Cory's "Laban" or "fight" party, rode statues of the Virgin Mary, carried, as in a religious procession, by hundreds of demonstrators. Here was another woman, another martyr's survivor, another invocation of a redemptive and conciliatory female: an echo, in short, of more mystical resonances that Aquino acquired.

Corazon Aquino was herself an evocative figure. As Ninoy's widow, she became, symbolically, the widow (mother, sister, etc.) of every martial law victim. Accordingly, her electoral platform focused on respect for human rights and civil liberties, all construed in terms of her husband's assassination. As leader of the popular movement, and initially as head of state, Aquino adopted the slogan "Ituloy ang laban ni Ninoy" ("Continue Ninoy's Fight"). In all this, Corazon Aquino came to represent her slain husband's resurrection in powerfully symbolic terms. More important, as the most visible leader of the anti-Marcos movement, Aquino came to personify the EDSA uprising, as both its unifying mother figure and its president-offspring.

The theme of redemption through resurrection has both Christian and distinctly Filipino resonances. While Christ's passion and resurrection typify this tradition, a parallel thread runs through Filipino mythology, from the patriotic Filipinized version of the Spanish epic, *Bernardo Carpio*, through many story lines in the popular Tagalog cinema. In such epics, the hero is usually killed or defeated and then spends a deathlike period accumulating martial or magical force. Eventually resurrected, the hero liberates the village, province, or nation.[3]

The resurrected figures of Filipino mythology—Bernardo Carpio, Felipe Salvador, Jose Rizal—are more commonly male than female. Yet throughout Philippine history, particularly at those moments dominated by a male redemptive figure, another, female figure, hovers in the background. Called either the *Inang Bayan* (mother of the land) or *Kalayaan* (usually "freedom," but at root the personification of an infant's bliss in its mother's arms), this female figure represented aspirations for independence or justice in the flags, slogans, poems, and popular mythology that animated nationalist and peasant uprisings in the nineteenth and early twentieth centuries. Nevertheless, if she appears in times of crisis and turmoil, the Inang Bayan plays a comparatively marginal role once turmoil passes. In *Pasyon and Revolution*, Reynaldo Clemeña Ileto refers to the popular and mythic spirit of revolt's cataclysmic sense of time: extranatural figures like Kalayaan and Inang Bayan emerge after long absences, in time of crisis. Male figures dominate the business of routine politics.[4]

The extraordinary dynamics that brought Aquino to power emphasized her gender: In casting aside Marcos and the vested interests that he protected, the antidictatorship movement rallied behind a leader who, down to her very gender, seemed an alternative to ruling politicians. Even Marcos' portrayal of his opponent as a "mere housewife" backfired: The label only worked to emphasize Aquino's differences with the incumbent and thus promised a break with the status quo. Indeed, Aquino's widowhood was so salient as to virtually obscure her elite family origin—and, thus, cast her as perhaps more of an "outsider" than she actually was. Aquino became a powerful opposition figure, not despite, but in some measure because of, her gender. One cannot, however, attribute Aquino's rise to her gender alone. More accurately, perhaps, the fact that a woman had achieved the presidency in a society as male dominated as the Philippines indicates the extent to which the crisis of 1983–1986 represented a cataclysmic period in Philippine politics.

As she entered the polity from its fringes, Aquino brought a fresh eye to politics, which allowed her, albeit briefly, to reevaluate all manner of policies, both domestic and international. However, like her mythic counterpart the Inang Bayan, Aquino was constrained by the routines of normal politics. In the face of emergent challenges from power blocs such as big business and the military, Aquino set about consolidating her political position, casting aside her activist persona as she did so. In the transition, gender grew less an explicit element of her public persona.

THE PEOPLE POWER PRESIDENT

On March 22, 1986, Aquino declared a revolutionary government, abolished such remnants of the Marcos political machinery as the national assembly, assumed special legislative powers (which allowed her to make law by decree), and constituted her cabinet as the main organ of government. Aquino's first year in office focused on restoring democracy and seeking a peaceful settlement to the fourteen-year armed conflict between the government and the underground National Democratic Movement–

Communist Party of the Philippines (NDF-CPP). Both policies were an extension of her campaign positions and a response to the popular call for peace and political stability.

In abolishing the formal structures of the Marcos regime, Aquino called attention to questions surrounding the form and policy direction that the future government might take. Such fundamental issues are never easily resolved, but Aquino's dilemma was compounded by her constituency's diversity. Her supporters included members of established power blocs who advocated a return to pre–martial law elite representation, as well as members of grassroots movements who favored a more participatory democracy. Moreover, this broad constituency contained divergent foreign policy agendas tied to economic and security matters. The traditionalists included big business and the military, both of which maintained and wished to protect close ties with the United States and other industrialized countries; this bloc placed a high premium on continuity in international relations. The popular constituency called for a more nationalist government willing to restructure international relations; this bloc saw the transition from dictatorial rule as an opportunity to change foreign policy. As such, perhaps no issue would determine the direction of the Philippine transition from dictatorial rule more than foreign policy, particularly regarding the country's association with its former colonizer, the United States.

Analysis of Aquino's effect on world politics begins by fixing the specific character of Philippine international relations. As an island nation, the Philippines need not greatly concern itself with issues of territorial protection and regulation. Hence, Philippine foreign policy often develops more from ties to global powers than from regional concerns: Tokyo and New York command more attention than do Jakarta and Kuala Lumpur. Specifically, Manila's major foreign policy concerns have tended to focus on international economic activity (particularly with respect to attracting investments and gaining access to markets), international indebtedness, and the (former) U.S. military bases in the Philippines.

Aquino's personal charisma, combined with the aura of the EDSA revolution, allowed her to step away from and critically analyze established foreign policies. Her gender contributed to this charisma (not by evoking any redemptive notions, as it had domestically), for it made her victory over Marcos seem all the more remarkable. At the outset, Aquino had comparatively little sense of obligation to foreign governments or multilateral agencies, particularly given her understanding that many of these had supported Marcos. Moreover, her appeals for international assistance at least initially rested on the heroism of EDSA itself, and had little to do with reciprocity or continuity in international relations; she enjoyed a relatively unencumbered mandate during her first year, with free play for personal initiative and experimentation.

Aquino briefly altered the tone of Philippine foreign policy on three essential issues. First, as promised, she granted amnesty to political prisoners detained under Marcos, including the leadership of the outlawed Communist party, despite objections from U.S. policy makers and her own military. Given strong U.S. concerns regarding the Communist insurgency, Aquino's decision to implement amnesty despite U.S. reservations had both domestic and foreign policy implications. Throughout 1986, Aquino insisted that apparently reluctant government negotiators craft a cease-fire and undertake peace negotiations with the communist movement. Second, Aquino, who as a candidate declared herself opposed to the country's U.S. military installations, maintained enough of that opposition to cause concern in the United States. Third, Aquino questioned the legitimacy of the Philippine government's foreign debt, and implied that the Marcos administration secured loans to finance repression and to plunder from complicit lenders.

This critical distance from which Aquino viewed established foreign relations did not, however, become the main theme of her policy agenda. Instead, priority went to gaining international aid to stabilize both her fledgling government and the country's devastated economy. In recruiting international support, Aquino emphasized the democratization process, an appeal that warred with stubborn impressions of the Philippine economy as a shambles and poor investment risk. To win support, she needed to convince foreign governments and businesses to suspend strict investment logic in order to sustain resurgent democracy. Her early state visits resembled nothing so much as sweeping goodwill tours.

Aquino's appeal to the world, at least initially, stemmed from the extraordinary spectacle of a televised popular uprising, viewed internationally. She toured the world's capitals as an untarnished international star of democracy—a thoroughly appealing hero. For a time, she was nothing short of the darling of international diplomacy. The contrast between Marcos's bombast and Aquino's retiring modesty, almost always described in feminine terms, played tremendously to Aquino's advantage. In May 1986, she undertook an official state visit to the United States that, according to one State Department official, "was staggeringly successful. She had hard-bitten politicians eating out of the palm of her hand." Gender was central to this appeal—a fact underscored by the report that at her address to a joint session of Congress there were several American legislators with "Cory" dolls; it is doubtful that a man in similar circumstances—such as Polish leader Lech Walesa—would have inspired this response.[5] By 1987, she was nominated for the Nobel Peace Prize. In the early days of 1987, she appeared as *Time*'s "Woman of the Year." It was only the third time that the magazine had accorded such an honor to a woman, and it was the first such honor to be given to a woman political leader. In June 1988, the Philippine government sponsored the First International Conference of Newly Restored Democracies.

Initially, for as long as the spectacle of EDSA remained fresh, Aquino relied on her considerable store of international goodwill to win support for her rule. Domestic efforts, such as the restoration of constitutional democracy, bolstered her international reputation. She stemmed the flight of capital from the Philippines, and, largely because of increased international confidence in her government, built capital reserves from a mere $200 million to $2 billion by the end of 1986. Similarly, international success, particularly support pledged by such influential figures as the U.S. president and the Pope, did much to increase Aquino's standing at home, and particularly to grant the country's first woman president the needed measure of formidability.

Not surprisingly, however, trouble for the Aquino government first emerged at home. Aquino, who had initially assumed a centrist position to accommodate divergent interests in and out of government, drew criticisms from the left and right. As early as the second year of her term, many erstwhile supporters, unhappy about the prolandlord agrarian reform passed by the new Congress, the continuation of counterinsurgency, and the apparent resurgence of elitist democracy, began to withdraw their support. Moreover, they viewed with suspicion the Aquino government's apparent dependence on foreign assistance. The greatest threat to her rule, however, came from big business and the military, whose power bases were virtually untouched by the EDSA uprising. The military establishment viewed the government's peace negotiations with leftist rebel groups as a sign of weakness from its first woman commander in chief. Military factions such as RAM, the Soldiers of the Filipino People (SFP), and the Young Officers Union (YOU) castigated the civilian government and the military establishment for corruption and elitist politics. In her first year as president, Aquino withstood at least four military coup attempts, some backed by key members of her administration. In 1987 and 1989, her government withstood two more serious and bloody adventures from military rebels, many of whom echoed U.S. calls for a more hard-line approach to the insurgency.

The names of many coup attempts (such as "God Save the Queen") suggest the military's opinion that Aquino was a naïve and weak leader, requiring masculine protection. If gender was one of Aquino's main assets during the popular rebellion, it proved a distinct liability when she needed to evoke loyalty and obedience from the military establishment. Aquino understood the implications of gender, however, and stood ready to play different parts as necessary. In the politically essential speeches that Aquino delivered following each coup attempt, for example, she moved back and forth between languages—first addressing her soldiers and government officials in crisp, short, and unequivocal English sentences, with which she meted out punishment and asserted resolve and then switching to a softer and lilting Tagalog, in which she spoke to her citizens, evoking her husband's sacrifice, the nation's collective struggle, and the need for national unity. Whatever other transitions occurred between these two segments of her speeches, they represented a switch from a firm and (perhaps) "masculine" presidential bearing to a more gentle and explicitly "feminine" appeal.

Aquino soon moved to position her government on a more stable foundation by allying with powerful vested interests; only such interests seemed powerful enough to protect her government from increasingly dangerous military coup attempts. After each putschist adventure, Aquino would punish the leaders of the coup, but largely acquiesced to the demands of the coup's constituency—a move that drove her government increasingly to the right. In the wake of an October 1986 attempt, for example, she fired Defense Minister Juan Ponce Enrile, seen as a key plotter, but also fired four "left-leaning" cabinet ministers, thus acquiescing to the coup coalition's demand. Among those fired was the head of the National Economic Development Authority (NEDA), Solita Monsod, who had advocated repudiation of unjustly incurred foreign loans and was one of the administration's most visible female appointees. In 1988, at the graduation of the Philippine Military Academy cadets, Aquino called on the military to "unsheathe the sword of war," a speech that deeply satisfied her military leaders and was said to have considerably increased her standing with the Philippine business community.

At around this time, Aquino also began to change the tone of her government's relations with international powers—and with the United States in particular. Aquino's insistent appeal for external assistance required closer adherence to established foreign policy relations. In her second visit to the United States in 1987, Aquino pledged that the Filipino people would honor their foreign debt obligations, a move that firmly tied her government to international financial institutions such as the International Monetary Fund and the World Bank. By taking a more military approach to the Communist movement, which, after an extended visit by retired CIA officer John Singlaub, included the formation of civilian anticommunist militia or vigilante groups,[6] Aquino did much to still Washington criticisms that her government had been soft on communism. By 1988, she also showed herself less inclined to seek the removal of U.S. bases from the Philippines, preferring instead to negotiate the best compensation deal possible.

Even as the character of Aquino's foreign policy changed, at least to the extent that she became a more tractable U.S. ally, the vast majority of foreign policy administration passed from her direct responsibility into the hands of a small group of technocrats. International economic policy revolved increasingly around the details of debt rescheduling, fiscal restructuring, and renegotiating the treaty for U.S. bases. The further such talks proceeded down technical avenues, the less visible a role Aquino herself occupied. Instead, a group of technocrats, well acquainted with and socialized into established norms of international institutions, took over negotiations. Many such individuals were either Marcos administration veterans or members of the once disenfranchised sections of big business. Thus, policies in international negotiations came to demonstrate more continuity with older policies and agreements than not, and the question of Aquino's gender became less and less relevant thereby.

By 1989, Aquino came to more clearly depend on U.S. assistance, both militarily and economically. Colonel Honasan's December 1989 coup attempt was only decisively foiled when U.S. fighter planes scrambled to intimidate the rebels. Similarly, Philippine economic recovery was, by 1990, largely seen to depend on the Philippine Aid Program, a so-called Mini-Marshall Plan initiated by a group in the U.S. House of Representatives. Not coincidentally, the increased salience of U.S. assistance coincided with firm and irrevocable support by Aquino for U.S. interests in her country, most especially those centered around foreign debt obligations and the U.S. military bases. In fact, in 1991, after the Philippine Congress refused to ratify a treaty extending the stay of the bases, Aquino herself spearheaded a move to launch a referendum, of dubious constitutionality, to override the Senate's veto. In respect to her foreign policy, at least, Aquino closely resembled Marcos by the end of her term. She was every bit the anti-Communist, pro–U.S. president her predecessor had been.

CONCLUSION

Despite the initial fervor for reform, Aquino's government soon passed from what one might call its revolutionary phase—and had certainly done so by mid-1987. After her first year, Aquino relinquished the rhetoric and ambition of social reforms for a more modest program of governance: the reconstitution of representative institutions, where long-standing political and economic interests, some dislocated by the popular uprising, reestablished themselves. Moreover, in the process of seeking support from international powers, Aquino made concessions to preexisting modes of international relations.

In combination, pressures from established domestic and international interests drove her toward positions that retraced paths trod by the Philippine landed dynasties. In consolidating her government, Aquino moved toward policies with a narrower base of support and came to act less as the leader of EDSA and more as a member of the elite with vested interests in maintaining the status quo.

Aquino's metamorphosis might be partly explained as her response to pressures almost certainly inspired by her gender: As the first woman head of state, she faced criticisms that she was softhearted and politically weak willed. Yet her decision to appease established power centers rather than pursue her original agenda of social reforms also reflects her class origins. Nowhere was this more evident than in her response to coup attempts, during which she told the aroused public to stay home and relied instead on behind-the-scenes accommodation and compromise. In foreign relations, Aquino used her political capital less to redefine international relations than to attain more loans and aid. Clearly, the routinization of politics changed Aquino, drove her activism—and with it an explicit sense of her gender—

into the background. Political routine developed the Cojuangco politician—largely respectful of established domestic alliances and international policies—who had always existed in Aquino, and such a routine narrowed the range of alternative policies that she could—or wished to—pursue.

Nevertheless, the Aquino presidency did affect Philippine politics in several ways, including the creation of a commission for the development of women in Philippine society. Women's representation in public office also increased, although often only marginally. While the 1984 legislature contained 5.4 percent women, over 8 percent of solons elected in 1988 were female. Two women held ministerial positions under Marcos, while three served in Aquino's Cabinet. Marcos appointees to Constitutional Commissions had always been men, but Aquino appointed one woman and two men. In the judiciary, women's representation in key positions increased from 7.5 percent to 9.6 percent, while in the foreign service it grew from 27.5 percent to 40 percent.[7]

Moreover, Aquino paved the way for other women who might aspire to the presidency. In the May 1992 elections, two women, the widow Imelda Marcos and Miriam Defensor-Santiago, were presidential contenders. The Defensor-Santiago candidacy in particular demonstrated the contributions that Aquino's presidency made to the status of women in Philippine politics. While Marcos (like Aquino) stood as something of a proxy for her husband, Defensor-Santiago was a candidate in her own right. Defensor-Santiago's strong candidacy testified to the extent to which the notion of a woman political leader had gained acceptance under Aquino. Hence, while Aquino's defense chief Fidel Ramos won the election, Filipino women won a no less significant victory: For the first time, a woman candidate made a significant run at the presidency on her own merits, rather than as surrogate for an indisposed man.

Corazon Aquino's influence on world politics remains an open question. The different attributes that she brought to the presidency—among them her gender—unfolded against powerful international and domestic structures. Perhaps the best way to conceive of the problem is as a tug of war, where the pressures of statecraft set themselves against the new impulses of women's leadership. Aquino's example seems to indicate that women's influence over world politics depends at least as much on interruptions of political routines as on the women themselves. Perhaps, then, one should not ask whether women bring new perspectives to politics, but if they can defend those perspectives—when they exist—against the established political order. If the same upheavals that bring women to power grant them space for policy innovation, does the return to routine strip innovation from them?

NOTES

1. For a discussion of the economic crisis that led to the protest, see Manuel S. Mayo, "Businessmen's Hopes Falling Like Confetti," *The Diliman Review* 32:1 (January–February 1984): 12–25.

2. David Wurfel, *Filipino Politics: Development and Decay* (Quezon City, Philippines: Ateneo de Manila University Press, 1988), 301.

3. Even today, throughout Luzon's southern Tagalog region, a sprinkling of "Rizalista" cults awaits the resurrection of Jose Rizal, a nationalist leader and author whom the Spanish executed at the end of the nineteenth century.

4. Reynaldo Clemeña Ileto, *Pasyon and Revolution: Popular Movements in the Philippines, 1840–1910* (Quezon City, Philippines: Ateneo de Manila University Press, 1979).

5. "Woman of the Year: Corazon Aquino," *Time Magazine* 129:1 (January 5, 1987): 14.

6. The links between Singlaub's activity and the construction of counterinsurgency vigilante units is detailed in a five-part investigative series entitled "The Singlaub File," in *The Manila Chronicle*, August 7–11, 1987.

7. Data is from the *National Commission on the Role of Filipino Women, Annual Report 1988* (Manila, Philippines: Filipino Government, 1988).

6

Women as Insiders: The Glass Ceiling at the United Nations

Kristen Timothy

Women have been important contributors to the work of the United Nations (UN)[1] since it was established in 1945, but have always represented a small percentage of the total professional staff, never exceeding 31 percent. While the UN *Charter* incorporated the principle of equality between men and women (Article 8), this has not been fully realized in practice by the UN itself. This situation has prevailed despite pressure from the women's lobby inside the UN and from supportive member governments. Only recently have a few women attained management level jobs.

Both a highly political and an intensely bureaucratic institution, the UN typifies the bureaucratic culture that feminists have argued is alien to women's experience.[2] But not until recently have women inside the UN had an overtly feminist agenda. Affirmative action was long considered too radical and was unlikely to succeed given the attitudes that prevailed in an environment dominated by men from largely patriarchal cultures.

In this chapter, I discuss the obstacles faced by women inside the UN in trying to improve their status, especially during the UN Decade for Women (1975–1985). In many ways, it is the story of pressuring the UN as an organization to practice what it preached on the issue of gender equality. Pressure came from women on the outside who were committed to change and who advocated improving women's status within the UN and in the world at large. At the same time, there emerged a strong women's lobby at the UN in the early 1970s that kept up the pressure from the inside.

Obstacles to women's advancement in the organization have included a persistent pattern of undervaluing women's potential to contribute on a par with men. Women have lacked networks to promote their interests. Men have often underestimated what women could and should do in the workplace. Screening that placed a premium on years of experience has worked against women who may have dropped out to raise children or languished in low-level jobs for longer periods than men with similar abilities. Married women have been obliged to give up career opportunities to follow their husbands, or because acceptable alternatives for their spouses were not available in the locations where UN jobs might have led them. Even with changes in the rules, women have fared worse than men in the competition for jobs and decision-making positions in the UN. Women have come up against a ceiling at mid–professional levels and have been recruited at a rate well below that of men.

The *Charter* of the UN, adopted in 1945, called for equality among men and women. Thanks to a handful of women who attended the initial Charter Conference in San Francisco, such as Minerva Bernardino from the Dominican Republic and Eleanor Roosevelt from the United States, Article 8 specified that both men and women should be eligible to participate on an equal basis in any capacity in the principal and subsidiary organs of the UN.

Bernardino, in an interview in 1992, said that in 1945 she was aware that women at the Charter Conference were making a revolution. They had to watch every detail. For example, she was proud to have been instrumental in changing the name of the *Declaration of the Rights of Man* to the *Declaration of Human Rights.*[3]

But since its inception, the UN has not been able to live up fully to the tenets of its *Charter.* Women have neither been treated equally nor given the opportunity to participate fully in the work of the UN at all levels. They have continued to represent a small though growing proportion of the staff but have been discriminated against in promotion and relegated for the most part to lower-echelon staff jobs.

Only in recent years has the advocacy of committed men and women representing Member States, nongovernmental organizations (NGOs), and women staff in the organization received some response. There has been incremental progress in getting women into decision-making positions and reducing not only the formal sources of discrimination, but also the informal behavior that has kept women largely in staff rather than line management jobs. By June 1992, the proportion of professional women in the UN Secretariat, one of the six principal UN organs, reached 31 percent. This was the target set by the General Assembly to be realized two years earlier. Only 37 of these women, however, were managers or directors, compared to 319 men. Figure 6.1 illustrates the low proportion of women at senior levels (P-5 and above in UN parlance) in the UN Secretariat in mid-June 1992. No women occupied the level of Undersecretary General (USG). Notably, the highest position in the UN, the Secretary General, has always been held by a man.

The situation in other organizations of the UN system was little better in 1992. Only the UN Development Programme (UNDP), the UN Fund for Pop-

Figure 6.1
Staff by Gender and Grade in Geographical Posts, June 30, 1992

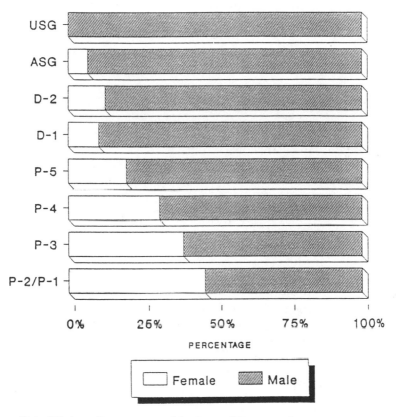

Source: United Nations, "Improvement of the Status of Women in the Secretariat," Report of the Secretary General, A/47/508 (October 1992), 5. USG is the abbreviation for Undersecretary General; ASG stands for Assistant Secretary General and is a level below USG. A post subject to geographical distribution is subject to the quota system created to ensure that all Member States have proportional representation on the staff according to a formula that includes their financial contribution to the organization.

ulation Activities (UNFPA), and the United Nations Children's Fund (UNICEF) had made notable strides to implement proactive policies to increase the number of women on their staff and to promote more of these women to top jobs. UN agencies with much poorer records included the regional economic and social commissions, the International Labour Organization, and the World Health Organization. All argued that there were not sufficient qualified women to hire or promote.

The UN agencies, delinquent in treating women equally with men, mirrored in many ways the experience in public life everywhere after World War II. There was a widely shared perception that women had no place in diplomacy, except perhaps in those arenas traditionally handled by women, like social issues, antislavery, and children's affairs. Both in the League of Nations and the UN, women and women's groups lobbied for women to play a more central role in the work of these organizations. Male-dominant attitudes stood in the way.

Sir Harold Nicholson, a well-known English diplomat in the 1940s, summed up a widely shared perception when he observed that diplomacy, including service in international organizations, was "men's business." Nicholson argued that there were three specifically "feminine" qualities that, unless kept under firmest control, were dangerous in international affairs: zeal, sympathy, and intuition. The ideal diplomat needed "masculine" qualities such as "impartiality and imperturbability; a diplomat needed to be a trifle inhuman."[4] Notably, the UN *Charter* in Article 101 states that its international staff should be impartial and neutral.

Those women who did go to work for the UN in the 1940s had, in many cases, been active in the humanitarian relief effort after the war. They were dedicated to the ideals of the UN and had perhaps somewhat lower expectations for their working lives than women do today. They did not openly challenge what were clearly inequities for women as far as benefits, promotion opportunities, and working conditions were concerned. Nor did they openly question the prevailing attitudes toward women that kept them in junior positions and supportive roles.

On the other hand, the NGOs that had fought so hard in San Francisco for the *Charter* provision on gender equality continued to lobby in the UN Commission on the Status of Women for the Secretary General to appoint high-level women. In 1954, Secretary General Dag Hammarsjköld went to the UN Commission on the Status of Women and pleaded with the members not to interfere in personnel practices. He argued that staff appointments and promotions were the prerogative of the chief executive. He said that women's emancipation had not progressed far enough to find highly qualified women for jobs in the Secretariat.[5]

Hammarsjköld also argued that more pressing considerations than gender dominated personnel decisions at the UN. One of these, geographical distribution, has continued to be a primary obstacle to recruiting more women into the ranks of the UN. Geographical distribution is a concept introduced in Article 101/3 of the UN *Charter.* This article called upon the Secretary General to achieve the highest standards of efficiency, competence, and integrity in appointing staff, but with the caveat that due regard be given to recruitment on a wide geographical basis.

The provision for geographical distribution was intended to permit the organization to profit from perspectives, values, and techniques from different parts of the world and to ensure that a certain percentage of nationals from each Member State was employed by the organization. A quota system was therefore introduced. The quota was derived from a somewhat arcane formula based roughly on contributions to the UN budget by which Member States are assigned a "desirable range" of positions to be filled by their nationals.[6]

Some Member States have filled their geographical quota for nationals with little regard for gender and in some cases with disregard for the technical qualifications needed as well. This practice tended to reinforce the traditional men's network among diplomats and Secretariat professionals. Women therefore face a double whammy: the quota system and the gender bias.[7] According to Suzan Habachy, the focal point for women in Secretariat posts in 1993, the Secretariat as a professional civil service is insulated from national influences in theory but not in practice: "Member States do get involved in nominating candidates, particularly for higher level posts, and overwhelmingly they tend to nominate men. Women coming through the system don't command the same kind of network and support."[8] Not surprisingly, a majority of governments did not recognize women as legitimate participants in public life until quite recently, and some still do not. In 1991, for example, the world average for women in parliaments (single or popular chamber) was only 11 percent.[9] Countries where women had little opportunity to enter the workplace or political life have found it difficult to find female candidates for jobs at the UN.

Other factors have also figured in recruitment decisions. For example, countries like the former Soviet Union successfully supported procedures that enabled them to loan a certain number of their citizens to the UN. Since women were rarely among those nominated despite the active role that women played in socialist societies, these UN jobs were effectively blocked.[10]

To this was added the view that women had family considerations that prevented them from being fully dedicated to the job, from traveling, or from making long-term careers in the UN. Some alleged that these constraints were not, as a rule, faced by their male colleagues. In practice, however, when given the opportunity, women proved to be as dedicated to their jobs and as available as men to travel and to make a long-term commitment to the organization. While attrition rates for women working at the UN were *perceived* to be higher than for men, this has not proved to be the case. A study conducted by the UN Institute for Training and Research demonstrated that of 254 men in 1951 at entry level, roughly 30 percent were still on the staff twenty years later. Of 93 women, a comparable percentage (29 percent) were still employed.[11]

In 1977, the Joint Inspection Unit (JIU), an independent body created by the General Assembly to audit UN practices, did a survey calling attention to the invisible barrier or "glass ceiling" for women in the UN at the mid–professional level. The survey pointed out that women who had broken the barrier tended to be much older than their male counterparts and had served longer. The JIU concluded that there was a need for top-level support to solve gender discrimination and stressed the need for mentors (usually sympathetic men) to help women climb the organizational ladder.[12] The JIU also considered such issues as dual-career couples and how to make the UN system more attractive to women. It found that women considered conditions of service such as availability of child care, maternity leave, spousal employment opportunities, and flexible hours when accepting a UN position. It recommended that policies be liberalized in those areas to accommodate women who combined career and family.

In 1975, *Ms.* magazine reported on the sorry state of affairs at the UN by pointing out that the UN had declared 1975 to be International Women's Year, with the threefold themes of equality, development, and peace, but that these were fine words that the UN did not uphold in its own "glass house."[13] In 1990, the United Nations was rated as one of the worst places where women could work.[14]

The formation of the Ad Hoc Group on Equal Rights for Women at the UN in 1971, later known simply as the Group on Equal Rights for Women, was the first significant effort by insiders to lobby for change. The efforts of the UN Commission on the Status of Women and the Ad Hoc Group converged as the pressure for women's rights grew in the Western industrialized countries. The Ad Hoc Group held its first meeting on April 6, 1971 at the initiative of Patricia Tsien, staff member of the Department of Political and Security Council Affairs, and decided to lobby against gender-biased staff rules and regulations.

The Group on Equal Rights for Women argued for eliminating all discriminatory conditions of service based on sex in the UN Staff Rules. Included were regulations governing official duty travel and pensions. For example, a male employee going on authorized leave was entitled to paid travel expenses for himself and his family regardless of his wife's employment situation. A female staffer, however, could not claim expenses for her husband unless he had no earnings of his own or his earnings did not exceed the lowest entry level of UN salary scales. The Ad Hoc Group fought this and other discriminatory regulations. In 1974 there were major revisions in the staff rules and regulations that were chalked up as a victory for the Group on Equal Rights for Women joined by the staff union.

The Group on Equal Rights for Women nevertheless realized that such changes had been wrought in the context of a highly conservative, unbending bureaucracy. Opposing such a bureaucracy was not easy. The established system for redressing grievances was dominated by the Administration, which in turn was controlled by men. The staff's union had little negotiating power, and the elaborate machinery for airing staff grievances was largely advisory to senior management. Too frequently, union decisions were either ignored or reversed by the Administration.

Diana Boernstein, a lawyer and feminist staff member, observed that most UN administrative decisions were made collectively. Many of the grievances resulted not from a specific administrative action but from a series of actions or inactions over the years that left women in a disadvantageous position in relation to their male colleagues. For instance, proving discriminatory intent from a form letter regretting that your promotion was not successful was very difficult. It had nothing to do with gender, they say. It was because poor Mabel was simply not up to snuff; she could not cut the mustard. She was stupid or incompetent; too aggressive or too passive; too fat or too thin. And, as the coup de grace, they might say confidentially that other women don't like her. Boernstein also maintained that women who filed gender discrimination charges faced massive and humiliating retaliation. Boernstein concluded that bringing a sex discrimination or sexual harassment case in the UN was an intolerable burden that took more courage than most had.[15] Only recently, following the publicity around the Anita Hill controversy in the United States on sexual harassment, have UN women succeeded in pushing through guidelines on sexual harassment with the help of some sympathetic men after studies showed the prevalence of harassment at the UN.[16]

While the pressure for equal treatment inside the UN grew, the numbers continued to tell the story of discrimination. The Administration of the UN continued to justify the low percentage of women in professional posts, repeating the hackneyed argument that not enough qualified women came forward or were proposed by Member States for UN jobs, particularly not for senior posts.

Under pressure from delegations and staff alike, the Administration decided to take the first concrete steps toward affirmative action in 1986. It decided that women's cumulative seniority would be taken into account when making promotions on the grounds that, on average, women spent more time than men at every level.[17] Men in the organization fought back arguing reverse discrimination.[18]

Some feminists have argued that bureaucracies are antithetical to women's experience and behavior. Feminist analysis has viewed contemporary bureaucracy as both structure and process characterized by patterns of dominance and subordination antithetical to women's experience of caretaking, nurturance, empathy, and connectedness.[19] This critique against bureaucracy began to have a noticeable effect in the Secretariat in the 1970s, resulting in a feminist discourse that opposed the bureaucratic forces that feminists saw as having marginalized women.

These forces have been challenged at the UN as a few women who were prepared to fight for women's rights, such as Dr. Nafis Sadik, head of the UN Fund for Population Activities (UNFPA), have succeeded in getting into more influential positions and have pressed for appointing and promoting more women. As more women have entered the managerial ranks, they have proved that they are as effective as men as managers in the multicultural environment of the UN. The stereotypes that had stood in the way for so long began to crumble. As women were given a chance to wield decision-making power in the UN, they also had a better chance of helping other women to advance. The oft-decried lack of solidarity amongst women has begun to give way to an increasingly influential and supportive "old girl" network.

At the same time, a few men have contributed their energies to the struggle, including William Draper III, Administrator of the UN Development Programme (UNDP) from 1989 to mid-1993, and the Secretary General himself, Boutros Boutros-Ghali. After one year in office, Boutros-Ghali supported a move to bring the number of women managers to 50 percent by 1995 and to have 50 percent of the professional category as a whole consist of women.

To reach the 50 percent targets, the Secretary General instituted special affirmative measures to achieve gender balance in policy-level positions. Acknowledging that it would take decades to achieve gender balance under normal procedures, he proposed measures to recruit, promote, and deploy women. He widened the pool of eligible women for vacancies; he upheld an earlier provision for cumulative seniority, and he called for vacancies to be filled with qualified women in departments and offices that did not meet the required percentages of women overall and at the higher levels. Posts would be available for male recruitment only after they had been vacant for twelve months, provided no qualified woman had been identified.[20]

To reach the target of 50 percent professional women by 1995, the fiftieth anniversary of the UN and the year of the fourth global UN Conference on Women, the Secretary General has had to prove himself to be doggedly committed to the goal and to demand that his senior managers be accountable for its achievement. Experience has shown that for reducing gender inequality, there is no substitute for the commitment of the chief executive officer.

At the same time, the widely diverse membership must also increase pressure for women's recruitment and advancement. In the post–cold war era, the competition for influence in the global organization will take new forms, but pressure by Member States to ensure that their nationals are employed by the organization is likely to continue. More of these must be qualified women, especially in senior positions, if the targets are to be met.

The fourth global UN Conference on Women is to be held in Beijing,

China, in September 1995. The Secretary General of the conference is Gertrude Mongella (Tanzania). The conference participants will examine achievements in improving the status of women around the world, including the 50 percent target for women in the UN Secretariat. The conference will also identify strategies for women's advancement, taking into account what worked during the UN Decade for Women and in the ten years subsequently. The record of the UN in eliminating the "glass ceiling" and in advancing women on a par with men will be reviewed and further steps recommended. In response to feminist concerns, the long-range goal may be to modify the very nature of bureaucracies in order to take into account the values, aspirations, and experiences of women.

NOTES

1. The views expressed in this chapter are the personal opinions of the author and do not represent the views of the United Nations Organization.

2. See Kathy Ferguson, *The Feminist Case against Bureaucracy* (Philadelphia: Temple University Press, 1984).

3. "An Interview with Minerva Bernardino," *INSTRAW News* 18 (Autumn 1992): 16.

4. *Spectator,* January 23, 1942, quoted in Carol Miller, "Conflicting Perceptions of the Role of Women in International Politics during the Interwar Years" (Paper presented to the Joint Annual Convention of the British ISA, London, 1989).

5. *United Nations Commission on the Status of Women,* Report of the Eighth Session E/2571 (April 1954), 17.

6. "Women in the Secretariat: Putting the Principle into Practice," *INSTRAW News* 18 (Autumn 1992): 19.

7. Lesley Parker, ed., "Strategies for Success," *Report of the Ad Hoc Group on Equal Rights for Women* (Vienna: United Nations, 1986).

8. "Women in the Secretariat," 19.

9. Interparliamentary Union, *Distribution of Seats between Men and Women in National Parliaments: Statistical Data from 1945 to 30 June 1991,* Series of Reports and Documents 18 (Geneva, 1991), 7.

10. See J. D. C. Jonah, "Independence and Integrity of the International Civil Service: The Role of Executive Heads and the Role of the States" (Paper for the First Mellor Conference, New York University Law School, November 1981); quoted in Thomas Franck, *Nation against Nation* (Cambridge: Oxford University Press, 1985), 106.

11. Alexander Szalai, *The Situation of Women in the United Nations,* UNITAR Report 18 (New York: UNITAR Publications, 1973), 15–16.

12. United Nations, "Women in the Professional Category and Above in the United Nations System," *JIU Report,* JIU/77/7–A/33/105 (1977), 43.

13. Pauline Frederick Robbins, "People in Glass Houses," *Ms.* 13 (January 1975): 48.

14. Ann Hornaday, "The 15 Worst Places to Work," *N.Y. Woman* 4 (June/July 1990): 76–83.

15. Diana Boernstein, "Enforcing Justice for Women in the UN," *Staff News* (April 1986): 3.

16. See United Nations, "Promotion of Equal Treatment of Men and Women in the Secretariat and Prevention of Sexual Harassment," *Secretary-General's Bulletin* ST/SGB/253 (October 29, 1992); see also United Nations, "Guidelines for Promoting Equal Treatment of Men and Women in the Secretariat," Information Circular, ST/IC/1992/67 (October 29, 1992).

17. United Nations, *Status of Women in the Professional Category and Above: Second Progress Report*, A/37/469 (September 21, 1982), 21.

18. "Profile, Kofi Annan, UN Personnel Chief," *Secretariat News* 63:5 (June 1987): 9.

19. Ferguson, *Feminist Case against Bureaucracy*, chap. 1.

20. United Nations, *Special Measures to Improve the Status of Women in the Secretariat*, ST/AI/382 (March 3, 1993).

7

In Their Own Words

Editors' note: In this chapter, four women who have been involved in world politics discuss what it has meant to them. First, Margaret Anstee of the United Kingdom speaks from her experience of a career in the United Nations diplomatic corps. Second, Benazir Bhutto describes her early life and entry into Pakistani politics. Third, Jeane J. Kirkpatrick reflects on her service as U.S. ambassador to the United Nations during the Reagan administration. Fourth, passages from writings and speeches of Golda Meir piece together her view on her experience as prime minister of Israel.

MARGARET ANSTEE

As an international civil servant of long standing, I can hardly be considered a "political" leader.[1] Nonetheless, the rank of Undersecretary General in the United Nations (UN) is considered to be at the "political" rather than the "professional" level, which means, in essence, that the incumbents are usually nominated by governments, among which there is keen competition for these posts. To be promoted from the ranks of career personnel to the political level is very much the exception, to be a woman so appointed even more so. When I was appointed Director General of the UN Office at Vienna at this level in 1987, it was a breakthrough in both senses, a "first." In that year, two women Undersecretaries General were appointed for the first time to established posts: myself and Thérèse Paquet-Sévigny, who came from outside the UN, nominated by the Canadian government. Five years later, we remain the only two women at this level in the core Secretariat, out of a total of twenty-seven. In the meantime, two other women have been appointed to posts at the Undersecretary General level in charge of separate UN organizations: Nafis Sadik (Pakistan) as director of the UN Fund for Population Activities (UNFPA) and Sadako Ogata (Japan) as Commissioner for the UN High Commission for Refugees (UNHCR).*

My own career at the UN began forty years ago, as a local staff member helping to set up one of the very first technical cooperation programs in the Philippines. How that came about is too long a story to tell here, but, of course, like so many women, I was undergraded[2] and underpaid in relation to my qualifications: I had a Double First Class Honours Degree from Cambridge University and had been a university lecturer and a diplomat; I had been one of the first women to be admitted to the British Foreign Service.

Other "firsts" were to follow. In 1956, I was sent to Colombia and became the first woman international field officer of the UN at the "professional" level. In 1957, I was posted to Uruguay and became the first woman Resident Representative of the UN Technical Assistance Board (which later evolved into what is now called the UN Development Programme, or UNDP), to head up the whole UN field team providing development cooperation to Colombia and Uruguay.[3] In 1977, I became the first (and so far only!) woman Assistant Administrator of UNDP, a post at the "political" level of Assistant Secretary General. In 1978, I was transferred to UN headquarters and became the first woman Assistant Secretary General of the core Secretariat to come up through the ranks, and only the second woman to be appointed at that level. In 1987, I became the first woman Undersecretary General, as I have already mentioned.

Over twenty years of my professional life were spent working in the field, on operational development programs. These involved residential assignments not only in the Philippines, Colombia, and Uruguay, but also in Argentina, Bolivia, Ethiopia, Morocco, and Chile. I also acquired considerable experience in disaster relief operations, most notably in Bangladesh in 1972–1973. As can be seen, it was a long haul to the top; and, after the breakthrough in 1957, I believe the tendency was for me to stay longer at each rung on the ladder than comparably experienced or qualified men.

This is only a bare outline of the milestones. What were the main factors in making it possible to attain them that I can pass on as tips to others? None of it would have been possible without a good sound education, the support of my family and of several farsighted male colleagues at the UN, my willingness to work hard, and my ability to keep my sense of humor.

First, my good formal education I owe to the dogged perseverance of my parents, especially my mother. I was born to very modest circumstances in a rural community where the village school headmistress used to tell us that we country children were not as bright as town children. If we happened to

*Sadik and Ogata continue in these posts as of June 1994. In addition, Elisabeth Dowdeswell (Canada) has been named Executive Director of the UN Environmental Program (UNEP), and Gillian Martin Sorensen (United States) has been appointed Special Adviser to the Secretary General for Information and Public Policy, to direct the observance of the UN's fiftieth anniversary. Melissa F. Wells (United States) served as Undersecretary General of Administration and Management from March 1993 to January 1994.

have the added misfortune of being girls, then we should more or less abandon hope of advancement. I suspect she wanted to protect us from disappointment, but the effect was hardly encouraging! Luckily, in my case, her protection was more than offset at home by the determination of my parents to ensure that their only child was given the education they had been denied, even if she happened to be a daughter (despite the often openly expressed censure and dismal forebodings of other villagers). So, by dint of my mother's refusal to let a series of seemingly insuperable obstacles deter us, and through my scholarships, the unimagined heights of Cambridge were scaled.

Another thing I owe to my mother was that she never allowed me to avoid challenges, and she always encouraged me to feel I could be up to them if I tried hard enough. Her favorite expression was, "Never say your mother had a jibber!" (that is, a horse that "jibs" or balks at a jump). So I jumped at all my fences even though sometimes coming seriously to grief. But without that advice ringing in my ears, I would not, for example, have even attempted the Foreign Service examination because the competition was so overwhelming. Hence, a second piece of advice, perhaps more difficult to follow, is: Choose your parents wisely, especially your mother!

Third, qualifications are of tremendous importance for women. I have known a number of brilliant men who have risen to high office, both inside and outside the UN, by their own talents and without a diploma to their name; incidentally, wars help in this regard. Women should not be deceived into thinking that the same path is open to them. I have found this to be true over and over again when trying to support the promotion of women in the UN who have shown excellent performance on the job (usually far better than men much higher placed) but who have no paper qualifications. I have invariably been told, quite bluntly, "But she isn't a professional." And when, as I equally invariably have done, I have asked whether "X" or "Y" (some of the men mentioned above) are not therefore to be considered not "professional," I have received first a vigorous affirmative, and then either a blank stare or a muttered, "Well, that's *different*."

So, qualifications are a must, and these must be acquired as early as possible: it is much, much more difficult to do so later in life, especially for a woman. And such qualifications must be kept up-to-date, and relevant, by further study as necessary. In my case, I acquired an external degree in economics at London University, by self-study while working flat out (full time) as Resident Representative in Bolivia in the early sixties, since I felt this study to be necessary for my job. Like many women of my generation, I had no career guidance before or at the university: the main objective was just to get there! I read modern languages and literature, which has stood me in very good stead, especially in understanding other cultures and other ways of life, which was essential to my field work in development cooperation, but was not of itself sufficient for an occupation outside the academic world.

After taking the Foreign Service examination, I was pushed in "at the deep end," as it were, when suddenly in 1956, at a very young age, I was left in charge of the UN Mission in Colombia, which was composed entirely of men older than myself. The experience and confidence that assignment gave me were invaluable: I feared I would sink, but instead found I could swim—and other people saw that I could, with the result that a year later, I was given my own post as head of the mission.

That this happened in Latin America thirty-six years ago is nothing less than remarkable, and tribute must be paid to a few farsighted men in the UN who saw that this was possible and right and who overcame government objections. I think particularly of two gentlemen who have passed on, David Owen (UK), then head of the UN Technical Assistance Board, who launched what has become the worldwide field network of the UN Development Programme in the early fifties, and James Keen (UK), who worked closely with him. Two others, still with us, who were also instrumental in making this breakthrough were Malcolm Adiseshiah (India), then Assistant Director General of the UN Educational, Social, and Cultural Organization (UNESCO) and Gustavo Martínez-Cabañas (Mexico), then an Assistant Secretary General in the UN.

So, fourth, it is important to get male backing too! Strident feminist "go it alone" tactics do not, in my experience, work. But it *is* necessary for women to assert themselves, to show that they *can* do the job. It is a source of continual regret to me to see so many highly qualified and capable women constantly underestimating themselves, lacking confidence, and underselling themselves. Having been the boss of many men of all nationalities for many years, I can vouch that they usually err on the opposite side!

Fifth, women invariably have to work harder, and do better, than men. The phenomenon is not quite as bad as in my young days, but it is still there. A positive feature in my own career, I think, was that I never declined an assignment or was "choosy." I became Resident Representative of the very important UN development program in Bolivia, the poorest country in South America, over thirty years ago simply because no one else (and all the others were men) wanted to go there on account of the altitude and the difficult living conditions. Not only did I consolidate my professional reputation there, but I had nearly six of the happiest and most satisfying years of my life in the country I intend to make my eventual home. From there I went on to work for nearly three years in Ethiopia, another invaluable and unforgettable experience. Later, I was the first UN woman head of a mission to work in an Arab country—Morocco—another breakthrough.

This brings me to another point. I have stressed that academic qualifications are essential. But they, on their own, are not enough. To succeed, women must also demonstrate what they *can* do on the job, and they must be *seen* doing it. Some women simply go on piling up the paper qualifications. This is fine if you aspire to an academic career, but it won't help you in public life if that is all you have to show.

The point I am making is that, even now in the 1990s, there are still a lot of myths around that women cannot do this or that. These myths must be dispelled, but one can only do so by proving that the myths are wrong. During my years as Resident Representative in various rather lively parts of the world, I several times had to deal, as head of the UN Mission, with major crises: armed revolutions, aircraft accidents, natural disasters, and other dangerous situations. In such cases, a woman in charge has to do more than a man, simply to show that she is capable of being "in the front line" and "cool under fire."

My general experience in my field assignments was one of reluctant acceptance, as I intimated earlier. Most governments to which I was accredited were considerably less than eager to give "agrément" (that is, their formal diplomatic acceptance of the nomination, without which the appointment cannot be made) when the UN proposed my name. This was understandable when I was young and relatively untried, but the initial reluctance reemerged every time I moved on to a new assignment, even when my curriculum vitae had grown much longer. So when diplomatic pressure had been exerted to get my appointment accepted, I found myself on arrival under severe scrutiny and very much on my mettle (having to prove myself). The first few months were very hard, always, but once that had been surmounted, then I suspect it was perhaps smoother sailing over the longer term for me than for a man who might have had an easier run at the beginning. Whether from surprise or relief, acceptance, once won, seemed to be total. And once that confidence is assured, I believe it is easier for a woman, say, to persuade a minister of state that it might be better to adopt a different approach to a program or project. Moreover, while every government to which I was accredited was apprehensive about my coming, they were all sorry to see me go—much better than the other way around.

Sixth, I think a sense of humor and a sense of proportion are indispensable. For a career woman to take herself *too* seriously is almost as bad as not taking herself seriously enough! Even nowadays, when occupying a relatively elevated position and meeting someone for the first time, I am still frequently mistaken for the secretary or wife of one of the male members of my accompanying staff, who is addressed as "Director General." I console myself that the embarrassment is much greater for the perpetrator of this anachronistic faux pas when he finds out (for it is almost always a "he"). And if, as usually happens nowadays, the man whose lucky spouse I am supposed to be is much younger than myself, then I firmly devise to take this as a compliment!

Apart from these aspects, it is hard to say whether a woman's way of handling such a post is different from a man's. In my own case, in the 1950s and 1960s I gave more emphasis to poverty and the social aspects of economic and technical development and to the role of women in bringing it about—long before either became fashionable or accepted doctrine. It may well be that greater sensitivity to such issues stems from being a woman.

As to management style, it is also difficult to judge if women differ from men, whether for myself or for anyone else. There may well be something in the suggestion made by some that women adopt a more conciliatory or consensual approach. At the same time, one can point to many cases where women are accused of adopting almost dictatorial attitudes. I think this reveals a basic dilemma: Many women do not want to be mirror images of men in similar positions, but at the same time they must show authority or they will simply be swept aside. This awareness may lead to overreaction. The key is to find a happy mean.

A final question, whether the fact of having a woman in an important position in the UN encourages greater participation by, or a change in, the political status of other women in the world community, is no easier to answer. To venture any assessment of this kind, one is entering the world of speculation and of the intangible. How do you measure such results? All I can say is that I have throughout my career tried to help and encourage other women, and I have also been told by a good many women that just the mere fact of my having held positions that were formerly male bastions has spurred them on to venture more daringly than they might otherwise have done. In other words, it has been shown to be possible.

By the same token, I think that when a woman acquits herself well in a very visible and demanding position, it must have a subtle influence on even the most entrenched prejudices of governments and individuals, though this may take a long time to work through to a general effect. Even one's failures can sometimes be of help in this regard. Some years ago, I was a candidate for the post of High Commissioner of Refugees. But then it began to be said in influential circles that a woman could not do this job because many of the refugees were in Muslim countries. My reply to this was that one might also apply the equally spurious argument that 80 percent of the refugees were women and children, so that only a woman could deal with them. It was of no avail, but I take comfort that this incident in some way contributed to the appointment of a woman—Sadako Ogata (Japan)—to the post several years later.

On another occasion, I was told by an ambassador from a Western country that a woman could never be in charge of a peacekeeping operation in the UN because it involved "dealing with the military." That myth has now been exploded: By an uncanny coincidence, while writing this autobiographical essay, I was telephoned by the new Secretary General, Dr. Boutros Boutros-Ghali, and asked if I would accept appointment as the Special Representative of the Secretary General for Angola and Chief of the UN Angola Verification Mission (UNAVEM II)—that is, to become the first woman to head a UN peacekeeping mission. Recalling my own advice to never be "choosy," I accepted. I am now in charge of a mission of over 1,000 people, including 350 military observers from twenty-four countries (headed by a Nigerian general), 12 police observers, and 400 electoral observers, with supporting administrative and logistical personnel. We are scattered in sixty-eight locations over this vast and wartorn country, which is as large as France, Germany, and Spain combined, and supported by the biggest air operation that the UN has so far mounted.

Our task is the daunting one of verifying, first, the confinement and then the demobilization of two opposing armies, totalling 200,000 soldiers; next, the creation of a single unified armed forces of 50,000, as well as a neutral police force; and finally, the holding of the first democratic and multiparty elections in Angola on September 29–30, 1992. *International observers agreed that the election was free and fair. The ruling MPLA (Popular Movement for the Liberation of Angola) won by a large margin, but the rebel group UNITA (National Union for the Total Independence of Angola), led by Jonas Savimbi, refused to accept the outcome and renewed the fighting. The Security Council adopted sanctions against UNITA in September 1993, imposing an oil and arms embargo. UNAVEM's mandate has been extended.*

There is always the danger that a successful woman may be considered an exception, a "flash in the pan" or some kind of gender abnormality. I can still remember my horror and indignation when the wife of an important minister once said to me: "My husband admires you very much. He says you have a man's mind!" This struck a particularly sore spot, because I have always felt myself to be very much a woman and have tried to conserve the essence of femininity which, it seemed to me, was an important element in any contribution I could make. This is not always easy, given all the pressures. It is, for instance, undoubtedly true that had I married and had a family, my career would simply not have been possible, at least not in my generation. The inescapable truth is that, as a woman, I had to make harder decisions about my personal life than did my male colleagues. And my personal life was subjected to much more intense scrutiny, particularly as a young, single woman in Latin America thirty years ago. Fortunately, much of this has changed radically, but it is still the case that women are faced with much more difficult choices, and have to make greater sacrifices, than men, particularly if their career is in the international sphere, which requires constant mobility. Yet, if women want to rise to high positions, they must somehow come to terms with this.

A related issue is that women, even if successful and given high posts, are all too often relegated to so-called women's areas. I was very fortunate that, from the beginning, I was given responsibilities traditionally considered "male." There must be much more of this if we are ever to get rid of the shibboleths of what women can and cannot do. It was only when I became Director General of the UN Office at Vienna that I had, for the first time, direct responsibility in the area of the advancement of women, since this was one of the various UN programs that was located in my office. There is no doubt in my mind, however, that the fact that I have spent many years in the "man's world," as it were, gives me insights not available to those who have spent a lifetime on women's issues alone.

One of our key mandates in this program was to monitor progress toward the attainment of the goals to which governments and the international community subscribed at the last UN Conference on Women in 1985: no less than equality by the year 2000. We are, I fear, far from that goal, and the main reason that we have detected in our analyses is the lack of women in political and policy decision making at all levels.

A major event we had planned in this connection was an Inter-Regional Consultation on Women in Public Life to be held last September [1993] in the Imperial Hofburg Palace in Vienna. Prominent women in government, diplomacy, business, and academia were to have come from all over the world to pool their collective wisdom, and a summit was to have been organized of women currently elected as heads of state or government. The UN General Assembly warmly endorsed the idea, but not the funding, saying that this must come from voluntary contributions. A few such were indeed forthcoming from a few governments, but were not sufficient—a somewhat ironic illustration that women's issues are not given prominence in male-dominated governments! But the idea is not dead, only postponed.

Such setbacks should not discourage us. As I look back over my own life, I am struck by the enormous and positive evolution in the situation of women that has taken place over time. We should always remember the words of the inspired graffiti writer, who, seeing the words, "Women are equal to men" written on a wall, scrawled underneath, "Women are equal to *anything*."

BENAZIR BHUTTO

Editors' note: At this writing, Benazir Bhutto holds office as the prime minister of Pakistan. She held the office once before, from December 1, 1988, to August 6, 1990. Her father, Zulfikar Ali Bhutto, was prime minister from 1971 to 1977. In her autobiography, she describes her early life in her family and community. Her story reveals much about gender relations in Pakistani society. For example, she relates how her father released her and her sister from traditional practices of marriage into the family and of wearing the burqa, *the gauzy head-to-toe veil worn by adult Pakistani women of the upper class,[4] and how he encouraged them to obtain an education.*

There was no question in my family that my sister and I would be given the same opportunities . . . as our brothers. Nor was there in Islam . . . [which] had been quite progressive toward women from its inception, the Prophet Mohammed (PBUH)[5] forbidding the practice of killing female infants . . . and calling for women's education and their right to inherit [property] long before these privileges were granted to them in the West.

. . . Muslim history was full of women who had taken a public role. . . . "I have found a woman ruling over them . . . and hers is a mighty throne," reads . . . the Holy Quran.[6]

Benazir Bhutto went to Radcliffe College at Harvard for her undergrad-

uate education in the fall of 1969, eventually majoring in comparative government. Upon graduating in 1973, Bhutto attended Oxford University at the urging of her father, who had studied law there two decades earlier.[7] She studied there four years, returning to Pakistan after a bitterly contested election returned her father to office. Part of the opposition to Zulfikar Ali Bhutto and the Pakistan People's Party (PPP) came from the religious right, which rejected her father's reforms regarding women. Bhutto notes that her father opened the foreign service, civil service, police force, and communications field to women, promoted women's education, and encouraged her mother to be politically active. Her mother, Nusrat Bhutto, served as Pakistan's representative to the UN Conference on Women held in Mexico City in 1975 as part of the Decade for Women.[8]

In 1977, her father was arrested and imprisoned in a military coup. Bhutto campaigned for his release and on behalf of her mother, who had been chosen as a compromise candidate by her father's party, the PPP, for scheduled elections. Here, she comments on how she felt preparing to give the first speech of her political career.

A woman standing on a political podium was not as strange to the crowd as it felt to me. Other women on the subcontinent had picked up the political banners of their husbands, brothers, and fathers before me. . . . Indira Gandhi in India. Sirimavo Bandaranaike in Sri Lanka. Fatima Jinnah and my own mother in Pakistan. I just never thought it would happen to me.[9]

The elections were postponed indefinitely, and her father was executed. Bhutto and the other members of her family were detained by the government. Upon her release, Bhutto took over the management of her family's farm, as her father was dead and her brothers were in exile. She explains that although women in rural areas rarely left their homes unescorted or without their burqas, *and rarely drove cars, she had to do these nontraditional things in order to fulfill her responsibilities at the farm.*

There was little room left in my life . . . for tradition.

In a way I had transcended gender. . . . Our tradition holds that women are the honor of families. To safeguard their honor, and themselves, a family keeps their women in *purdah*, behind the four walls and under the veil.

My four aunts . . . formed part of this tradition. . . . They were the old generation. I was the new.[10]

Since neither her ailing mother nor her exiled brother could do so, after spending some time abroad, Bhutto returned to Pakistan to lead the PPP her father had founded in a campaign against Zia ul-Haq's government. A victory for the PPP in parliamentary elections would make Bhutto prime minister, as her father had been at the time of his arrest. She describes her campaign effort to convince the Pakistanis that a woman could lead them. Here, she recounts a campaign speech in the city of Peshawar.

"People think I am weak because I am a woman," I called out. . . . "Do they not know that I am a Muslim woman. . . . I have the patience of Bibi

Khadija . . . the perseverance of Bibi Zeinab . . . [and] the courage of Bibi Aisha. . . . I am the daughter of the martyr Zulfikar Ali Bhutto, the sister of martyr Shah Nawaz Khan Bhutto, and I am your sister as well. I challenge my opponents to . . . democratic elections."[11]

Bhutto continued her campaigning against Zia's government. Zia finally called elections in 1988, as Bhutto was expecting her first child. On August 17, 1988, Zia died in a plane crash. On November 16 and 19, 1988, the PPP won majorities in National Assembly and provincial elections. As a result, on December 1, 1988, the president of Pakistan named the PPP leader, Benazir Bhutto, as prime minister. Her administration was a short one, lasting only until August 6, 1990. Bhutto was charged with corruption, dismissed as prime minister, and detained but eventually acquitted on all charges.

In 1993, Bhutto once again campaigned for prime minister. This time, her opposition included her brother, Mir Murtaza Bhutto, and her mother, Nusrat Bhutto, who supported her brother as the rightful heir of the Bhutto political legacy. Her brother returned from exile and was charged with terrorism for his militant antigovernment activities. From his jail cell, he ran against PPP candidates for seats in the parliamentary elections. While his mother urged the government to withdraw the charges, Benazir Bhutto worried that if her brother did not clear himself "in normal judicial procedures," there would be a political scandal that would hurt the PPP.[12] In a recent interview, Benazir Bhutto describes the conflict she has experienced between the gendered roles of dutiful daughter/loyal sister and of political leader.

. . . I love my mother dearly. I was always an obedient daughter. . . . But in our family it was always a joke that my mother had a soft spot for my brother. We all knew that he was her favorite, that she spoiled him.

. . . all my life I was such a dutiful daughter. And perhaps my mother found it difficult to accept that when the time came for a decision between political responsibility and obedience as a daughter, I chose political responsibility. . . . Right now I'm trying to reconstruct my relationship with her.

As for my brother, I think he has to familiarize himself with Pakistan because at the moment he still thinks of me as "a sister." He doesn't think of me as a political leader who stayed behind and waged a political battle and triumphed.[13]

In the same interview, Bhutto also describes the circumstances of her much-criticized decision to enter into an arranged marriage with Asif Ali Zadari in 1987.

I *couldn't* have a love match. I was under so much scrutiny. If my name had been linked with a man, it would have destroyed my political career. Actually, I had reconciled myself to a life without marriage or children for the sake of my career. And then my brothers got married. I realized I didn't even have a home, that in the future I couldn't do politics when I had to ask permission . . . [to use] the telephone. I couldn't rent a home because a woman living on her own can be suspected of all kinds of scandalous associations. So keeping in mind that many people in Pakistan looked to me, I decided to make a personal sacrifice in what I thought would be a loveless marriage, a marriage of convenience. The surprising part is that we are very close. . . . [14]

Bhutto and Zadari have three children: Bilawal (age 5), Bakhtawar (age 4), and Asifa (age 1).

JEANE J. KIRKPATRICK

Editors' note: Jeane Duane Jordan Kirkpatrick[15] received her Ph.D. from the University of Paris and has taught at Trinity College and Georgetown University, becoming a full professor at the latter in 1978. She was a Senior Fellow at the American Enterprise Institute before serving as the U.S. ambassador to the United Nations from 1981–1985. [The current U.S. ambassador to the United Nations is Madeleine Korbel Albright.]

The Situation Room is a small room underground, in the basement of the White House West Wing. There's a small table in the Situation Room around which eight or nine people gather fairly regularly to discuss major questions of foreign policy: the President, the Secretaries of State and Defense, the Chief of the Joint Chiefs, the National Security Advisor, the Director of the CIA and, when I was United Nations Ambassador, me. In the course of a meeting one day, I looked across the room and saw a mouse making its way slowly across the floor. Someone else noticed it about the same time: "It's a mouse." They said, "A mouse? In the Situation Room?" And there he was: a mouse in the Situation Room. I thought to myself later, "It might be that that mouse was no more surprising a creature to see in the Situation Room than I was."

There are people who come and go in the room, and among them is almost invariably a woman or two—fetching and carrying papers to the people who are sitting at the table. Has there ever been a woman as near to the center of decision making in U.S. foreign policy as I was? I rather doubt it. Not under President Carter, not under Ford or Nixon, not in the Johnson administration.

The arena of foreign affairs—diplomacy and defense—has been at its very top levels, in all countries, a very peculiarly, particularly male bastion. And it matters. This is where the very biggest decisions are made, the decisions that shape the destiny of the world. Margaret Thatcher is, of course, inside that arena, and there have been a few others—Indira Gandhi, Golda Meir, and a few queens like Elizabeth I and Isabella. But women have been present only when they were heads of state.

It came as something of a shock to me to discover after being appointed to the United Nations that I was not only the first woman ever to head the United States Mission to the United Nations, but that I was the first woman to be a chief of mission of a country that falls in the category of Western civilization.

These facts alone make it clear that the United Nations, like the Situation Room, has been a male preserve. Male preemption of international affairs is so ubiquitous, so "normal," so taken for granted that it is invisible even to most women accustomed to thinking unthinkable thoughts about sex roles. But as someone who has read and written about women in power,[16] I am convinced that this pattern of sex role distribution *is* distinctive and important, conceivably even to the future of the world. We can't be certain that women would make different decisions than men, but they might if there were enough of them to affect the decision process and its environment.

I feel quite sure that a significant portion of my experience as U.S. Permanent Representative to the U.N. was gender-based, was a result of the fact that I was a woman in a place where women are so very rare. I encountered some special sex-related problems, and perhaps some special benefits, that were directly related to being a woman. The problems came as something of a surprise to me; most were almost wholly unanticipated. I had assumed that as a woman who has succeeded sufficiently to be appointed to a top-level job in politics, I had demonstrated not only professional skills, but some survivor skills as well. I had no reason to suppose that the quality of my experiences in this job should have been different. I was wrong.

One of the first big surprises I encountered was what I might call the process of dequalification—a sort of systematic inattention to my substantial academic background and success. I was never called "Doctor" or "Professor," but always "Mrs." I think "Mrs." is an honorable title; certainly it's an earned title, like "Doctor" and "Professor." But it's a nondifferentiating, nonprofessional title, while *academic* titles are regularly attributed to the likes of Henry Kissinger, Zbigniew Brzezinski, or any one of the dozen men I could name, who come from universities to occupy significant posts at the upper levels of U.S. politics.

There was another variety of sex-related, symbolic denigration, which I noticed repeatedly, and about which I do not think I was hypersensitive. I was continually described as "school-marmish" or as a "schoolteacher," rather than "professional" or a "professor." I was almost never described as a scholar, a term that is regularly applied to males with similar vitae.

I was, however, described as "confrontational," a label I never heard before I went to the United Nations. It was a little while before I noticed that *none* of my male colleagues, who often delivered more "confrontational" speeches at the U.N. than I, were labeled as "confrontational." In thinking about this, I have concluded that it is unlikely that *any* woman who arrives at a very high level in any public activity is confrontational. If she were, she would have long since been eliminated. To achieve significant recognition in our society, it is necessary to pass through doors to which males are the gatekeepers. It is highly unlikely that any woman with a confrontational style would make it through more than one of those doors.

I now think that being tagged "confrontational" and being a woman in a high position are very closely related. At a certain level of office, the very fact of a woman's occcupancy poses a confrontation with conventional expectations. Similarly, I think being described as "tough" and being a woman in public life are very closely related. Again, this is an adjective that was *never* applied to me before I entered high politics. Yet it was not long before the French were calling me the *"Femme de Fer,"* and our own papers were describing me repeatedly as "Reagan's Iron Woman." I've thought about that, too, and I've come to see a double bind: If a woman seems strong, she is called "tough"; and if she doesn't seem strong, she's found not strong enough to occupy a high-level job in a crunch.

Terms like "tough" and "confrontational" express a certain surprise and disapproval at the presence of a woman in areas in which it is necessary to be what, for males, would normally be considered assertive.

This leads me back to the ultimate questions of whether there are identifiable male and female sensibilities and social styles. I tend to think that the patterns of interaction in high politics are particularly unattractive to women—as unattractive to women as they are inhospitable to them. I find myself thinking of the great number of women who withdrew from high politics and government by personal decision—not because they can't hack it, but because they don't choose to. High politics involves a weirdly unbalanced kind of life-style, which requires continuous involvement with power. It is not simply necessary that one work eighty- or ninety-hour weeks; this is true of many vocations. It is that the whole enterprise resembles that described by the philosopher Thomas Hobbes: "the restless striving after power which [one suspects] ceases only in death."

None of these tendencies portends a rapid influx of women into top positions in government, least of all in foreign policy. And it's unfortunate: Being a woman in international politics has special benefits. I think that, particularly with foreign political leaders, and with some of our own as well, a woman is less threatening. It may therefore be easier, perhaps, to have long conversations, because there exists a more hospitable environment for them to talk freely.

What do I want to say about it all? I want to say that I think sexism is alive in the U.S. government; it's alive in American politics. It's alive at the United Nations; it's bipartisan. And I also want to say that sexism is not unconquerable if one can avoid getting and staying angry and wasting one's energies on rage. In *A Room of One's Own*, that beautiful essay that remains my favorite feminist classic, Virginia Woolf talks about the pitfalls of anger for women, of wasting one's energy, one's self, on rage. I think that's very important, because if one is angry much of the time, that anger unbalances judgment, consumes one's energy. If you can avoid the pitfalls of rage and paranoia and can hang in long enough to prove your seriousness and competence in the diplomatic world and American high politics, then you can develop good relations based on mutual respect with almost all your colleagues.

GOLDA MEIR

Editors' note: Golda Mabovitch (Meyerson) Meir[17] was born in Russia in 1898 to an impoverished Jewish family and immigrated to the United States in 1906. As an adult, she returned to what would become Israel and became an influential political figure. After Israel became independent in 1948, she served in a variety of positions, including ambassador to the USSR (1948– 1949), foreign minister (1956–1966), and prime minister (1969–1974). She died in 1978. In her autobiography—from which we have drawn most of the following extracts—she describes how she became involved in politics and what her gender meant to her as a political actor.

Her childhood in Russia was intensely political. She recalled the preparations her community made to ward off periodic pogroms against Jews. Her sister Sheyna, nine years her senior, "was a revolutionary, an earnest, dedicated member of the Socialist-Zionist movement. . . . Not only were she and her friends 'conspiring' to overthrow the all-powerful czar, but they also proclaimed their dream to bring into existence a Jewish socialist state in Palestine."[18]

The family left Russia and finally settled in Milwaukee, Wisconsin. As a teenager, Meir had to balance her parents' demands that she work in their chronically failing grocery shop, her love of school where she excelled, and her desire to be independent. She early learned the power of organization in politics and her effectiveness in such organizations. In Milwaukee, while public school was free, poor students could not afford to purchase the textbooks. Meir and a group of friends organized a public meeting on the issue.

Having appointed myself chairman of the society, I hired a hall and sent invitations out to the entire district. Today it seems incredible to me that anyone would agree to rent a hall to a child of eleven but the meeting took place . . . and dozens of people came. The program was very simple: I spoke about the need for all children to have textbooks whether they had money or not, and [her sister] Clara, who was then about eight, recited a socialist poem in Yiddish. . . . A considerable amount of money was raised.[19]

The Mabovitch house became a part of the political and intellectual ferment for Jews who had the goal of creating a Jewish state in Palestine following its liberation from the Turks during World War I. Golda Mabovitch became a socialist and a Zionist. She tried to persuade American Jews to support Zionist political goals.

If you wanted to campaign among Jews, I decided, the logical place to locate yourself was the neighborhood synagogue, particularly around the time of the Jewish High Holidays, when everyone went to the synagogue. But since only men were allowed to address the congregation, I put up a box just outside the synagogue, and people walking out on their way home had no alternative other than to hear at least part of what I had to say about the Labor Zionist platform. I suppose I had more than my fair share of self-confidence in this respect, if not in others, and when a great many people actually stopped to listen to me outside the synagogue, I thought I ought to try it again in another place. But this time my father learned about my plans, and we had a terrible row. Moshe Mabovitch's daughter, he stormed, was not going to stand on a box in the street and make a spectacle of herself. It was out of the question, a *shadeh* (a disgrace). . . . My mother stood between us like a referee at a fight, and we went on arguing at the top of our voices.

In the end neither of us gave in. My father, red in the face with fury, said that if I insisted on going, he would come after me and publicly pull me home by my braid. I had no doubt that he would do so, because he generally kept his promises. But I went anyway. I warned my friends on the street corner that my father was on the war path, got up on my soapbox and made my speech—not without some panic. When I finally got home, I found my mother waiting up for me in the kitchen. Father was already asleep, she told me, but he had been at the street corner meeting and heard me speak. "I don't know where she gets it from," he said to her wonderingly. He had been so carried away listening to me perched on my soapbox that he had completely forgotten his threat! Neither of us ever referred to the incident again but I consider that to have been the most successful speech I ever made.[20]

Golda Mabovitch married Morris Meyerson in December 1917. (Nearly forty years later, she took the name "Meir" in response to an injunction from the leader of the Labor party that Israelis have Hebrew names.) She and her husband immigrated to Palestine in 1921, now under British occupation. Meir joined a kibbutz, a pioneer settlement run on socialist principles, but one barely eking out an existence.

There was very little to eat, and what was available tasted dreadful. . . . When my turn came to work in the kitchen, to everyone's astonishment I was delighted. Now I could really do something about the frightful food.

Let me explain that in those days kibbutz women hated kitchen duty, not because it was hard (compared to other work on the settlement, it was rather easy), but because they felt it to be demeaning. Their struggle wasn't for equal "civic" rights, which they had in abundance, but for equal burdens. They wanted to be given whatever work their male comrades were given—paving roads, hoeing fields, building houses, or standing guard duty—not to be treated as though they were different and automatically relegated to the kitchen. All this was at least half a century before anyone invented the unfortunate term "women's lib," but the fact is that kibbutz women were among the world's first and most successful fighters for true equality. But I didn't feel that way about working in the kitchen. I couldn't for the life of me understand what all the fuss was about and said so. "Why is it so much better," I asked the girls who were moping (or storming) about kitchen duty, "to work in the barn and feed the cows, rather than in the kitchen and feed your comrades?" No one ever answered this question convincingly, and I remained more concerned with the quality of our diet than with feminine emancipation.[21]

Meir left the kibbutz unwillingly after three years because her husband was ill and rejected the discipline of kibbutz life. She soon found a job with the General Federation of Jewish Labor (Histadrut), which was, in addition to a labor union, a founder of economic enterprises owned by all the members of the union and the care provider for the growing number of Jewish immigrants and refugees. Her job and her traveling continued to erode their marriage; Meir and her husband stayed legally married (he died in 1951) but went their separate ways, loving each other and their two children, Menachem and Sarah, but unsuccessful in their own relationship.

In the 1930s and 1940s, Meir became increasingly involved in the struggle to create a Jewish state free from British control, against the wishes of many Arab Palestinians and Arab nations surrounding what would become the State of Israel. Meir's frequent assignment as a delegate to conferences abroad and her success as a fund-raiser reflected her growing influence within the Zionist movement. Her postindependence official positions are evidence of both influence and her skills. Meir's involvement in Israeli politics led her to reflect on being a woman in that male-dominated political world.

The fact is that I have lived and worked with men all my life, but being a woman has never hindered me in any way at all. It has never caused me unease or given me an inferiority complex or made me think that men are better off than women—or that it is a disaster to give birth to children. Not at all. Nor have men ever given me preferential treatment. But what is true, I think, is that women who want and need a life outside as well as inside the home have a much, much harder time than men because they carry such a heavy double burden. . . . And the life of a working mother who lives without the constant presence and support of the father of her children is three times harder than that of any man I have ever met.

To some extent my own life in Tel Aviv . . . is an illustration of these dilemmas and difficulties. I was always rushing from one place to another—to work, home, to a meeting, to take [her son] Menachem to a music lesson, to keep a doctor's appointment with [her daughter] Sarah, to shop, to cook, to work and back home again. And still to this day I am not sure that I didn't harm the children or neglect them, despite the efforts I made not to be away from them even an hour more than was strictly necessary.[22]

In an interview, Meir expanded on her sense of herself in the political realm.

All my adult life I have worked among men, and they have treated me on my merits. I never knew a man who gave in to an argument of mine because I was a woman—except one, my husband—and they had the open-mindedness and the manliness to accept my idea if they thought it was right. I always tried to reciprocate—I didn't expect privileges because I was a woman, and if the majority was against me, I accepted it, even if I knew it as a man's idea . . . and wrong.

I think women often get not so much an unfair deal as an illogical one. Once in the Cabinet we had to deal with the fact that there had been an outbreak of assaults on women at night. One minister (a member of an extreme religious party) suggested a curfew. Women should stay at home after dark. I said: "But it's the men who are attacking the women. If there's to be a curfew, let the men stay at home, not the women."[23]

We end these excerpts with a joke that was well known in Israel, and Meir's comment about it.

A story—which, as far as I know, is all it was—once went the rounds of Israel to the effect that [Prime Minister David] Ben-Gurion described me as the "only man" in his cabinet. What amused me about it was that obviously he (or whoever invented the story) thought that this was the greatest possible compliment that could be paid a woman. I very much doubt that any man would have been flattered if I had said about him that he was the only woman in the government![24]

NOTES

1. The views expressed here are the personal opinions and observations of Margaret Anstee and do not represent the views of the United Nations Organization.

2. That is, assigned to a lower job grade or level than merited based on education and experience.

3. Resident Representative is a quasi-ambassadorial position that involves being accredited to a government.

4. Benazir Bhutto, *Daughter of Destiny: An Autobiography* (New York: Simon & Schuster, 1989), 42–44, 46–47.

5. PBUH means "Peace Be Upon Him," written in the original text. Ibid., 44.

6. Ibid.

7. Ibid., 67–68.

8. Ibid., 23.

9. Ibid., 124–25.

10. Ibid., 168–69.

11. Ibid., 332–33. The legendary Muslim women named here were well known to Bhutto's audience. For example, Bibi Aisha, wife of the Prophet Muhammed, led the Muslims into battle against foreign invaders.

12. See Henry Kamm, "Battle Among the Bhuttos: From Politics to Gunfire," *New York Times*, January 6, 1994, A3, and Kamm, "With Blood Ties Sundered, Blood Divides Bhuttos," *New York Times*, January 12, 1994, A4.

13. "Benazir Bhutto," interview by Claudia Dreifus, *New York Times Magazine*, May 15, 1994, 38.

14. Ibid., 39.

15. Originally published as "Why I Think More Women Are Needed at the Pinnacle of World Politics," *Glamour* 83 (September 1985): 178–79. Reprinted with permission.

16. Notably J. Kirkpatrick, *Political Woman* (New York: Basic Books, 1974); see also Jeane Kirkpatrick *The New Presidential Elite* (New York: Russell Sage, 1976).

17. Excerpts are from Golda Meir, *My Life* (New York: Putnam, 1975), except as noted. Reprinted by permission of the Putnam Publishing Group and Weidenfeld & Nicolson Limited from *My Life* by Golda Meir. Copyright © 1975 by Golda Meir.

18. Ibid., 22.

19. Ibid., 39.

20. Ibid., 60–61.

21. Ibid., 88–89.

22. Ibid., 115.

23. From an interview, reported in Marie Syrkin, ed., *Golda Meir Speaks Out* (London: Weidenfeld & Nicolson, 1973), 240.

24. Meir, *My Life*, 114.

8

Gender and the Political Beliefs of American Opinion Leaders

Ole R. Holsti and James N. Rosenau

The past half century could accurately be called the age of public opinion polling. The many surveys during the period have provided us with immense amounts of information about public attitudes, but one of the anomalies of public opinion research is that we have relatively little information about the political beliefs and attitudes of opinion leaders—the elites who hold important positions in various institutions and who are more likely than the average citizen (1) to be interested in and informed about public affairs; (2) to make their political views and policy preferences known, be it by a speech to the local service club, a letter to the editor of a newspaper, or active participation in electoral campaigns; and (3) to serve as the recruitment pool for policy-making positions.

The Foreign Policy Leadership Project (FPLP) was established in the mid-1970s with the goal of filling this gap by gaining better evidence-based insight into the foreign policy views of opinion leaders in a broad spectrum of U.S. institutions and occupations. The first survey was conducted in 1976. A sample of almost 4,000 names was drawn from such general directories as *Who's Who in America* and *Who's Who of American Women*, as well as more specialized directories of clergy, labor leaders, political leaders, State Department and Foreign Service officials, media leaders, military officers, and foreign policy experts outside government. The 1976 survey elicited responses from 2,282 leaders. That initial study has been replicated at four-year intervals. The sampling design for each survey has been the same, but the procedures for selecting the random sample mean that relatively few persons are likely to have appeared in more than a single study.[1] The proportion of women taking part in the four surveys ranged from 10 percent in

1976 to 13 percent in 1988. A similar survey was conducted in 1992, but the results were not available at the time that this chapter was completed.

Why should we be interested in political beliefs and, more especially, in exploring the possible differences in the beliefs of women and men? People act on their beliefs, and those in leadership positions are more likely to do so with significant consequences. If women's beliefs differ from those of men and if women were to carry their beliefs into positions of power or insist that policy makers respond to their beliefs, public policies themselves would be affected by gender, as might the way in which issues are framed, the way in which they are discussed, and the way in which they appear on the agenda. Of course, the process by which such beliefs affect policy, as well as the extent to which they might do so, is also affected by the broader political context. Even if one could get systematic data on the views of Saudi Arabian or Malawian women, such beliefs would have much less effect than those of women in the Scandinavian countries or the United States. All of the data presented in this chapter are drawn from U.S. citizens. Before turning to that evidence, we summarize very briefly what we know—and what is more controversial—with respect to gender and political beliefs.

Stereotypes often seem to have more lives than the proverbial cat. Decades ago, one of the pioneers of public opinion research wrote: "More women than men seem to be ignorant of or apathetic to foreign policy issues."[2] More than thirty years later, Donald Regan, President Reagan's hapless chief of the White House staff, made similar observations about women being more interested in shopping than in foreign affairs. But the ignorance-apathy thesis is not the only such stereotype. A strong and systematic correlation between gender and "warlike" or "pacifist" attitudes is often alleged but much less frequently supported with systematic evidence. Although such stereotypes may still be found even in serious literature, there are also signs that interest in the effect of gender on politics has grown substantially in recent years. One obvious reason is that more women are playing an important, if not yet equal, leadership role in politics. Margaret Thatcher was England's longest-serving twentieth-century prime minister, and women have led governments in countries as diverse as Sri Lanka, Norway, Israel, France, Pakistan, Iceland, the Philippines, Nicaragua, Yugoslavia, and India. At the same time there is a growing sense among students and observers of political behavior that much of the received wisdom, such as the stereotypes cited above, requires serious empirical examination. However, the growing interest in and literature about gender politics has not yielded a consensus. For example, differences exist on such basic questions as the following:

1. Is there a "gender gap" (strong and consistent differences in attitudes between men and women) or, more precisely, which issues give rise to such differences?[3]

2. Have gender differences increased or decreased during recent years?[4]

3. To the extent that there is a gender gap, is it the result of changing attitudes and behavior among women? Conversely, does the gender gap arise as a result, for example, of growing conservatism among men?[5]

4. When we find differences between women and men, are they the result of gender or of some other factor such as party, ideology, occupation, or age?

5. Are gender differences more pronounced among the mass public or among elites?[6]

There is, in short, a rather striking lack of consensus among those who have pondered these issues, even though most of the evidence is drawn from recent surveys in a single country: the United States.

Gender differences can arise in several domains of political behavior, including both overt actions (e.g., voting and other forms of political participation) and in values and opinions. This chapter focuses on an area that has received very limited attention—namely, the opinions held by women and men in leadership positions. An earlier analysis of data from the first survey in 1976 found that the foreign policy beliefs of women in leadership did not differ significantly from those held by men in comparable roles. Women and men differed in a few areas but similarities far outweighed the differences. A gender gap was notably absent on questions dealing with the use of force in international affairs. Moreover, when occupation was introduced into the analyses, the already limited effect of gender was further reduced. Thus, military officers, whether men or women, tended to hold similar opinions, as did educators, business executives, media leaders, and others.[7]

FPLP surveys in 1980, 1984, 1988, employing the same sampling design and many of the same questionnaire items, provide a much more substantial base for further exploring the effect of gender on opinions. The additional surveys not only increase the data base, but they also permit some assessment of trends. In this chapter, we will first compare the attitudes of men and women on a broad range of international issues and will then undertake multivariate analyses that introduce four control variables: ideology, party, occupation, and age.

BELIEFS ABOUT WORLD POLITICS

In examining individuals' beliefs about world politics, it is helpful to use two broad categories: (1) how individuals perceive world politics operating and (2) the kinds of responses they believe the United States should make in such a world. We shall start with persons' perceptions of world politics, beginning with how they think about two central problems of international relations: (1) the causes of war and (2) approaches to peace. We will then consider their opinions regarding the Soviet Union, U.S. foreign policy goals, U.S. commitments abroad, the military and the use of force, arms control, and international economic relations.

The results summarized in Table 8.1 reveal relatively stable views about

Table 8.1

Gender and Political Beliefs among American Leaders, 1984–1988: Causes of War

Survey question: How much importance do you attach to each of the following as a cause of war?	Percent of respondents selecting "very important":			
	1984		1988	
	Men	Women	Men	Women
Particular leaders (Napoleon, Hitler, Stalin, etc.)	60	66	64	61
Aggressive nations that seek to dominate others	49	65*	51	58
Nationalism	47	44	50	46
Power politics	42	58*	42	58*
Ignorance, misunderstanding and inadequate communication among peoples	36	50*	38	48
Economic rivalries among nations	37	44	38	46
Human nature (aggressive, irrational, selfish, etc.)	32	35	35	34
Ideology	28	31	34	39
An international system in which there is no central authority to settle disputes	24	26	19	25

* Gender differences significant at the .001 level.

the causes of war. In 1984, for example, 35 percent of women leaders said that human nature was a "very important" cause of war; in 1988, 34 percent held this view. The major change during the four-year period was a tendency to attribute greater potency to ideology in the 1988 survey. The evidence also indicates that men and women agree more than they diverge in their diagnoses of international conflict. Both groups are most inclined to attribute war to the policies of such aggressive leaders as Napoleon, Hitler, Stalin, and to "aggressive nations that seek to dominate others." Compared to men, women generally assign somewhat greater weight to these explanations of international conflict, as well as to "ignorance, misunderstanding, and inadequate communication among peoples." They are also significantly more inclined to locate the roots of war in "power politics."[8] Conversely, the structural explanation that lies at the heart of Realist theories of international relations—that war is inevitable in an international system lacking any central

Table 8.2
Gender and Political Beliefs among American Leaders, 1984–1988:
Approaches to World Peace

Survey question: How effective do you consider each of the following as an approach to world peace?	Percent of respondents selecting "very effective":			
	1984		1988	
	Men	Women	Men	Women
Better communication among peoples and nations	49	56	48	64*
Trade, technical cooperation, and economic interdependence	44	57*	46	52
Collective security through alliances	31	39	35	41
Military superiority of the United States	34	26	34	25*
Arms control	33	42	30	43*
Political efforts to achieve a balance of power within regions and between the superpowers	25	36*	24	32
Narrowing the gap between rich and poor nations	32	37	27	38
Strengthening the United Nations and other international organizations	19	29*	18	32*

* Gender differences significant at the .001 level

authority to settle disputes—receives little support from either men or women. Stated differently, both men and women adhere to what Kenneth Waltz has called "image 1" (bad leaders cause war) and "image 2" (aggressive nations cause war) diagnoses, while largely ignoring "image 3" (structural anarchy causes war) reasoning.[9]

Although questions about the causes of war yielded generally similar responses from women and men, the question about the effectiveness of various approaches to peace gave rise to more substantial gender differences (Table 8.2). Both men and women assigned top ranking to "better communication and understanding among peoples and nations" and to "trade, technical cooperation, and economic interdependence," but a higher proportion of women did so. Conversely, neither group expressed much confidence in the effectiveness of "military superiority of the United States," but the gender gap on this approach reached a significant 9 percent difference in the most recent survey. Indeed, in both surveys women ranked military superiority last among the various prescriptions for peace. On the other hand, women were significantly more inclined than men to ascribe effectiveness to arms control and to international organizations. Thus, although there was considerable convergence on identifying the causes of war, those similarities did not completely carry over to evaluating the effectiveness of prescriptions for dealing with the problem.

FUTURE THREATS TO AMERICAN NATIONAL SECURITY

Among the more dramatic changes in the views of opinion leaders during the 1980s were their assessments of threats to U.S. national security during the remainder of the century. Surveys by the FPLP included an item that asked respondents to select the two most potent threats from among a list of six options. A declining perception of threat from the Soviet military buildup and growing concern for domestic threats are the most striking features of responses to the 1980, 1984, and 1988 leadership surveys.

When the data are analyzed according to gender (Table 8.3), they indicate that, compared to men, women have consistently been less inclined to include an increase of Soviet military strength among the list of top threats. But a similar gap does not exist with respect to another item dealing with the USSR. Perceptions of threat arising from "Soviet expansion into Third World areas" declined only modestly during the 1980–1988 period, without any visible differences in the judgments of men and women.

A second pair of options, focusing on the United States, gave rise to considerable gender differences. Both women and men consistently judged several domestic problems to represent a major threat, but women gave them greater emphasis. The finding that concern for domestic threats has increased sharply during recent years parallels that emerging from polls of the general public, including the Americans Talk Security surveys of 1987–1988.[10] Similarly, women typically expressed greater fears about "American interventions in conflicts that are none of our business."

Finally, two future threats with a strong Third World focus—the rich nation–poor nation gap and population growth—evoked stronger concern from men than from women. Perhaps somewhat surprisingly, men were consistently more inclined to include "uncontrolled growth of the world's population" among the two most important future security threats. Whereas in 1980 the "rich nation–poor nation" gap was cited more frequently by women as a threat, the last two surveys revealed that there has been a gender reversal on this item.

Although Table 8.3 indicates that men and women differed somewhat in their appraisals of future security threats, overall gender differences are typically modest rather than dramatic except on the issue of the Soviet military build-up.[11] Moreover, the pattern of responses during the eight-year period reveals that changes in women's and men's assessments of threat generally moved in tandem.

Further insight into assessments of the Soviet Union can be derived from

Table 8.3

Gender and Political Beliefs among American Leaders, 1980–1988: Future Threats to American National Security

<u>Survey question</u>: During the remaining years of this century which <u>two</u> of the following are likely to pose the greatest threats to American national security?

Percent of respondents checking each threat:

	1980		1984		1988	
	Men [N=2,173]	Women [N=289]	Men [N=2,124]	Women [N=313]	Men [N=1,909]	Women [N=219]
an increase of Soviet military strength relative to that of the U.S.	51%	38%	38%	30%	22%	13%
a growing gap between rich nations and poor nations	25%	30%	44%	39%	49%	45%
an inability to solve such domestic problems as the decay of cities, unemployment, inflation, racial conflict, and crime	49%	54%	37%	50%	59%	66%
uncontrolled growth of the world's population	13%	10%	25%	17%	25%	17%
American interventions in conflicts that are none of our business	7%	17%	20%	30%	16%	28%
Soviet expansion into Third World areas	34%	35%	34%	33%	25%	26%
C coefficient	.10		.09		.10	

Table 8.4

Gender and Political Beliefs among American Leaders, 1984–1988: Soviet Foreign Policy

Survey question: Here are some statements about Soviet foreign policy. Please indicate how strongly you agree or disagree with each statement.

	1984		1988	
	Men	Women	Men	Women
Soviet foreign policy is essentially guided by Marxist-Leninist ideology	.06	.18	.22	.23
Soviet foreign policy goals do not differ significantly from those of all major powers	-.31	-.28	-.10	-.03
The Soviets will seek to expand only when the risks of doing so are relatively low	.43	.21*	.44	.24*
Soviet foreign policy actions often stem from genuine fears for Russian security	.34	.13*	.37	.16*
Soviet foreign policy goals are inherently expansionist and will not change until there is a fundamental transformation of the Soviet system	.33	.36	.20	.20
The Soviet Union and the U.S. share a number of foreign policy interests such as prevention of war, arms control, and stabilizing relations between them	.54	.35*	.63	.55
The Gorbachev regime in the USSR is sincerely seeking to stabilize relations with the United States	--	--	.47	.43
The Soviet invasion of Afghanistan was one step in a larger plan to control the Persian Gulf area	.22	.37*	.12	.16

Scale: Scores may range from 1.00 (all respondents "agree strongly") to -1.00 (all respondents "disagree strongly").

*Gender differences significant at the .001 level.

an item that asked respondents to assess the sources and motives of Soviet foreign policy by expressing agreement or disagreement with several propositions that have been at the core of the almost perpetual debates on the question, "What are the Russians up to now?" Responses to these items reveal a consistent, if not always significant, tendency on the part of women to hold a more suspicious view of the Soviet Union and its foreign policy (Table 8.4). They were less inclined to attribute Soviet international actions to "genuine fears for Russian security," or to view the Soviets as low risk takers, or to believe that the two superpowers share a number of important foreign policy interests, and they expressed greater skepticism about the sincerity of the Gorbachev regime's efforts to stabilize relations with the United States.

These findings concerning assessment of the Soviet Union seem to run counter to the conventional view of how men and women view adversaries, but in fact they parallel the results of recent surveys of the general public. One of the striking findings of the dozen Americans Talk Security surveys of the general public in 1987–1988 is the extent to which women, especially those over forty-years old, consistently expressed a greater degree of skepticism about virtually all aspects of Soviet domestic and foreign policy, assessments of President Gorbachev, and the significance of his reforms.

MILITANT AND COOPERATIVE INTERNATIONALISM

Several recent studies have demonstrated that the isolationist-internationalist dimension that dominated opinion analysis for several decades during and after World War II is no longer adequate for describing American public opinion. Although a consensus has yet to emerge on the precise nature and number of dimensions needed to identify the main contours of opinion on foreign affairs, there is a growing body of systematic evidence that attitudes toward *militant internationalism* (MI) and *cooperative internationalism* (CI) are necessary for describing the foreign policy orientations of the American public and leaders. Militant internationalism focuses upon strategic/military issues and the threats arising from the goals of adversaries in an anarchic international system; in contrast, cooperative internationalism emphasizes the possibilities for and potential shared gains from cooperation among nations and other important global actors, not only on security but also on a much broader range of issues. Crossing these two dimensions yields four types: *isolationists* (who oppose both militant and cooperative internationalism), *internationalists* (who support both forms of internationalism), *hard-liners* (who support militant internationalism and oppose cooperative internationalism), and *accommodationists* (who support cooperative internationalism and oppose militant internationalism).[12]

Table 8.5 reveals the distribution of men and women within the four quadrants of the MI/CI scheme in each of the FPLP surveys. The results reveal moderate gender-based differences in the 1976 survey, with a trend toward convergence between women and men in 1980 and 1984; in none of the four groups did differences between men and women exceed 2 percent in 1984. However, that trend was broken in 1988. Although the distribution of men across the four categories was a virtual carbon copy of that of four years earlier, the proportion of women classified as accommodationists increased by 8 percent. It would be overstating the results summarized in Table 8.5 to conclude that a substantial gender gap has developed, because such large proportions of both men and women are classified as accommodation-

Table 8.5

Gender and Political Beliefs among American Leaders, 1976–1988: Hard-Liners, Internationalists, Isolationists, and Accommodationists

			COOPERATIVE INTERNATIONALISM					
			Oppose			Support		
			HARD-LINERS			INTERNATIONALISTS		
			Men	Women			Men	Women
I			1976	21%	12%	1976	31%	25%
N			1980	20%	15%	1980	33%	36%
T	Support		1984	17%	15%	1984	25%	27%
E			1988	17%	12%	1988	25%	21%
M R								
I N								
L A								
I T								
T I			ISOLATIONISTS			ACCOMMODATIONISTS		
A O								
N N			Men	Women			Men	Women
T A			1976	8%	6%	1976	40%	57%
L			1980	7%	3%	1980	40%	45%
I S	Oppose		1984	7%	6%	1984	51%	53%
M			1988	8%	5%	1988	50%	61%

Correlations [C coefficient] between gender and foreign policy attitudes were: .11 for 1976, .06 for 1980, .03 for 1984, and .08 for 1988.

ists, but to the extent that a gender-based difference may be emerging, it is clearly the result of shifting attitudes among women rather than men.

We can gain further insight into these results by examining responses to the fourteen questionnaire items that were used to construct the militant internationalism and cooperative internationalism scales. The seven items on the MI scale focus on a cold war view of the international system (the domino theory, a zero-sum view of the world), Soviet expansionism, and how best to respond to the threat (Table 8.6). On balance, between 1976 and 1988 both men and women have shown a decreasing inclination to agree to the seven militant internationalism propositions, but consistently significant gender differences have emerged on only a single item; except in 1984, women have been notably more opposed to the proposition that "there is nothing wrong with using the C.I.A. to try to undermine hostile governments." However, by 1988 women were also less supportive of the other six items on the MI scale, although none of the differences was statistically significant.

Table 8.7 summarizes responses to the seven questions that define the cooperative internationalism scale. These items emphasize the role of international organizations, arms control, efforts to deal with critical Third World

Table 8.6
The Militant Internationalism Scale: Responses by Gender in the 1976, 1980, 1984, and 1988 Foreign Policy Leadership Surveys

	Scale	1976		1980		1984		1988	
		Men	Women	Men	Women	Men	Women	Men	Women
There is considerable validity in the "domino theory" that when one nation falls to communism, others nearby will soon follow a similar path	a	.25	.15	.17	.14	.04	.02	-.10	-.12
Any communist victory is a defeat for America's national interest	a	-.13	-.13	-.06	-.03	-.17	-.12	-.10	-.18
The Soviet Union is generally expansionist rather than defensive in its foreign policy goals	a	.59	.46	.62	.50	.47	.47	.36	.33
There is nothing wrong with using C.I.A. to try to undermine hostile governments	a	.02	-.37*	.11	-.13*	-.12	-.23	.05	-.17*
The U.S. should take all steps including the use of force to undermine the spread of communism	a	-.27	-.41	-.22	-.26	-.29	-.30	-.22	-.33
Containing communism [as an important foreign policy goal]	b	.29	.13	.32	.23	.26	.27	.23	.13
It is not in our interest to have better relations with the Soviet Union because we are getting less than we are giving to them	a	-.32	-.36	-.36	-.34	-.66	-.62	-.72	-.75
AVERAGE		.06	-.08	.08	.02	-.07	-.07	-.07	-.16

a Scores may range from 1.00 (all respondents "agree strongly") to -1.00 (all respondents "disagree strongly").

b Scores may range from 1.00 (all respondents rate as "very important") to -1.00 (all respondents rate as "not important at all").

* Gender differences significant at .001 level.

Table 8.7
The Cooperative Internationalism Scale: Responses by Gender in the 1976, 1980, 1984, and 1988 Foreign Policy Leadership Surveys

	Scale	1976		1980		1984		1988	
		Men	Women	Men	Women	Men	Women	Men	Women
It is vital to enlist cooperation of the U.N. in settling international disputes	a	.18	.40	.28	.45*	.13	.32*	.13	.39*
The U.S. should give economic aid to poorer countries even if it means higher prices at home	a	-.04	-.11	.02	-.12*	.19	.01*	.12	-.01
Helping to improve the standard of living in less developed countries [as an important foreign policy goal]	b	.30	.31	.36	.38	.57	.53	.48	.41
Worldwide arms control [as an important foreign policy goal]	b	.62	.76*	.47	.58	.66	.72	.64	.67
Combatting world hunger [as an important foreign policy goal]	b	.44	.50	.45	.51	.51	.57	.51	.61
Strengthening the United Nations [as an important foreign policy goal]	b	-.09	.18*	.03	.29*	-.12	.13*	-.06	.19*
Fostering international cooperation to solve common problems, such as food, inflation, and energy [as an important foreign policy goal]	b	.68	.77	.70	.79	.62	.70	.67	.74
AVERAGE		.30	.40	.33	.42	.37	.43	.36	.43

a   Scores may range from 1.00 (all respondents "agree strongly") to -1.00 (all respondents "disagree strongly").

b   Scores may range from 1.00 (all respondents rate as "very important") to -1.00 (all respondents rate as "not important at all").

*   Gender differences significant at .001 level.

problems, and international cooperation on economic issues. Women have consistently scored somewhat higher on the CI scale, but that gap arises almost wholly from more supportive responses by women to the two items that focus on the United Nations. In all four surveys, women have expressed significantly greater agreement for employing the UN to settle international disputes, and they have ascribed greater importance to the goal of strengthening that international organization. On the other hand, the proposition that "the U.S. should give economic aid to poorer countries even if it means higher prices at home" has never generated much enthusiasm among women. The two most recent surveys revealed that men have also been somewhat more inclined to regard "helping to improve the standard of living in less developed countries" as an important foreign policy goal.

BELIEFS ABOUT AMERICAN FOREIGN POLICY

Since 1974 the Chicago Council on Foreign Relations (CCFR) surveys have asked respondents to assess the importance of several foreign policy goals for the United States. That cluster of questions has also appeared in each of the FPLP surveys although, as has been the case with the CCFR surveys, some of the specific goals have changed from survey to survey. Several striking patterns emerge from the results summarized in Table 8.8. Although the 1976–1988 period witnessed dramatic changes, most notably in the tenor of relations between the superpowers, the assessment of many goals has not varied greatly. For example, the period in question encompassed the erosion of détente, a resumption of cold war hostilities, and the flurry of Reagan–Gorbachev summit meetings during the late 1980s, but the importance ascribed to the goal of containment remained relatively stable. The data reveal some gender-based differences on goals, notably with respect to the United Nations, protecting the jobs of American workers, promoting human rights abroad, extended deterrence, and protecting the global environment, although by 1988 the gender gap regarding the protection of the environment had narrowed to a point where it was no longer statistically significant. However, these differences are less striking than the level of agreement in assessing the most important goals for American foreign policy. For example, responses to the most recent survey indicate that both men and women judge international cooperation on economic issues, environmental protection, and energy security as the three most important goals. Moreover, there is also agreement that the next three most important goals are arms control, combatting hunger, and redressing the trade imbalance. Among the entire set of goals in Table 8.8, there were fewer significant gender differences in 1988 (four) than had been the case twelve years earlier (six).

When asked to assess the importance of "defending our allies' security," that is, U.S. commitments abroad, women consistently ascribed less importance to that foreign policy goal than did their male counterparts (Table 8.8).

Table 8.8
Gender and Political Beliefs among American Leaders, 1976–1988: Foreign Policy Goals

Survey question: Please indicate how much importance should be attached to each goal:	1976 Men	1976 Women	1980 Men	1980 Women	1984 Men	1984 Women	1988 Men	1988 Women
Containing communism	.29	.13	.32	.23	.26	.27	.23	.13
Matching Soviet military power	--	--	--	--	.28	.18	.21	.09
Helping to improve the standard of living in less developed countries	.30	.31	.36	.38	.57	.53	.48	.41
Keeping peace in the world	.69	.80	.73	.80	--	--	--	--
Worldwide arms control	.62	.76*	.46	.58	.66	.72	.64	.67
Defending our allies' securities	.35	.20*	.44	.25*	.46	.37	.50	.38*
Promoting and defending our own security	.86	.71*	.89	.87	.83	.84	--	--
Promoting the development of capitalism abroad	-.50	-.57	-.35	-.39	--	--	--	--
Securing adequate supplies of energy	.70	.76	.76	.75	.84	.88	.75	.70
Helping to bring a democratic form of government to other nations	-.35	-.32	-.24	-.27	-.02	-.02	.13	.06
Protecting the interests of American business abroad	-.10	-.25	.00	.00	.06	.16	--	--
Maintaining a balance of power among nations	.38	.30	.51	.50	.35	.39	--	--
Combatting world hunger	.44	.50	.45	.51	.51	.57	.51	.61
Strengthening the United Nations	-.09	.18*	.03	.29*	-.12	.13*	-.06	.19*
Strengthening countries who are friendly toward us	.16	.01*	.34	.23	--	--	--	--

Fostering international cooperation to solve common problems, such as food, inflation, and energy	.68	.77	.70	.79	.62	.70	.67	.74
Worldwide population control	--	--	.33	.30	.45	.44	.45	.46
Promoting and defending human rights in other countries	--	--	.02	.16	.19	.30	.29	.45*
Protecting the global environment	--	--	.37	.53*	.46	.61*	.66	.72
Averting financial crises arising from Third World debts	--	--	--	--	.37	.43	.41	.44
Reducing the U.S. trade deficit with other countries	--	--	--	--	--	--	.61	.59

Scale: Scores may range from 1.00 (all respondents rate as "very important") to -1.00 (all respondents rate as "not important at all").

* Gender differences significant at the .001 level.

Evidence about security pledges to specific nations abroad confirms the existence of a consistent gender gap. Compared to men, women are generally less enthusiastic about American commitments abroad, and their support for many such undertakings has tended to decline during the twelve-year period covered by the four FPLP surveys. Agreement with American pledges to protect the security of Israel and South Korea has remained high; however, although such support has stayed virtually unchanged among men, there has been a marked erosion of support among women for these commitments. In the case of Israel, the explanation is probably not to be found in opposition to Tel Aviv's policy on the Palestinian issue; both men and women support a homeland for the Palestinians, but the former exceed the latter in this respect by a margin of 78 percent to 69 percent. Men also expressed greater support for a U.S. obligation to protect the security of Taiwan. The proposition that the United States should withdraw its troops from Europe is the only exception to this pattern of significant gender differences on American commitments to extended deterrence; this proposition received little support from either men or women.

Among the most consistent findings on the attitudes of the mass public on the military and the use of force in pursuing foreign policy goals is that women are more skeptical of the military and more opposed to the use of force in international affairs. An earlier analysis of the 1976 FPLP survey data found limited evidence of this tendency at the level of opinion leaders, especially after occupation had been introduced into the analysis.[13]

Data on seven items that appeared in all four of the FPLP surveys yield some evidence of gender-based differences, but not on all aspects of military power and force (Table 8.9). The strongest and most consistent evidence that women take a dimmer view of the use of force emerges from three questions on the adverse consequences of military aid programs, the proper role of military advice in the conduct of foreign affairs, and the efficacy of graduated escalation in interventions abroad. Support for the military was consistently and significantly lower among women, especially on the first two of these items. On the other hand, relatively limited gender-related differences can be detected in responses to questions about stationing American troops abroad—a type of international undertaking that is judged with considerable jaundice by majorities among both men and women—the proper balance of military and political considerations in decisions to use force, the efficiency of military power, and the proposition that when force is used, "it is necessary to strike at the heart of the opponent's power." The data thus yield some support for the thesis of a gender gap on the uses of force, but, except for the question on military-aid programs, it is not consistently of a significant magnitude.

The 1976 FPLP survey revealed that while substantial majorities of both women and men rated arms control as a "very important" foreign policy goal for the United States, by a margin of 12 percent women ascribed even greater

Table 8.9

Gender and Political Beliefs among American Leaders, 1976–1988: Military Power and the Use of Force

Survey question: Please indicate how strongly you agree or disagree with each statement:	1976 Men	1976 Women	1980 Men	1980 Women	1984 Men	1984 Women	1988 Men	1988 Women
Military aid programs will eventually draw the United States into unnecessary wars	-.15	.20*	-.31	-.02	-.17	.17*	-.21	.15*
The conduct of American foreign affairs relies excessively on military advice	-.01	.22*	-.14	.06*	.09	.29*	.12	.26
Stationing American troops abroad encourages other countries to let us do their fighting for them	.13	.28	.06	.08	.17	.21	.22	.20
Rather than simply countering our opponent's thrusts, it is necessary to strike at the heart of the opponent's power	.02	-.09	-.02	.14	-.18	-.05	-.09	-.13
The efficiency of military power in foreign affairs is declining	.17	.17	.17	.31*	.17	.27	.17	.25
When force is used, military rather than political goals should determine its application	-.20	-.27	-.29	-.17	-.30	-.22	-.33	-.33
If foreign interventions are undertaken, the necessary force should be applied in a short period of time rather than through a policy of graduated escalation	.56	.47	.59	.47*	.53	.45	.52	.35*

Scale: Scores may range from 1.00 (all respondents "agree strongly") to -1.00 (all respondents "disagree strongly").

* Gender differences significant at the .001 level.

significance to it than men. By 1988, however, that gender difference had disappeared, as approximately two-thirds of both men and women gave the top importance rating to arms control (Table 8.8).

The 1988 survey also included a cluster of items concerning the Intermediate-range Nuclear Forces (INF) Treaty, the most far-reaching and only disarmament agreement up to that time between the two superpowers. Strong majorities among both men (84%) and women (82%) agreed that the treaty established a good precedent for negotiations on reducing strategic nuclear forces. However, men expressed significantly stronger support for two key propositions relating to the treaty: The agreement is in the interests of the West because it requires the Soviets to scrap more weapons than the West, and it should be ratified without amendments by the Senate—the treaty was in fact ratified with only five negative votes shortly after the 1988 FPLP survey. The margins on the issues were 10 percent and 17 percent respectively. Men also disagreed significantly more strongly than women that the agreement works to the detriment of NATO because it leaves the Warsaw Pact forces with conventional superiority. Perhaps a partial explanation for this pattern of responses may be found in predictions of likely Soviet actions in connection with the INF agreement; women (58%) were slightly more inclined than men (55%) to believe that "although the INF Treaty includes stringent verification procedures, the Soviets are likely to violate it." On one point there was absolutely no difference. Only 22 percent of women and men wished to award the Nobel Peace Prize to Presidents Reagan and Gorbachev for the INF Treaty.

These findings suggest at least two possible explanations for gender differences in evaluating the INF Treaty. First, although women are no less supportive of arms control in general (Table 8.8), their somewhat more negative assessment of the USSR (Table 8.4) constrained their enthusiasm for this specific arms control treaty. An alternative explanation focuses on partisanship. Among women in the 1988 FPLP sample, Democrats outnumbered Republicans by a margin of 19 percent, whereas the comparable figure for men was only 5 percent. The INF Treaty was closely associated with a stridently Republican president and, further, a president who had been a vocal critic of arms control until his second term in the White House.

Evidence presented earlier indicates that, compared to men, women were somewhat more likely to regard economic rivalries as an important cause of war (Table 8.1) and that they were also significantly more inclined to believe in the effectiveness of "trade, technical cooperation, and economic interdependence" as an approach to world peace (Table 8.2). These differences notwithstanding, international economic relations clearly ranked among the more important causes of war and approaches to peace among both men and women. Moreover, in 1988 well over 60 percent of men and women rated "reducing the U.S. trade deficit with foreign countries" as a "very important" foreign policy goal (Table 8.8).

Against this background, one might assume that women who participated in the FPLP leadership surveys would express stronger support for free trade and be more critical of the protectionist sentiments that have grown dramatically among the general public during recent decades. However, that expectation is not supported by the evidence. Offered a series of options on how to deal with the chronic U.S. trade deficit, the proportion of women (16%) supporting the use of tariffs and quotas to restrict imports was double that of men (8%), and a proposal to "reduce tariffs, quotas and other barriers to free trade among all nations" received considerably greater support from men than from women, by a margin of 37 percent to 24 percent. Responses to two other items provide further corroboration of a consistent pattern on trade policy. More women than men described "protecting the jobs of American workers" as a "very important" foreign policy goal (Table 8.8); and support for President Reagan's threat to veto a protectionist trade bill, should it be passed by the Congress, won greater approval from men by a margin of 20 percent (Table 8.11 below). Finally, compared to men, significantly fewer women expressed disapproval of "erecting trade barriers against foreign goods to protect American industries and jobs."

It should be noted that none of these items evoked a protectionist response from a majority of women leaders. Nevertheless, differences between men and women are of a magnitude and consistency that clearly point to trade as an issue on which there exists a genuine gender gap.

FOREIGN POLICIES OF THE REAGAN ADMINISTRATION, 1984 AND 1988

The 1984 FPLP survey included a cluster of items assessing fifteen foreign and defense policy actions undertaken during the first Reagan administration. A consistent pattern of gender-based differences emerges from the data in Table 8.10, as men expressed greater approval on thirteen policies; moreover, differences were of a sufficient magnitude to be statistically significant on over half of them.

Several further patterns may also be discerned. Women were consistently less inclined to favor U.S. military undertakings abroad, whether in El Salvador, Nicaragua, or Grenada, or the introduction of medium-range missiles in Europe. On the other hand, women expressed greater approval for the use of economic sanctions against South Africa, the Soviet Union, and Poland. Indeed, the economic sanctions against the Soviet Union and Poland by the Reagan administration were the only actions that elicited stronger agreement from women than men. Greater opposition among women to withdrawal from UNESCO is consistent with other findings, noted at several earlier points, that they are more inclined than men to view the United Nations favorably. Finally, the several arms control items in Table 8.10 yielded mixed responses; while taking a pro–arms control stance on two

Table 8.10

Gender and Political Beliefs among American Leaders, 1984: U.S. Actions

<u>Survey question</u>: Please indicate how strongly you agree or disagree with these recent U.S. foreign policies:

	<u>Men</u>	<u>Women</u>
Deploying new American missiles in Western Europe	.19	.03
Sending U.S. military advisors to El Salvador	-.03	-.26*
Supporting rebels fighting the Sandinista government in Nicaragua	-.15	-.36*
Preventing American firms from selling non-strategic equipment to the Soviet Union	-.07	.01
Sending American forces into Grenada	.25	-.06*
Supporting Great Britain after the invasion of the Falkland Islands by Argentina	.55	.37*
Continuing arms control negotiations after the Soviets shot down the Korean civilian airliner	.59	.49
Increasing U.S. contributions to the International Monetary Fund in the hope of averting a debt default by Third World nations	.28	.22
Opposing a "nuclear freeze"	-.08	-.31*
Giving higher priority to a defense buildup than to arms control	-.21	-.33
Placing sanctions on Poland after the imposition of martial law	.12	.17
Restoring grain sales to the Soviet Union	.33	.13*
Failing to impose economic sanctions on South Africa for its policy of apartheid	-.05	-.23*
Preventing the media from covering the landing operation in Grenada	-.07	-.20
Withdrawing from UNESCO	.18	.00*

Scale: Scores may range from 1.00 (all respondents "agree strongly") to -1.00 (all respondents "disagree strongly").

* Gender differences significant at the .001 level.

items, women were also more critical of the Reagan decision to continue arms negotiations with the Soviets in the wake of the downing of the Korean airliner.

A similar cluster of items asked opinion leaders who participated in the 1988 survey to evaluate actions undertaken by the Reagan administration during the previous four years. Once again the data indicate that women were consistently, and often significantly, less inclined to support these actions (Table 8.11). Only the imposition of sanctions on South Africa—an action undertaken as a result of veto-proof congressional votes, despite,

Table 8.11
Gender and Political Beliefs among American Leaders, 1988: U.S. Actions

Survey question: Please indicate how strongly you agree or disagree with these recent U.S. foreign policies:

	Men	Women
Selling arms to Iran in the hope of freeing American hostages	-.78	-.73
Sending U.S. military advisors to El Salvador	.05	-.32*
Supporting rebels fighting the Sandinista government in Nicaragua	-.07	-.35*
Preventing American firms from selling non-strategic equipment to the Soviet Union	-.10	-.14
Increasing U.S. contributions to the International Monetary Fund in the hope of averting a debt default by Third World nations	.17	.16
Giving high priority to a defense buildup	-.14	-.32*
Signing an agreement with the USSR to eliminate both American and Soviet intermediate range missiles	.69	.65
Imposing economic sanctions on South Africa for its policy of apartheid	.18	.42*
Supporting the "contra" rebels in Nicaragua with funds gained from the sale of arms to Iran	-.66	-.69
Helping to replace the Marcos government in the Philippines with that of Corazon Aquino	.67	.50*
Refusing to invoke the War Powers Act after American naval forces were deployed in the Persian Gulf	.08	.00
Insisting that the Strategic Defense Initiative ("Star Wars") program cannot be included in arms control negotiations with the USSR	.00	-.10
Aiding anti-communist rebels in Angola	.06	-.19*
Threatening to veto a protectionist trade bill if it is passed by the Congress	.52	.27*
Bombing Libya in the spring of 1986	.20	-.07*
Selling arms to Saudi Arabia	.28	-.15*

Scale: Scores may range from 1.00 (all respondents "agree strongly") to -1.00 (all respondents "disagree strongly").

*Gender differences significant at the .001 level.

rather than with, the approval of the administration—gained significantly greater approbation among women. Women were also slightly less outraged by the covert arms sales to Iran. Each of the other fourteen actions garnered stronger support among men. That was especially true of U.S. military interventions and other types of undertakings abroad, including those in El Salvador, Nicaragua, Libya, Angola, and Saudi Arabia. Even U.S. pressure to replace the corrupt Marcos regime in the Philippines with that of Corazon Aquino received significantly greater support from men. As in 1984, questions with arms-control implications yielded a mixed pattern. The policy of barring the Strategic Defense Initiative from negotiations received somewhat less support from women, whereas men were significantly stronger supporters of the INF Treaty. The latter finding confirms the gender differences summarized earlier.

Because all of the policies that appeared in Tables 8.10 and 8.11 are associated with a single administration, the possibility that gender gaps are in fact rooted in partisan differences arises again, especially with respect to the military interventions abroad. In stating disagreement with these actions, are women exhibiting a gender-based opposition to the use of force, or are they expressing party-based disapproval of actions undertaken by a highly partisan Republican president? The answer can only be supplied by multivariate analyses, undertaken below, that incorporate party as well as gender.

THE EFFECT OF GENDER COMPARED TO OTHER BACKGROUND ATTRIBUTES

The foregoing analyses confirm the existence of modest gender differences among opinion leaders, but they also leave unanswered a number of questions that arise from the fact that women and men in the FPLP samples differed on a number of background attributes.

- Compared to men, women are consistently more inclined to identify themselves as Democrats. In 1988, the margin was 9 percent (46%–37%).

- Women are consistently somewhat more liberal than men, with differences among those identifying themselves as liberal to some degree ranging between 6 percent and 16 percent during the 1976–1988 period.

- Leadership positions in several occupations are clearly linked to gender. There are relatively few women among the military, clergy, and, until 1988, labor leaders. Conversely, the proportion of women among media leaders, public officials, and health care providers has tended to exceed that of men.

- Age differences between men and women in the four FPLP surveys are very substantial. Women are clearly and consistently younger than their male counterparts.

- By any standard, the level of education among both men and women in the FPLP samples was exceptionally high in 1976, and it has increased in each of the subsequent surveys. By 1988, 56 percent of the women and 75 percent of the men had earned some type of graduate degree.

These differences give rise to two questions. First, how does the effect of gender compare with that of other respondent attributes for which data from the leadership surveys are available: ideology (liberal-conservative), party, occupation, and age?[14] For instance, does one's party identification as a Republican or a Democrat influence one's political beliefs perhaps even more than gender seems to do? Second, can we tell if gender differences are really involved? Questions were raised earlier about whether women's less enthusiastic responses to some issues—for example, some foreign policy undertakings of the Reagan administration (Tables 8.10 and 8.11) or the INF Treaty—reflected gender-based differences or whether they were the result of women's identifying more with the Democratic party than the men did. More generally, how do multivariate analyses affect the results reported in Tables 8.10 and 8.11?

A technique called one-way analysis of variance provides one way to assess how important a factor is. Such an analysis was applied to all questions on the 1988 questionnaire, excluding only a small number of items for which this method is inappropriate. The results reveal that significant gender differences emerge on fewer than 30 percent of the 169 questions. The comparable figures for ideology (92%), party (83%), and occupation (86%) clearly indicate that these are the dominant background correlates of political beliefs. These aggregate results not only support findings of earlier FPLP surveys, but they also confirm more general analyses of American foreign policy that point to ideology and partisanship as the dominant lines of foreign policy cleavages in post-Vietnam America.[15] In contrast, although the terms "gender gap" and "generation gap" are well established in the American political lexicon, they appear to be much less potent factors in defining contemporary political fault lines. Nevertheless, the evidence cited earlier does suggest that on some kinds of issues there are systematic gender differences. It remains to be seen to what extent those differences are sustained, magnified, or eroded when gender is paired with other background attributes in multivariate analyses.

What happens when we pair gender with each of these other four background attributes? Does gender remain important or is its connection to political beliefs spurious? Two-way analysis of variance allows us to examine these questions. For example, each of the FPLP surveys includes a seven-point ideology scale on which respondents were asked to place themselves: "far left," "very liberal," "somewhat liberal," "moderate," "somewhat conservative," "very conservative," "far right." Because there were very few who identified themselves as "far left" or "far right," their responses were combined with the "very liberal" and "very conservative" groups. Two-way analyses of variance then compared mean scores for each of ten groups (men

Table 8.12
The Effect of Gender on Leadership Survey Responses, 1988, Controlling for Ideology, Party, Occupation, and Age (comparison of mean scores by two-way analysis of variance)

	Questions with significant differences:	
Paired background variables:	Number*	Percent (%)
Gender & ideology		
Gender	44	26.0
Ideology	152	90.0
Gender & party		
Gender	47	27.8
Party	142	84.0
Gender & occupation		
Gender	49	29.0
Occupation	147	87.0
Gender & age		
Gender	59	34.9
Generation	55	32.5

* This analysis is based on 169 items in the 1988 leadership survey. This total includes all questionnaire items, not only those reported in Tables 8.1 to 8.11. The first column reports the number of questions for which differences in mean scores were significant, and the second column reports the percentage (N divided by 169).

in the five ideological categories and women in those five) for the full set of 169 questions.

The results reported in Table 8.12 largely confirm rather than overturn those of previous analyses. Ideology tends to eclipse gender as a source of differences in responses to most questions. However, ideology fails to undermine systematically the effect of gender on questions that evoked gender-based differences, including such questions as the INF Treaty, the United Nations, China's foreign policy motivations, the role of genuine security fears in Soviet foreign policy, shared interests between the superpowers, support for the Contras in Nicaragua, and South African sanctions. In each case, significant ideological cleavages also appeared, but they did not erase gender differences. Moreover, wide differences between men and women on trade protectionism not only survived multivariate analysis, but were also found to be independent of ideology and other background attributes as well.

Results of similar two-way analyses of variance reveal that the effect of party generally overshadows that of gender. Earlier analyses uncovered significant gender differences on such questions as interventions abroad, arms control and the INF Treaty, assessments of adversaries, and the like. Almost without exception these differences survived multivariate analyses that controlled for party membership. For example, the pattern of responses on sixteen foreign policy undertakings of the Reagan administration was unchanged in any respect by the introduction of party into the analysis. As in Table 8.11, significant gender differences appeared on the same nine policies even though partisan cleavages, as well as ideological ones, emerged on all sixteen items. The gender gaps that emerged on the three questions relating to the INF Treaty were also replicated in the gender-party analyses.

Earlier explorations of the 1976 FPLP survey data revealed that occupational differences generally dominated those based on gender in explaining responses to a broad range of questions on foreign affairs. The same tendency persisted in the 1988 data. Occupation ranks alongside ideology and party as primary correlates of political beliefs.

Opinion leaders taking part in FPLP surveys were classified into four generational groups defined by three major twentieth-century American wars: World War II generation (born before 1924), Korean War generation (born 1924–1932), interim generation (born 1933–1940), and Vietnam generation (born since 1940). Analyses of earlier FPLP surveys failed to confirm hypotheses of strong generational differences.[16] Nevertheless, there are also some reasons for further exploration of generation in conjunction with gender. First, as noted earlier, age differences between men and women in the 1988 sample of opinion leaders are quite substantial. Second, evidence from some surveys of the general public, including the 1987–1988 Americans Talk Security studies, indicate the existence of generational differences among women on such questions as assessments of the Soviet Union and the importance of changes undertaken there during the Gorbachev era. While women were generally more skeptical and wary of the Soviet Union, this was especially true of older women. Two-way analyses of variance involving gender and age generally confirm the results reported earlier. They also reveal that on questions relating to the Soviet Union and China, age differences were generally more pronounced among women than men.

CONCLUSION

The multivariate analyses of survey responses generally confirmed the findings reported in earlier sections of this chapter. Although gender does not rival ideology, partisanship, or occupation as an explanation for foreign policy beliefs, neither does it disappear once these other attributes are introduced into the analysis. The term *gender gap* is insufficiently precise, however, unless it is further identified with specific issues. Several patterns emerge from the present data.

First, although the results are not reported in Tables 8.1 to 8.11, responses to most environmental issues gave rise to a gender gap, with women expressing a greater degree of concern for the environment. Given the plethora of evidence from surveys of the general public that environmental issues are competing with drug trafficking at the top of the nation's current security concerns, as well as the increasing significance of the environment as a world politics issue, this is a far from trivial finding. To the extent that there is some narrowing of the gender gap in this respect, it is important to reiterate that this trend is largely due to men's catching up with women in environmental sensitivity, rather than a declining interest among women. At least on this cluster of issues, the results run counter to the hypothesis that the gender gap arises from men's having moved toward more conservative positions during the 1980s. The issue of nuclear power actually gave rise to a widening gender gap, with opposition growing faster among women. The prospect of materially high prices for oil and gas, increasing dependence on foreign oil, and environmental problems that arise from burning coal suggest that nuclear power will be one of the more contentious issues of the next several decades.

Second, opinion leaders are less protectionist than the general public regarding trade, but women are consistently more inclined toward efforts to protect jobs and industries by imposing trade barriers. Trade policy stands out as one of the few issues on which there are neither partisan nor ideological differences among opinion leaders; and, thus, the consistently strong gender gap on this issue stands out rather sharply.

Third, on issues that involve the possibility of projecting U.S. power abroad, women are generally less likely to support the use of military force, but they are also more inclined toward the use of economic sanctions. However, the evidence also suggests that the gender gap arises less from a general aversion to the use of force (Table 8.9) and more from a greater skepticism among women about American foreign commitments and interventions (Tables 8.10 and 8.11) that might entangle the United States in undertakings abroad.

Fourth, hypotheses about a greater sensitivity among women to "compassion issues" such as world hunger receives some support from the FPLP data, but that was more consistently true on domestic issues than on those involving foreign assistance.

Fifth, the initial finding that women are somewhat more wary of America's cold war adversaries survived even when the data were subject to multivariate analyses. Moreover, the most recent survey, which was undertaken three years after Gorbachev assumed leadership of the Soviet Union, actually found some evidence of growing rather than declining gender differences with respect to the USSR. This greater wariness among women carried over into responses to specific issues such as the INF Treaty.

Finally, are there some higher-level generalizations that may be drawn from the data under scrutiny here? A thread that seems to run through many of the observed gender differences is a greater aversion among women to foreign entanglements that includes, but is not limited to, military interventions abroad. Consider some of the evidence that supports this hypothesis.

- Women were less inclined to accept American responsibility for the defense of allies (Table 8.8) or to support commitments to specific nations.

- Women showed a greater opposition not only to military intervention in Central

America and elsewhere, but also toward involvement in the replacement of the Marcos regime with that of Corazon Aquino (Tables 8.10 and 8.11).

• Women consistently showed greater support for the United Nations (Tables 8.7 and 8.8). At first glance this would appear to be an expression of internationalism. However, could it be that at least some respondents regard the United Nations as a *substitute* for an active American involvement in crises and conflicts abroad? That is, if the UN deals with a crisis, for example, by sending in peacekeeping forces, it will reduce the likelihood that the United States will become actively involved. Unfortunately none of the four FPLP surveys includes questions that will permit this speculative interpretation of support for the United Nations to be tested.

• Women expressed less support for both military aid (Table 8.9) and economic-assistance programs abroad (Table 8.7).

• Women were more inclined to support imposition of economic sanctions (Tables 8.10 and 8.11). Because economic sanctions reduce or eliminate trade, aid, and related interactions with the target country, choice of that policy instrument can also be viewed as one of withdrawal from foreign entanglements.

• There is considerable evidence of greater support for protectionist economic policies among women (Tables 8.8 and 8.11).

Among the more obvious objections to this line of reasoning is that Table 8.5 gave no evidence of disproportionate isolationism among women in any of the four FPLP surveys. However, the speculative interpretation offered here not only goes beyond the questions used to construct Table 8.5—the fourteen items that defined "militant internationalism" and "cooperative internationalism" (Tables 8.6 and 8.7)—but it also suggests a somewhat different way of interpreting strong support for the United Nations. This type of post hoc explanation hardly qualifies as theory testing, but it offers some leads for further exploration.

NOTES

This research was supported by National Science Foundation Grant No. NSF-SES-87-22646. We are grateful to Ralph Carter and Jean O'Barr and the editors of this volume for thoughtful comments and suggestions on earlier drafts of this chapter, to Daniel Harkins for programming and many other kinds of assistance, and to Alice Dorman and Rita Dowling for secretarial assistance.

1. For further information on methods used in these surveys, see Ole R. Holsti and James N. Rosenau, *American Leadership in World Affairs: Vietnam and the Breakdown of Consensus* (London: Allyn & Unwin, 1984). The 1980, 1984, and 1988 surveys yielded completed questionnaires from 2,502, 2,515, and 2,226 opinion leaders, respectively.

2. Gabriel Almond, *The American People and Foreign Policy* (New York: Harcourt, Brace, 1950), 121.

3. Much of the research on gender differences has focused on militarism and the uses of force, as well as compassion issues. For a sampling of the relevant evidence

and alternative interpretations, see Sandra Baxter and Marjorie Lansing, *Women and Politics: The Invisible Majority* (Ann Arbor: University of Michigan Press, 1980); Tom W. Smith, "The Polls: Gender and Attitudes Toward Violence," *Public Opinion Quarterly* 48:1B (Spring 1984): 384–96; Robert Y. Shapiro and Harpeet Mahajan, "Gender Differences in Policy Preferences," *Public Opinion Quarterly* 50:1 (Spring 1986): 42–61; Susan Welch and Sue Thomas, "Explaining the Gender Gap in British Public Opinion," *Women & Politics* 8:3–4 (1988): 25–44; Pamela Johnston Conover, "Feminists and the Gender Gap," *Journal of Politics* 50:4 (November 1988): 985–1010; Ofer Zur and Andrea Morrison, "Gender and War: Reexamining Attitudes," *American Journal of Orthopsychiatry* 59:4 (October 1989): 528–33; Ronald B. Rapaport, Walter J. Stone, and Alan I. Abramowitz, "Sex and the Caucus Participant: The Gender Gap and Presidential Nominations," *American Journal of Political Science* 34:3 (August 1990): 725–40; David Fite, Marc Genest, and Clyde Wilcox, "Gender Differences in Foreign Policy Attitudes: A Longitudinal Analysis," *American Politics Quarterly* 18:4 (October 1990): 492–513; Elizabeth Adell Cook and Clyde Wilcox, "Feminism and the Gender Gap: A Second Look," *Journal of Politics* 53:4 (November 1991): 1111–1122; and Nancy Gallagher, "The Gender Gap in Popular Attitudes toward the Use of Force," in Ruth Howes and Michael Stevenson, eds., *Women and the Use of Force* (Boulder, CO: Rienner, 1992).

4. For evidence of a widening gap, see Baxter and Lansing *Women and Politics*; Shapiro and Mahajan, "Gender Differences"; and Ethel Klein, *Gender Politics* (Cambridge: Harvard University Press, 1984).

5. The opposing views are spelled out in Barbara Ehrenreich, "The Real and Ever-Widening Gender Gap," *Esquire* 101:6 (June 1984): 213–17; Louis Boyce, "The Role of Gender in Recent Presidential Elections: Reagan and the Reverse Gender Gap," *Presidential Studies Quarterly* 15:2 (Spring 1985): 372–85; and Daniel Wirls, "Reinterpreting the Gender Gap," *Public Opinion Quarterly* 50:3 (Fall 1986): 316–30.

6. Contradictory evidence emerges from Vicky Randall, *Women and Politics: An International Perspective* (New York: St. Martin's, 1982), and Ole R. Holsti and James N. Rosenau, "The Foreign Policy Beliefs of Women in Leadership Positions," *Journal of Politics* 43:2 (May 1981): 326–47.

7. Holsti and Rosenau, "Beliefs of Women."

8. When we say something is significant at the .001 level, we are trying to estimate the odds of being wrong in making an inference about an entire population from a sample of information. In these cases, there is one chance in a thousand (or less) that differences of this magnitude would be found if in fact there were no gender differences among all opinion leaders. Strictly speaking, since we cannot be sure that our sample is a random representation of all U.S. opinion leaders—defining elites is an issue that has generated countless and inconclusive debates among social scientists—it is debatable that we can generalize from our sample to a population. However, it can still be useful to provide a summary statistic.

9. Kenneth Waltz, *Man, the State, and War* (New York: Columbia University Press, 1958).

10. *Americans Talk Security: Twelve National Surveys on National Security Issues Conducted from October 1987 to December 1988* (Winchester, MA: Americans Talk Security, 1989).

11. The C (or contingency) coefficient is a measure of the association or correlation between two sets of attributes. It is especially useful when one or both of the attributes

is a category—for example, men and women—rather than an attribute, such as income or years of education, that can take on many values along a single scale. The higher the C coefficient, the stronger the association between the variables; its values may range from 0.00 (no association) to an upper limit that is set by the number of categories. A disadvantage is that the C coefficient cannot reach 1.00, as is true of some other measures of association.

12. This scheme was developed by Eugene Wittkopf; see his *Faces of Internationalism* (Durham, NC: Duke University Press, 1990). Its applicability for surveys of opinion leaders is tested in Ole R. Holsti and James N. Rosenau, "The Structure of Foreign Policy Attitudes among American Leaders," *Journal of Politics* 52:1 (February 1990): 94–125.

13. Holsti and Rosenau, "Beliefs of Women."

14. None of the surveys asked respondents to provide information about income, race, religion, marital status, or children, thus eliminating the possibility of introducing these as additional control variables.

15. See I. M. Destler, Leslie Gelb, and Anthony Lake, *Our Own Worst Enemy* (New York: Simon & Schuster, 1984), and Ralph Carter, "Senate Defense Budgeting, 1981–1988," *American Politics Quarterly* 17:3 (July 1989): 332–47.

16. Ole R. Holsti and James N. Rosenau, "Does Where You Stand Depend on When You Were Born?" *Public Opinion Quarterly* 44:1 (Spring 1980): 1–22.

9

Organizing for Change: International Women's Movements and World Politics

Deborah Stienstra

Imagine this scene:

February 1972, United Nations offices, Geneva, Switzerland

The thirty-two representatives to the United Nations Commission on the Status of Women and their assistants are milling about the room. At the very back of the room the "unofficial" women, representatives from international nongovernmental organizations, have decided to make their approach during the next coffee break.

Women from the Women's International Democratic Federation based in Berlin, the International Federation of Business and Professional Women, the International Council of Women, and others stand together trying to get the attention of the Romanian delegate. Florica Andrei, the representative from Romania, comes over to the group. She accepts the piece of paper they hand her, listens, nodding thoughtfully. Finally, she leaves and talks to Helvi Sipila, the representative from Finland. They laugh, agree, and write something on the paper. Florica Andrei returns to the small group of women. "Yes," she says, "we will do it." When the meeting begins again, she proposes that 1975 be made the International Year for the Advancement of Women.

This may not have been exactly how the 1975 International Women's Year was first introduced, but we do know that the people who brought forward the idea that a full year of attention should be given to the situations of women were women representing nongovernmental organizations (NGOs). They were not representatives of their governments, but had been working as volunteers, usually unpaid, attending meetings of the United Nations (UN), trying to present their views on women's situations. They believed, and continue to believe, that in order to bring about change in those situations they had to work within the international system by lobbying, providing information, and submitting statements based on their experiences of working with women around the world.

Their actions in promoting an international year for women led to a full decade (1976–1985) dedicated to promoting the equality of women, ensuring the full integration of women in development efforts, and securing the participation of women in efforts for international peace and cooperation. At the end of that decade for women, 15,000 women came together in Nairobi, Kenya, to celebrate the progress that had been made and to call for new measures to improve the situation of women around the world.

These nongovernmental women were active in changing the UN system for the benefit of women. The methods they used have been called *mainstreaming*. Groups that practice a *politics of mainstreaming* seek to reach the largest possible audience by working within or together with the existing social structures such as governments, educational institutions, and international organizations.

Other women have organized in different ways to bring about change in women's situations. Imagine another scene:

March 1976, Palais des Congrès, Brussels, Belgium

Over 2,000 women from forty countries are crowded into this large auditorium, listening attentively to the woman at the front telling how she was raped and the unwillingness of the police to press charges against her attacker. Another woman tells how she was unable to get an abortion, and then an older woman speaks of the abuse she has suffered. In different languages, these and many other accounts of crimes against women are told to the 2,000 women who see themselves as judges constituting the International Tribunal on Crimes against Women. Their judgment is unanimous: In every country, women are oppressed in different ways as a result of their gender— and this has to change. The judges offer assorted strategies including the development of an international feminist network to provide solidarity to women who have had specific crimes committed against them.

The International Tribunal on Crimes against Women was a unique and empowering act by many women to bring international attention to the ongoing struggles that women have to face. The organizers feared that the International Women's Year would lead women to believe that their governments had women's best interests in mind and would thus blunt the anger of women at their own situations, making them less willing to act. The women who organized and participated in the tribunal rejected cooperation with national governments and international organizations and opted to create an alternative—based in feminist practice and ideas. This approach of creating alternatives outside of the existing structures is called *disengagement*. Groups that practice a *politics of disengagement* offer a critique of the ways in which governments and other social structures address issues and offer their own alternatives.

These stories illustrate two examples of how women have been actors at the global level. Since the mid-1800s, women have joined together at the global level to raise questions about the role of women in the areas of antislavery activity, suffrage, and conflict resolution.[1] More recently, feminists across the globe have organized international networks in many areas. Women from the Third World came together in 1984 to discuss how analyses of women's work, especially of poor women's situations, could be used to transform our understanding of economics and development. Women who were concerned about the rise of prostitution in Southeast Asia as a result of the Vietnam War and the increase in export-processing zones came together to develop a network against female sexual slavery. Women concerned with the rise of new reproductive technologies, like sex selection of fetuses, in vitro fertilization (test-tube babies), and surrogate or contract mothering, organized a network to address these concerns.

These international women's movements, both past and present, have worked with the League of Nations and the UN, but they have also organized their own alternative nongovernmental conferences for discussion and for creating new global groups and networks. Many of the groups established since the International Women's Year in 1975 consider themselves feminist, while others are formed on the basis of their shared gender, with little or no analysis of the underlying causes of the different treatment of women. The international women's movements also differ in the issues they consider and the organizational structures they use. Some are hierarchical, bureaucratic, international organizations. Others are structured less formally including networks, coalitions, and alliances among individuals or groups. They may also take the form of periodic conferences or international meetings. We can refer to all of these activities more generally as international women's movements.

Women's movements can be discussed in terms of the strategy they adopt: those that work within the international system and follow the practice of *mainstreaming* and those that remain outside the established system and follow a practice of *disengagement.* Most movements practice both mainstreaming and disengagement at some point, and thus these two practices should be seen as two ends of a continuum of political practice.

MAINSTREAMING WITHIN THE UNITED NATIONS

At least forty-five women's groups have nongovernmental consultative status within the UN.[2] "Consultative status" means that a group's representatives may attend and make statements at UN meetings. These groups provide information about the opinion of their constituencies to the UN and member states and provide information about the activities of the UN to their memberships. They lobby representatives of member states and members of the UN Secretariat to ensure their policy positions are taken into account. The primary location for their action is through the Economic and Social Council (ECOSOC) of the UN, although a number of groups also work with the UN organizations that deal with what have been considered "traditional" women's issues: education, food, children, labor, and health. Only the oldest and most active international women's groups, such as the International Council of Women, the International Alliance of Women, and the International Federation of Business and Professional Women, have gone beyond these organizations associated with "women's issues" into UNIDO (UN Industrial Development Organization), UNCTAD (UN Conferences on Trade and Development), UNEP (UN Environmental Programme), UNDP (UN Development Programme), and UNFPA (UN Fund for Population Activities).

Since at least 1970, the ongoing presence of NGOs with consultative status at UN meetings on the advancement of women, as well as in areas not traditionally associated with women, has sustained the pressure on governments and the UN to incorporate in their work an analysis of women's situations from a nongovernmental perspective. The NGOs persisted in pursuing the idea of an international conference on women in 1972 and were able to get an international year for women adopted. The International Women's Year in 1975 and the United Nations Decade for Women have been major catalysts in international activities related to women at the governmental and nongovernmental levels. In the context of these events, NGOs have also been able to encourage governments to continue to address issues related to the advancement of women in the UN system. As a result of their many volunteers and institutional resources, these groups were also able to organize major nongovernmental conferences on women in 1975, 1980, and 1985, which gave women who had little or no contact with the United Nations an opportunity to meet and to exchange ideas and strategies. Another opportunity will come at the next UN-sponsored conference in 1995 in Beijing, China.

More generally, the strengths of the mainstreaming groups during this period have been their constancy and persistence, as well as the volunteer labor and institutional and organizational resources they have brought to international organizing. But their work remains extremely limited for a variety of reasons. The historical structures of their own organizations and their access to resources constrain their work. As well, by opting to work within the framework of the consultative status of the UN, they remain bit players in the overall production of intergovernmental activities on women.

The primary purpose of many of the groups working within the UN system has been to promote international cooperation among women or to organize women who share a similar identity. These groups have continued to pursue issues as they come up, either through their memberships, the interests of an individual or leader within the group, or in response to activities of other groups or agencies, rather than in response to the growing feminist consciousness around the world. Their relatively broad mandates give the international representatives the opportunity to comment on a wide variety of issues, but the broad mandates also mean that the goals or strategies for change in women's lives pursued by these groups remain vague. This limits their ability to act effectively and with the full support of their memberships.

Many of these groups are also constrained by their organizational structures. Many groups have an elaborate bureaucratic and hierarchical organizational structure, with local chapters, national bodies, and an international federation. The impetus for action at the international level comes every three, four, or five years from international meetings that give policy direction. Yet the implementation of these directions as well as the response to immediate situations comes from the international executive, the Secretariat, and the representative to the UN. Most of the organizations have a difficult time maintaining the links between their memberships at the local level and their leadership.

Another problem related to NGO structure is representation in group leadership. While some organizations have allocated at least one seat on the executive for a woman from the Third World (the South), most of the executive positions are filled by white, middle-class women from First World (the North) countries. Most of the presidential and international representative positions in these groups remain volunteer jobs located in cities in the First World. These features prevent many women from Third World countries from participating in these decision-making positions, except for those who have some external financial support. This has created an elite of increasingly elderly, married, middle- or upper-class women who represent their organizations at the international level and provide the direction to NGO activities around women in the UN. These women usually do not have experiences living in the Third World, working in Southeast Asian export-processing zones, or deriving their living as farmers in Africa. Thus, any support they may be able to give to the women in these situations is as an outsider, rather than on the basis of their own experience. The elite of these organizations remain unrepresentative of women around the world, who are primarily women of color, women who have to work to ensure that their families survive, and poor women. When the limitations of this elite are combined with the vague mandates, these organizations remain unable to provide the vitality and feminist direction needed at the international level.

The groups working within the UN framework also remain constrained at the international level by the sources of their funding. For most, the funding they receive comes from their membership, which is disproportionately located in North America and Europe. The Women's International Democratic Federation (WIDF), by contrast, receives much of its support from individuals and governments in Eastern Europe as well as from socialist movements in the South. WIDF remains active even with the recent changes in the communist governments in Eastern Europe.

The funding received shapes the type of participation of these groups. Governmental funding, especially that from the East European countries, has often been suspect and seen to link groups to promoting an official line.

Funding from international aid agencies is usually used for travel for women from the Third World or for specific development project work. Most groups have been unable to raise large sums of money for other types of work, such as research or network building.

A final constraint on the effectiveness of the international women's groups is the structure of the UN arrangements with NGOs. Even though the NGOs have some access to the decision-making processes, they continue to rely on volunteer labor to prepare the necessary documentation. But more importantly, NGOs within the UN framework remain at the margins of decision making, performing only lobbying and information-exchange functions rather than decision making. As well, their work must be tailored to the agenda of the international organizations. It is difficult to encourage the discussion of new issues or different approaches within these organizations, especially if access to the process is limited to written or oral statements and corridor lobbying.

In spite of these limitations, the international women's groups work actively to sustain the presence of nongovernmental women within the UN. Their limited activities have precipitated the nongovernmental conferences during the UN Decade for Women which gave women unprecedented opportunities to coordinate across national boundaries. Their constant presence and pressure has continued to encourage national governments to consider issues of concern to women.

DISENGAGEMENT AND INTERNATIONAL WOMEN'S MOVEMENTS

Since 1970, feminists have organized a large number of international women's groups, networks, and meetings that have focused on specific issues such as communications, health, reproductive rights, peace, prostitution and the exploitation of women, and the environment. Between 1970 and 1990, at least twenty-seven new feminist issue-oriented networks were initiated and well over fifty international meetings were held, with between 10 and 15,000 participants. Most often these groups practiced a *politics of disengagement* from the UN and the international system more generally.

These groups have made it their priority to mobilize women and to coordinate local and national activities through *networking*. Networking for many of these may simply be a regular exchange of information through telephone, fax, or published magazines or newsletters. The DAWN network (Development Alternatives with Women for a New Era) established a fax information exchange in 1992, wherein each participating group sends in a fax form on what they are doing every month, and every six months an evaluation fax is sent with an assessment of how useful the information was. But networking has come to mean more than information exchange in the international feminist community; it also refers to groups that coordinate their actions or initiate quick responses to issues around the world. One example of network action was the worldwide protest by women and women's groups to Egypt when, in 1991, the Egyptian government banned the Arab Women's Solidarity Association (AWSA). The AWSA is an organization for women in the Muslim world.

The networks often take a different organizational structure than earlier women's groups. Many of the networks "have rejected rigid and heavy bureaucratic structures in favor of informal, non-hierarchical and open structures and ways of operating. This gives networks a flexibility and possibility to respond and take action quickly when necessary."[3] Often these networks have organized around specific issues or actions. For example, the international network on women and health issues has been at the forefront of identifying women's health concerns since 1977. A network, formed in 1984, that links women in Africa, Asia, and other parts of the world is the Women under Muslim Laws network, which works to support the struggles of women who live where Islam is the basis for the state structure. A significant part of women's organizing has also taken place through international and regional conferences, tribunals, and workshops.

At different times, women's international organizing has focused on different needs. In the first half of the 1970s, at a time when women, especially in North America and Europe, were reforming feminist movements, women began to develop a foundation for international communication among themselves. A number of networks have been established to promote communication among women and to distribute information about women across the world. These include Isis (International Women's Information and Communication Service), the Women's International Network (WIN), and the International Women's Tribune Centre (IWTC). All were initially based in the North, and while all developed communication systems, their goals and approaches to feminism differ. Some, like Isis, seek to promote development and to empower women and are explicitly feminist, while others, like WIN, provide information on women's international activities, job opportunities, and technical information.

At the same time that these communication networks were organized, women began to debate what feminism meant. These debates, while often divisive, were an important development in women's international organizing. The debates challenged the Western domination of feminist thinking. They also resulted in greater participation of women from the South in feminist organizing. Women's organizing took on a more global character, and women began to identify how their individual and national struggles could be linked to those of other women around the world, thus allowing for greater international cooperation.

At the 1975 Mexico City nongovernmental conference, a number of the participants assumed that the feminism they knew provided a common framework to describe women's concerns. In one instance, a number of predominantly Western women, as part of a caucus led by Gloria Steinem, prepared a feminist manifesto that put forward their vision of women's situation. It lacked input from Third World women and therefore failed to reflect their experiences and to express their hopes. The differences in the importance or priority given to feminism between women from First and Third World countries were significant. Many Latin American women rejected the primacy of "women's issues" put forward especially by U.S. feminists, wanting instead to emphasize the economic relations that affected their lives.

At an international women's workshop in 1979 with women from the Third and First World, the issue of whether feminism was the goal and basis for women's organizing at the international level was addressed in a systematic fashion and, for the first time, a definition of the long-term goals of feminism was given:

First, the freedom from oppression for women involves not only equity, but also the right of women to freedom of choice, and the power to control their own lives within and outside of the home. Having control over our lives and our bodies is essential to ensure a sense of dignity and autonomy for every woman. . . .

The second goal of feminism is therefore the removal of all forms of inequity and oppression through the creation of a more just social and economic order, nationally and internationally. This means the involvement of women in national liberation struggles, in plans for national development, and in local and global strategies for change.[4]

This definition provided the basis for much international feminist organizing during the 1980s.

Women in the Third World were increasingly organizing regional feminist networks during the 1980s. In 1981 in Bogotá, Colombia, the first Latin American feminist meeting was held with 270 women from ten Latin American and other countries. These women chose to name themselves as feminists and to create space for an autonomous feminist movement in their region. Latin American and Caribbean feminist meetings have continued and have grown in strength. By 1990 these meetings attracted 3,000 women.

With increasing participation of women from the South, the global character of feminism was also strengthened. In a 1982 declaration, participants of international women's movements more clearly described what unified and diversified feminists around the world: "Feminism is international in defining as its aim the liberation of women from all types of oppression and in providing solidarity among women of all countries; it is national in stating its priorities and strategies in accordance with particular cultural and socioeconomic conditions."[5]

These articulations of feminism in the global context remain at the foundation of much of contemporary feminist organizing at the international level and have shaped the ways in which feminists have practiced disengagement. For example, in 1984, women from different regions of the Third World came together in Bangalore, India, to examine development policies and economic and environmental crises from the vantage point of poor women in the Third World. From this initial meeting came the network DAWN, mentioned earlier. DAWN brings together women from the Third World to do research and to initiate action based on women's experiences, and it links feminist analysis with other types of analysis such as socialism.

During the 1980s, regional and international networks on research on women and women's studies were also developed. AAWORD, the Association of African Women for Research and Development, however, had been established in 1977 in Dakar, Senegal, and continues to be a strong research and networking organization for women in Africa.

The growth of feminist research and women's studies is seen in two events organized at the international level on a regular basis: the International Interdisciplinary Congresses on Women and the biannual international feminist book fairs. Although the numbers of women attending continues to increase with each congress, participation remains limited to primarily women academics from North America and Europe. In contrast, the book fairs make the connection between women's actions and women's words, celebrate women's writing, and provide workshops on feminist thought. In 1988, when the book fair was held in Montreal, at least 6,000 women from around the world attended.

Women have organized in response to global changes, including changes in the form and location of production, the influx of technological changes that affect industrial, service, and agricultural sectors. They have also organized in response to changing medical and biological practices and to social changes that have resulted from these economic and technological changes. At the local and national levels, women have protested and joined together to research and to strategize around these changes. At the international level, they have joined with other women to share information and analysis of problems, to provide support for those on the front lines, and to strategize about how to tackle these issues on a global scale.

Several groups, like the Third World Movement against the Exploitation of Women (TW MAE W) and the International Feminist Network against Forced Prostitution and other forms of Female Sexual Slavery, were organized to call for increasing government intervention in the globalization of prostitution and the resulting victimization of these women. With the presence of primarily U.S. military forces in Asia, there was an increasing demand for prostitutes who would be at "rest and relaxation" locations. More businessmen from the United States, Japan, and Korea bought tourist packages with prostitutes included; this is also called sex tourism. These changes have altered the nature of prostitution and the response of women's groups.

Technology in the area of reproductive health is changing rapidly and providing new opportunities for responses to male and female infertility through practices like in vitro fertilization or contract mothering. Feminists argue that these practices leave poor women to be "breeders" for rich women and warn that genetic manipulation could result in aborting fetuses of the "wrong" sex. To fight these practices, women have organized the Feminist International Network of Resistance to Reproductive and Genetic Engineering (FINRRAGE). This network has called for greater research on the causes of infertility, more control by women over the contraceptives that are available to them, and withdrawal of genetic manipulation that seeks to control life.

Women have also organized themselves around issues related to the international military order and the effects this has had on women's lives. Women have been organizing around peace and against specific international conflicts for many years. During the 1980s, however, organizing took a new form through the women's peace camp. Best known is Greenham Common, organized initially in opposition to cruise missiles on military bases in Great Britain. Other camps include the Women's Encampment for Peace at the Seneca Army Depot in the United States. Even though few of the camps remain, they have become a network of women's peace groups and a movement around feminist nonviolent action. In 1985 at the Nairobi nongovernmental conference, women established a peace tent as a space for women to speak about their differences in a safe place. Arab and Israeli women tried to deal with their differences on the Palestinian issue, and women from the United States and the then Soviet Union gathered to talk about cold war tensions. Women have also organized around the superpower summits of the late 1980s through the network Women for Mutual Security (WMS).

All of these efforts—international feminist communication networks; women's research conferences and book fairs; attempts to define feminism in a global context; and the multitude of different groups, meetings, and networks responding to global changes—are examples of women intensely engaged in world politics. These women have chosen to remain outside the formal international system and to work on their own terms. At the international level, women have created alternatives to traditional international organizations, alternatives usually based in feminist theory and practice. They have been able to raise for women the profile of emerging issues of concern such as genetic engineering, but also have provided information, have shared strategies, and have created solidarity among women around the world. These actions have created alternative spaces where women speak with authoritative voices about their situations and suggest responses to the world problems that affect their lives.

CONCLUSION

Over the past decades women have been actors at the international level through international women's movements. The forms and goals of these movements have differed. But perhaps the clearest difference is between groups that pursue a strategy of *mainstreaming* within the UN and those that follow *disengagement* practices. Groups with formal organizational structure and access to sufficient resources have used these to obtain representation at the UN and have lobbied governmental and international officials. These groups have successfully kept public attention focused on issues of concern to women throughout the UN Decade for Women and beyond. They have been less successful in having emerging issues put on the agenda of intergovernmental negotiations. International women's movements that have followed the practice of disengagement have had less of a clear influence on the policies and practices of governments. But their primary goals have not been to affect change within government but to create alternative spaces where women can pursue feminist practices and share information and strategies. This, they argue, will create change among women.

In spite of the differences between mainstreaming and disengagement discussed throughout this chapter, all international women's movements remain involved in activities aimed at both mainstreaming and disengagement. Women's organizing follows the entire spectrum of politics, with more formally organized groups spending more time on mainstreaming, and networks and conferences spending more time on disengagement. Yet even the networks have sought to have an effect from time to time on international organizations or the international media and to raise the profile of issues of concern to women.

The women who are active in the leadership of international women's movements, however, remain an elite of women throughout the world. Many movements are led by white, middle-class women from the First World. But there has been a continuous rise in the leadership from women in the Third World since 1970, which has resulted in the increasing orientation of international women's activities provided by women in the Third World. Yet even many of these women are well educated, often academics, who have established international connections. Few international movements have regularly included grassroots and community-based women in decision making or activities at the international level.

International women's movements have and will continue to shape the world that we live in. Whether by lobbying national governments to include legislation on the situation of elderly women or by creating alternative feminist health networks, these movements will continue to bring women together around issues of concern to them. The movements have created an unprecedented solidarity and communication among women across the world. This has had the effect of increasing information about the research on women's situations throughout the international community. It has also meant that women have not had to rely exclusively on governments for action but can turn to feminist alternatives. Thus, these women's movements have changed the face of world politics by becoming an alternative voice outside of states or international organizations. Governments and international organizations have only minimally responded to international women's movements; but with women becoming increasingly organized, we may see greater changes in the lives of women around the world.

NOTES

1. Two articles on women's early international organizing are E. Hurwitz, "The International Sisterhood," in R. Bridenthal and C. Koontz, eds., *Becoming Visible: Women in European History* (New York: Houghton Mifflin, 1977), and R. L. Sherrick, "Toward Universal Sisterhood," *Women's Studies International Forum* 5:6 (1982): 655–61.

2. These are women-only groups. While many women are involved in international nongovernmental organizations that have women and men as members, it is the women-only groups that consciously identify themselves with their gender and may be more involved with women's issues within the UN.

3. Marilee Karl, "Networking in the Global Women's Movement," M. Karl and X. Charnes, eds., *Women, Struggles, and Strategies: Third World Perspectives* (Rome: Isis International, 1986), 10.

4. Charlotte Bunch and Shirley Castley, *Developing Strategies for the Future: Feminist Perspectives*, Report of the International Feminist Workshop held at Stony Point, New York, April 20–25, 1980 (New York: International Women's Tribune Centre, 1980), 27.

5. Charlotte Bunch and Roxanna Carrillo, "Feminist Perspectives on Women in Development," in Irene Tinker, ed., *Persistent Inequalities: Women and World Development* (New York: Oxford University Press, 1990) 80.

10

Jane Addams: The Chance the World Missed

Sybil Oldfield

I have never been sure I was right. I have often been doubtful about the next step.

Jane Addams (1935)

In 1910, the fifty-year-old U.S. citizen Jane Addams—pioneer of social transformation via settlements in the inner city and successful campaigner against child labor, sweat shops, slum housing, and the political persecution of refugees—was listed in U.S. newspapers as "the greatest woman in America." In 1915 the American press labeled her "a silly, vain, impertinent old maid." By 1917 she was called a traitor.[1] What caused the considerable difference between these judgments? Was it because Jane Addams had tried, as a private citizen, to influence world politics in significant ways? How do women who are not governmental officials affect world politics? A study of Jane Addams' efforts provides us with some important clues.

BEFORE 1914

Before World War I Jane Addams had established not merely a national but an international reputation. In 1913, at the World Conference of the International Union of Women's Suffrage Associations in Budapest, Hungary, the leaders of the women's movement who were present "realized that [Addams] was the one that was known to the whole world."[2] That worldwide reputation was based both on Jane Addams' practical work and on her writing. Her work became an inspiration to reformers in different nations because it was so diverse. She helped organize garbage collection in poor urban districts, worked to provide public libraries and play spaces, and supported

Jane Addams

the rights of women, children, political dissidents, trade unionists, and peoples of color. Because her work was grounded in constructive cooperation among the many immigrant communities in the cities—Italian, German, Russian, Jewish, Polish, Greek, Arab—these efforts became known in the homelands of those immigrants. In addition, Jane Addams' published books, articles, and speeches before 1914 had established her as an important thinker throughout the English-reading world on questions of how to improve the quality of city life, how to emancipate women, and how to achieve world peace.[3] It was inevitable, therefore, that when World War I broke out, the "peace-minded" women of the world should have looked to Jane Addams as their leader. But before tracing what Jane Addams did at that catastrophic moment in world history, it is necessary to understand what she thought.

Jane Addams' early thoughts on war and peace in her first book on the subject, *Newer Ideals of Peace*, written between 1902 and 1907, could not have been more optimistic. In this she resembled her male counterparts in the peace movement, such as Norman Angell, author of *The Great Illusion*, who argued that a world war was impossible. Her years of experience among immigrants from many mutually hostile nationalities in downtown Chicago had proved, she thought, that it was possible to "break through the tribal bond." For had she not herself witnessed how often out of "primitive pity" the poor would insist on sharing the little they had with those who had still less? Moreover, these same people, however disparate their origins, were the first to recognize their *common* need for communal baths, libraries, schools, and open spaces. Therefore, Jane Addams had concluded hopefully in 1907 in *Newer Ideals of Peace*:

It is possible that we shall be saved from warfare by the "fighting rabble" itself, by the "quarrelsome mob" turned into kindly citizens of the world through the pressure of a cosmopolitan neighborhood. It is not that they are shouting for peace—on the contrary, if they shout at all, they will continue to shout for war—but that they are really attaining cosmopolitan [i.e., international] relations through daily experience. . . . Below their shouting, they are living in the kingdom of human kindness. They are laying the simple and inevitable foundations for an international order.[4]

There were three strands in Jane Addams' antimilitarist vision before World War I. First and most fundamental was her basic anti-Hobbesian perspective on human nature. She could not accept Thomas Hobbes' view of humans as warring brutes who would always require repressive control by force from above.[5] Instead, Jane Addams stressed what were to her the experiential realities of human pity, kindness, and altruism in addition to the realities of human egoism and survivalism. Secondly, there was her conviction, spelled out in the passage above, that progress toward international peace is socially determined and will evolve from perceived practical social needs. Finally, there was her liberal faith in irreversible progress that promised her that the global establishment of peace was inevitable. As late as 1913, Jane Addams (like the "Realist" Vladimir Lenin) was still confident that working people the world over would reject a world war—but August 1914, of course, was to prove her and her fellow pacifists terribly mistaken. The "tribal bond" was apparently the strongest bond of all.

THE GREAT WAR OF 1914–1918

Given Jane Addams' immense standing as a practical reformer and as a high-minded thinker, it followed that an elite band of women reformers and thinkers, both within the United States and outside, should now turn to her for leadership regarding the war in Europe. By the end of 1914, after the battles of the Marne and Ypres, each side had already suffered over half a million casualties and the deadlocked enemy lines faced one another from the Belgian coast to Switzerland to compete in massacring one another for the foreseeable future. Such a "reality" was so insupportable that on January 10, 1915, Jane Addams presided at the founding of the Woman's Peace Party at a congress in Washington attended by 3,000 people.[6] She was made chairwoman of a political party whose central plank was the advocacy of continuous mediation by neutrals to try to bring the war to a negotiated early end. In supporting this women's initiative, Jane Addams was taking her first, tentative step in transnational idealist intervention. She would soon literally be crossing most of the borders in Western Europe in her efforts to appeal to the world's leaders. The ideal—our sense of how humans *ought* to behave toward one another—was, she believed, what we *must* invoke if we are to find any alternative to the killing fields.

In February 1915, Jane Addams received the following cable from the Netherlands:

Call to the Women of All Nations

From many countries appeals have come asking us to call together an International Women's Congress to discuss what the women of the world can do and ought to do in the dreadful times in which we are now living.

We women in the Netherlands, living in a neutral country, accessible to the women of all other nations, therefore, take upon ourselves the responsibility of calling together such an international congress of women. We feel strongly that at a time when there is so much hatred among nations, we women must show that we can retain our solidarity and that we are able to maintain a mutual friendship.

Women are waiting to be called together. The world is looking to them for their contribution towards the solution of the great problems of the day.

Women, whatever your nationality, whatever your party, your presence will be of great importance.

The greater the number of those who take part in the congress, the stronger will be the impression its proceedings will make.

Your presence will testify that you, too, wish to record your protest against this horrible war, and that you desire to assist in preventing a recurrence of it in the future. Let our call to you not be in vain!

The cable was signed by a Dutch woman, Dr. Aletta Jacobs, pioneer in women's education, suffrage, medicine, birth control, and antimilitarism. Among other voices pressing Jane Addams to lead an American delegation to the Women's Congress at The Hague were those of the British suffragette leader Emmeline Pethick Lawrence, the Hungarian pacifist feminist Rozika Schwimmer, the German radical feminist Lida Gustava Heymann, as well as all the leading figures in the American peace movement. Initially, Jane Addams had misgivings: Might not an international peace conference of women in the midst of a world war be futile if not outright harmful? She had no illusions that the women could be miracle workers, but she did believe it was fitting for women at least to meet and take counsel to see what could be done.

The women who attended or supported this Women's International Congress at The Hague in April 1915 were a quite extraordinary group of gifted, courageous, and altruistic pioneers. The American contingent included a professor of economics, Emily Greene Balch, later a Nobel Peace Prize winner; Dr. Alice Hamilton, medical specialist in industrial diseases; Julia Grace Wales, a university English teacher; Madeleine Doty, a lawyer and investigator of juvenile courts; and Elizabeth Glendower Evans, a trade-union organizer. The English supporters included women lawyers, artists, mathematicians, classicists, theologians, midwives, radical social reformers, writers, doctors, trade unionists, musicians—the most famous names among them being probably Olive Schreiner and Sylvia Pankhurst. The English press had a mocking field day, calling these women "Pro-Hun Peacettes," "feminine busybodies," and a "shipload of hysterical women." Theodore Roosevelt called the whole undertaking "silly and base." Winston Churchill actually closed the North Sea to shipping, thus preventing most of the British delegates from attending the meeting. Meanwhile the American women aboard the *Noordam* had to risk possible U-boat attack on the Atlantic only to meet a British gunboat training a machine gun on them when the British Admiralty forced them to anchor off the coast of Britain. Finally, however, the Americans were allowed to sail for a Dutch port, arriving just in time for the opening speeches at The Hague. Delegates to the congress had arrived from Austria, Belgium, Britain, Canada, Denmark, Germany, Hungary, Italy, Netherlands, Norway, Sweden, and the United States and joined 1,000 Dutch women at The Hague. Messages of support came from women in India, Brazil, Spain, Serbia, Poland, and South Africa. Only Frenchwomen, still enduring German occupation in northern France, were largely hostile. It was agreed beforehand that there should be no opportunity for accusations and counteraccusations concerning the belligerents' guilt. All minds were to be concentrated on how international affairs must be organized in the future to prevent a similar cataclysm.

The original objects of the Women's International Congress had been (1) to demand that international disputes shall in the future be settled by some other means than war and (2) to claim that women should have a voice in the affairs of the nations. The congress did rather more than demand some bland, nonspecified alternative to war: The women worked out a number of very practical alternatives to competitions in massacre. Their final resolutions included several that focused on war prevention via a more just and cooperative regulation of international commercial, nonmilitary trade; open diplomacy instead of covert intrigue and secret treaties; and self-determination for small nations. They also supported the creation of international bodies for arbitration and conciliation once conflicts had broken out. Almost all these resolutions anticipated and even influenced Woodrow Wilson's famous Fourteen Points.

At the end of the congress's business, Rozika Schwimmer took the rostrum to declare that "paper expressions of pious wishes" were not enough. There must be action. She moved that the congress immediately send women envoys to all the war capitals and all the neutral nations, asking the foreign ministers of the belligerents to state their war aims and the neutral governments to act as mediators to bring about a cease-fire and a negotiated end to the war. "Brains, they say, have ruled the world. But if brains have brought us to where we find ourselves today, it is time that our hearts spoke also. . . . We must send our women as envoys. To these crowned male heads we must send the women crowned with thorns."[7]

If the holding of the Women's International Congress in the middle of a world war was an act of unparalleled antimilitarist resolve,[8] the dispatch of women envoys to all the belligerent and neutral capitals of Europe was even more transnationally idealistic and audacious. "I know how wild [the plans] must sound in the U.S.A.," Jane Addams admitted to her lifelong friend Mary Smith. "I don't think I have lost my head. There is just one chance in ten thousand." She was deputed to go with Dr. Aletta Jacobs and Dr. Alice Hamilton to the foreign ministries in London, Berlin, Vienna, Budapest, Bern, Rome, Paris, and Le Havre (the home of the Belgian government in exile). She found the Austrian foreign minister the most ready to envisage a mediated settlement, his French counterpart the least. All the belligerents claimed they were fighting in self-defense and must carry on to the bitter end. To be seen willing to negotiate would look like weakness. The message from the neutrals seemed to be that they were waiting for a signal from the belligerents and above all from the United States before attempting to intervene. The Germans, however, did not believe in the Americans' good faith, being convinced that they were not really neutral but on the side of a Britain that was deliberately starving German noncombatants by blockading Germany.[9]

Jane Addams, tired and ill, returned to the United States early in July 1915 and sought to rouse public opinion behind an American effort to end the war, putting her case to President Wilson that he should head such an effort, which neutral governments were encouraging. However, the very opposite of what she had hoped for ensued. Far from winning over public opinion in America, Jane Addams alienated it; far from trying to stop the war, Woodrow Wilson led the United States into it; far from ending as soon as possible with a just, negotiated peace, the war dragged on through the slaughter of the Somme, Verdun, and Passchendaele to the punitive, doomed Treaty of Versailles.

Jane Addams alienated American public opinion by daring to question the "heroism" of war. Even though the people of the United States were not yet actually dying in World War I, they were already fighting, in their imagination, Germany, one of whose submarines sank the *Lusitania*. And as Jane Addams herself remarked with rueful wisdom, "Even to seem to differ from those she loves in the hour of their affliction has ever been the supreme test of a woman's conscience."[10] It is the supreme test because it may make those she loves hate her.

Jane Addams and her fellow envoys from The Hague congress had been unique among American women in 1915 in that they had actually seen the "barricaded cities, bombed-out buildings, wounded and crippled soldiers of Europe"[11] as they crossed many frontiers to hold their unsuccessful interviews with the foreign ministers of the belligerent powers. What had struck Jane Addams most poignantly on her travels, as she reported at Carnegie Hall on July 9, 1915, was the sheer horror of militarism as expressed by young soldiers of *all* nationalities. More than anything, the soldiers who were sensitive could not bear the command to participate in a bayonet charge: "We were told in several countries that in order to inhibit the sensibilities of this type of man, stimulants were given to the soldiers before a bayonet charge was ordered. The men had to be primed with rum or absinthe."[12]

Jane Addams was instantly accused of besmirching the heroism of men dying for "home, country, and peace itself." As usual, war was valorized by the dying that it involved, not invalidated by the crazy killing that it legitimated. Jane Addams' conviction, based on her interviews in many European military hospitals, that men are *not* natural killers, was twisted by the American press to imply that she believed men to be incapable of heroic self-sacrifice. On the contrary, of course, it was the refusal of many of the young men in the trenches to be absolutely ruthless that Jane Addams held to be truly self-sacrificial and truly heroic. It was for this that she was labeled a "silly, vain, impertinent old maid," "a foolish, garrulous woman," "one of the shrieking sisterhood," and "poor bleeding Jane."[13]

Jane Addams did not relish such personal abuse and the attacks were made worse by the fact that she was suffering from exhaustion, pneumonia, and tuberculosis of the kidney after her return from Europe. Nevertheless, having failed to persuade Wilson to act on his wish to be the pacific mediator in

Europe (he was more swayed by the militarist advice of Secretary of State Lansing), Jane Addams went on doggedly, agreeing to testify at a hearing before the House Committee on Military Affairs in January 1916. The House was dealing with a bill to increase the efficiency of the military establishment, and Jane Addams, representing the Women's Peace party, testified that in her view America was suffering from irrational "war contagion." She opposed the advocates of "preparedness" who wanted a massive increase in spending for the Navy. However, she did not make any utopian plea for actual *disarmament* by the United States; she merely urged that the U.S. government pause and consider the matter for six months rather than rush into a rearmament drive that could foster an arms race with Japan and prevent America from having any moral influence in a postwar-weary Europe desperately needing to substitute proportional disarmament for its old habit of building rival standing armies. She lost the military preparedness debate; and as she predicted, a lethal and renewed arms race, with Japan and within Europe, took place.

Even after the United States entered the war in April 1917, Jane Addams maintained her principled commitment to pacifism. But she was increasingly isolated in taking such a stance. Those very Americans, either themselves immigrants or else the children of immigrants, whom she had so recently believed to be evolving into "kindly citizens of the world," now became superpatriots overnight. Far from transcending nationalism they overcompensated for the suspicion that they might be less than 150 percent American. Jane Addams was publicly denounced and ostracized and even placed under surveillance by the Department of Justice. She confessed that she now learned, when totally isolated, how a pacifist "finds it possible to travel from the mire of self-pity straight to the barren hills of self-righteousness and to hate herself equally in both places."[14] By March 1918 the *Los Angeles Times* described Jane Addams' eyes, sanguine no more, as "very earnest, very tragic."[15]

JANE ADDAMS AND THE POSTWAR WORLD

In January 1919, two months after the guns at last stopped firing in Europe, Jane Addams' name headed a list compiled by Archibald Stevenson, a lawyer employed by Military Intelligence, of Americans holding "dangerous, destructive, and anarchistic sentiments." Addams was soon branded a Communist. In May 1919, refusing to be intimidated by this growing hostility and distrust from the American press, Jane Addams went to Zurich to preside over a second Women's International Congress, again consisting of women from the recently warring nations as well as of neutrals. That congress was a second remarkable achievement in transnationalism, and it founded the Women's International League for Peace and Freedom. Its main work was a detailed, prophetic critique of the punitive clauses of the Treaty of Versailles, and Jane Addams delivered that critique in person to the deaf ears of the U.S. ambassador in Paris.

In July 1919, Jane Addams joined a Quaker relief mission to Germany to see the conditions of the defeated for herself; for although the war was over, the Allies were still blockading Germany in order to enforce the Treaty of Versailles. She saw the sick, apathetic, skeletal babies and children, and she ate their "ersatz" diet of watery soup and black bread made partly of sawdust and tree bark. On her return to the United States, she wrote and spoke in public about the food crisis in Europe and tried to raise money to feed German children. For this she was called un-American and a traitor. In Detroit alone she was heckled for forty-five minutes before being allowed to speak.

By 1920, Jane Addams' only preoccupation was how to organize postwar reconstruction so that future wars would be prevented, and her thoughts on this problem were published in 1922 as *Peace and Bread in Time of War.* In this book, which might have been more aptly entitled *Peace* through *Bread,* Jane Addams formulated a contrasting, alternative version of real-politik to that favored by Bismarck and all his militarist heirs. To her—and, she insisted, to all ordinary people—the fundamental human reality is not the struggle for power, a struggle only resolvable intermittently by a threat-ened or actual infliction of death, but rather the reality of our experienced *life* needs—above all, the need for food. A concomitant reality is our pity for those whom we know to be without food and our resulting urge to feed them. A third reality *could* be the enactment of that pity and that urge to feed the starving through an organized cooperative internationalism. "There [is] something primitive and real about feeding the helpless as there [is] about . . . fighting. . . . In the race history, the tribal feeding of children an-tedated mass fighting by perhaps a million years. Anthropologists insist that war has not been in the world for more than 20,000 years."[16]

It was at this point in her life that Jane Addams turned to women for hope of a new, more peaceful world order. Because of the age-old social role of women in growing and preparing much of the world's food each day, it seemed to Jane Addams during World War I that "millions of American women might be caught up into a great world purpose, that of conservation of life: there might be found an antidote to war in woman's affection and all-embracing pity for helpless children."[17] Out of her faith in the possibility of feeding the world's children through a collective international effort organ-ized primarily by women, came Jane Addams' vision of the possibility of a new, humane, international world order: "[During] the winter of 1916–17, I . . . came to believe it possible that the more sophisticated questions of national grouping and territorial control would gradually adjust themselves if the paramount human question of food for the hungry were fearlessly and drastically treated upon an international basis."[18]

She was, of course, to be tragically disappointed yet again. Fridtjof Nan-sen's pleas to the League of Nations in September 1921 for a coordinated international effort to relieve 25 million starving Russians was rejected. Jane Addams did not lose all hope for the world at that point, but she did lose hope for the League of Nations. "If the coal, the iron, the oil and above all the grain had been distributed under international control from the first day of the armistice . . . the League could actually have laid the foundations of that type of government towards which the world is striving."[19]

From our own perspective at the end of the twentieth century, with another order dying and another new order yet unborn, perhaps we should give serious thought to Jane Addams' advocacy of adequate international aid as the essential prerequisite for a more just and, therefore, a more peaceable world.

Internationalism, Jane Addams believed, is much too vital to the life of the world to be left to the rulers of the world, for they, in fact, are the very last people on earth capable of conceding the necessary diminution of their "tribal" powers. Our only alternative, according to her, is to rely upon *non*-governmental agencies to practice internationalism for life's sake, thereby creating an international order through the "internationalism of the deed" rather than the internationalism of abstract rhetoric. There should be fewer pious invocations of "human rights" and rather more practical carrying out of our own "duties of humanity" in Mazzini's phrase, thought Jane Addams, social worker from downtown Chicago, whose "turf" was finally the world. As John Dewey, the child-centered educationalist and philosopher, commented in 1945 in his essay "Democratic Versus Coercive International Organization—the Realism of Jane Addams," "It has become customary to give the name 'realistic' to the kind of organization that is based upon opposition to an enemy and that relies upon armed force to maintain itself. In contrast the road indicated by Miss Addams is . . . infinitely more 'realistic.' "[20]

Jane Addams had to live to witness both the Great Depression and the rise of fascism. Appalled, and increasingly exhausted, she continued nevertheless to testify to the eventual viability of alternatives to militaristic nationalism, that is, to the practical world organizations that would be rooted in "the oneness of humanity and the interdependence of nations." Of the two central issues of American foreign and defense policy during the 1920s and early 1930s, she persistently advocated the recognition of the Soviet Union by the United States and the withdrawal of U.S. Marines from all foreign bases.

JANE ADDAMS' EFFECT ON WORLD POLITICS

Jane Addams' life as an actor in world politics may seem to have been a total failure. All her unprecedented and unparalleled attempts at intervention were foiled. She did not succeed in helping to shorten World War I by persuading President Wilson or any other head of state to initiate continuous mediation by neutral powers in 1915; she did not persuade the House Committee to postpone, let alone cut, massive increases in the naval budget in

1916; she did not persuade the victorious world powers after 1919 to practice "internationalism of the deed," pooling and distributing the essentials of life—grain, coal, iron, and oil—according to the devastated countries' needs. Nevertheless, her efforts were not without some effect. The Final Resolutions of the Women's International Congress in 1915 did influence Woodrow Wilson's Fourteen Points, especially on the issues of national self-determination, arms control, open diplomacy, fairer trade, and the pacific settlement of disputes. The organization that Jane Addams helped to found and over which she presided—the Women's International League—is still functioning today (with national sections in every continent) and is also a respected nongovernmental organization of well-informed professional women at the UN.

Above all, Jane Addams' ideas are still alive. She was the prototype of the "social feminist," a woman who, while never idealizing women as being essentially pacific,[21] still respected women's brains and workaday experience sufficiently to insist that women do have a necessary contribution to make to the joint struggle against war. Women have a clear responsibility to extend their life-nurturing work in the private world to the larger public world, and they should be given the opportunity to exercise such responsibility. "There is obviously great need," she wrote in the middle of World War I, in *Women at The Hague*, "that women should attempt, in an organized capacity, to make their contribution to . . . governmental internationalism and to the long effort to place law above force . . . in the great experiment of living together."[22]

In accepting her share of the Nobel Peace Prize in 1931, Addams expressed her version of Martin Luther King's dream: "It was the mothers who first protested that their children should no longer be slain as living sacrifices upon the altars of tribal gods. . . . I should like to see the women of civilization rebel against the senseless wholesale human sacrifice of warfare."[23] The "women of civilization"—modern, educated women, no longer victims of mass irrationality—were the women in whom Jane Addams put her hope.

That Jane Addams should have been granted a hearing on the subject of world politics by so many men in power was owing to the fact that she was a quite exceptional woman. And paradoxically, it was easier for her to gain that hearing precisely because, as a woman, she was an unenfranchised outsider who did not have to compete against men, on men's terms. Because she was acknowledged to be exceptional, men could make her an exception. But because she was, in the last resort, "only" a woman—however exceptional and however closely linked to other exceptional women—men in power did not *have* to heed her. That men in power did not in fact heed her was, in my view, entirely owing to their limitations, not hers. The timid, old-fashioned, cynical "realism" of men in power dared not contemplate acting on her alternative "realism" based on an acknowledgment of our common human needs and our capacity to want to answer such needs. Leonard Woolf's *International Government* (1916) divided the world into "practical men" and "amiable cranks," pointing out that those who regard themselves as the former have often been led into the most hideous and disastrous errors while laughing at the latter. Among the amiable cranks he included Socrates, Jesus Christ, and Jane Addams.

Jane Addams' legacy to us today is best understood if we look at one woman activist now alive who most carries on her legacy. Inga Thorsson, veteran Swedish economist and former United Nations Special Expert on Disarmament for Development, carries on Jane Addams' advocacy of peace through bread. Thorsson tirelessly reminds both governments and international organizations that the world's resources must and can be redistributed "so that the fundamental necessities of human life—clean water, food, elementary health care and schooling—are available to all people throughout the world" as set forth in the UN *Charter*. Inga Thorsson has done much detailed work on the economic conversion strategies necessary to change from weapons production to "civilian" production without incurring mass unemployment. She has also spelled out the change we need to make in our thinking so that we no longer automatically identify the term "security" as necessarily meaning military security against military attack, but rather as precisely the reverse—nonmilitary security from nonmilitary scourges: destitution, hunger, disease, unemployment, homelessness, and illiteracy. By tackling the conservation of human life and the enrichment of the quality of human life in an internationalist spirit, Inga Thorsson, like Jane Addams seventy years before her, tells us we shall find that we are also, in fact, saving the life of the world from war.[24]

Given our current situation at the end of the twentieth century, with the revival of warring tribalisms in Europe, the growing inequality between nations North and South, and West and East, the lack of effective arms control, the manifold threats to the global ecology, and the rise of increasingly intolerant fundamentalisms—each claiming a monopoly of truth and all of them oppressive to women—Jane Addams may be envied her rest in peace. But in her time, she had her full share of the world's evils to grieve over and to try to counter and alleviate. Despite the fluctuations in her standing in the American popular press, to almost all who worked with her, Jane Addams was the wisest human being they ever knew. It is just possible that her faith in "the internationalism of the deed" may be vindicated yet.

NOTES

1. See Allen F. Davis, *American Heroine: The Life and Legend of Jane Addams* (New York: Oxford, 1973), chap. 14.

2. Maude Royden's Address at the Memorial Service for Jane Addams, London, June 4, 1935.

3. Jane Addams' prewar publications included *Democracy and Social Ethics* (1902), *Newer Ideals of Peace* (1907), *The Spirit of Youth and the City Streets* (1909), *Twenty Years at Hull House* (1910), and "Why Women Should Vote" (1910).

4. Quoted in Christopher Lasch, ed., *The Social Thought of Jane Addams* (New York: Bobbs-Merrill, 1965), 227–28.

5. See Thomas Hobbes, *Leviathan*, pt. 1, chaps. 11 and 15.

6. See Daniel Levine, *Jane Addams and the Liberal Tradition* (Madison: State Historical Society of Wisconsin, 1971), chap. 14; see also Davis, *American Heroine*, chap. 12.

7. From the report of the Women's International Congress held in the Fawcett Archive, City of London University.

8. How unthinkable it would have been during the Gulf War for antimilitarist women from Iraq, Iran, Saudi Arabia, the United States, Israel, Kuwait, Western Europe, Libya, Jordan, and so forth, to have gathered for a Women's International Congress in Stockholm in 1991.

9. For accounts of the congress and its activities, see Lela B. Costin, "Feminism, Pacifism, Internationalism, and the 1915 International Congress of Women," *Women's Studies International Forum* 5:34 (1982): 301–5, and Anne Wiltsher, *Most Dangerous Women: Feminist Peace Campaigners of the Great War* (London: Pandora, 1985).

10. Jane Addams, Emily Balch, and Alice Hamilton, *Women at The Hague* (New York: Macmillan, 1915), 125.

11. Ibid., 73.

12. Quoted in Davis, *American Heroine*, 226.

13. Ibid., 229 and 223.

14. Ibid., 247.

15. Ibid., 250.

16. Jane Addams, *Peace and Bread in Time of War* (1922; reprint, Boston: Hall, 1960), 75.

17. Ibid., 82–83.

18. Ibid., 89.

19. Ibid., 213.

20. Ibid., xviii.

21. In *Women at The Hague*, Jane Addams wrote: "The belief that a woman is against war simply because she is a woman and not a man cannot, of course, be substantiated. In every country there are women who believe that war is inevitable and righteous; the majority of women as well as men in the nations at war doubtless hold that conviction" (127–28).

22. Ibid., 138–41.

23. Emily Cooper Johnson, ed., *Jane Addams: A Centennial Reader* (New York: Macmillan, 1960), 324.

24. For more on Inga Thorsson, see Sybil Oldfield, *Women against the Iron Fist: Alternatives to Militarism, 1900–1989* (Oxford: Basil Blackwell, 1989), chap. 9.

11

Women and the Global Green Movement

Petra Kelly

Editors' Note: Petra Kelly agreed to contribute to this anthology but did not complete her manuscript before her untimely death in October 1992. Using materials she had sent us, we have put together her analysis of an important transnational movement of women, using her own words wherever possible. Our additions appear in italics.

Petra Kelly helped found the West German Green party in 1979 and served as one of its representatives in the West German Parliament, the Bundestag, from March 1983 to December 1990. Her program of ecofeminism saw an interconnection between respect for all people and respect for all nations, and between human rights, women's rights, and environmental activism. Her inclusive vision and leadership were often challenged within the German Green party itself, but the larger Green movement that she helped to establish built a transnational network with grassroots connections around the world. In the selection below,[1] she describes the relationship between women and the environment.

"To think globally and to act locally" is one of the mottos of the Green party and of the feminist movement in Europe. Among the principles of the Green Movement are the enhancement of a cooperative relationship between human beings and nature and nonviolence toward the Earth and all people.

Also important are the dismantling of the nuclear, defense, and chemical industries, which are destroying the Earth, as well as the eradication of nuclear power and nuclear weapons, and unilateral disarmament, and civilian-based and nonmilitary forms of defense.

Petra Kelly

Greens also work for the establishment of a free society guaranteeing economic, social, and individual human rights, as well as the equal distribution of wealth and power. We also work to reduce our consumption so that we consume only our share of the Earth's resources.

Global Green feminist politics have never had such an opportunity as that available today. While men's revolutions have often been based on the concept of dying for a cause, feminist-conceived transformation is about daring to live for a cause!

When I speak about Green feminist-based transformation, I am thinking about the nuns in the Philippines who nonviolently brought about the fall of dictator Ferdinand Marcos; about the women of the Chipko (Save the Tree) Movement in India; about the Argentinian Mothers of the Plaza de Mayo who search for their "disappeared"; about the women in the Swords into Plowshares Movement in the United States; about Katya Komisaruk, a San Francisco peace activist who was sentenced in January 1988 to five years imprisonment in order to pay $500,000 restitution for destroying three navigational computers designed for nuclear warmaking at Vandenburg Air Force Base.

And I think about women and sisters like Maneka Gandhi, the new Indian forest and environment minister, who is courageously trying to block dam projects and wants to set up environmental courts! I think of the women, the brave and courageous women, who have struggled in nonviolent revolutions in East Germany, Czechoslovakia, Poland, Hungary, the Soviet Union, Bulgaria, and Romania.

Women represent half the global population and over one-third of the labor force, and we log two-thirds of all working hours. Yet we women receive only one-tenth of the world's income and own less than 1 percent of the world's property. Not only are females most of the poor, the starving, and the illiterate, but women and children constitute more than 90 percent of all refugee populations. Women outlive men in most cultures and, therefore, are the elderly of the world as well as being the primary caretakers of the elderly. In industrialized countries, we women still are paid only half to three-quarters of what men earn at the same jobs, we are still ghettoized into lower-paying, female-intensive job categories, and we are still the last hired and the first fired!

Women in the developing world are responsible for more than 50 percent of all food production, 50 percent of all animal husbandry, and 100 percent of all food processing.

Toxic pesticides, herbicides, chemical pollution, leakage from nuclear wastes, and acid rain, usually take their first toll as a rise in cancers of the female reproductive system, and in miscarriages, stillbirths, and congenital deformities. Furthermore, it is women's work that compensates for the destruction of the ecological balance. For example, deforestation results in a lowering of the water table, which in turn causes parched grasslands and erosion of topsoil. Women, as the world's principal water haulers and fuel gatherers, must walk further to find water, to find food for animals, and to find cooking fuel. This land loss has caused a major worldwide trend—rural migration to the cities and that has had a doubly devastating effect on women.

The overlooked factor in the power of women as a world political force is the magnitude of suffering combined with the magnitude of women: Women constitute not an oppressed minority but a majority—of almost all national populations and of the entire human species. We can feminize power! We must dare new political and bold initiatives.

As our human species approaches the capacity to eradicate all life on this planet, *we must be mobilizing!* The goal is not only to change drastically our own powerless status, but to redefine all existing social structures and modes of existence and to transform nonviolently these patriarchal structures. The recent nonviolent revolutions in Eastern Europe have shown us in the West that it is possible to nonviolently transform repressive and barbaric communist systems and secret services and to use the people's power against the useless power of guns, tanks, secret service, and oppression.

The most pernicious of all patriarchal tactics is to keep women a divided world caste. I believe that indigenous feminism has been present in every culture in the world and in every period of history since the suppression of women began. How many of us know that, for example, Mahatma Gandhi's nonviolent resistance strategies were acknowledged by Gandhi to have been copied from a nineteenth-century Indian women's movement? Or that it was women's action that inspired the *Solidarność* movement in Poland? Feminism, nonviolence, and ecology are profound revolutionary ideas. I think, for example, about the attempts of Israeli and Palestinian feminists who have dared to open and continue a dialogue as women—and toward a genuine peace, since their lives as women reflect each other more than politics in the region would admit.

Many times, I have noticed that women, often bearing experiential scars from the way most men have used power, want no part of established power themselves. Thus, we must try to transform the concepts of power and to transform the way in which men use that power. What a world these men in power have left behind for their children! Their legacy includes acid rain, Bhopal, the Alaska oil spill, global warming, Chernobyl, toxic waste, and useless scrap heaps of weapons. The whales and the elephants are endangered and nearly six hundred Soviet cities have advised people to drink bottled water.

When we try to rid the world of the oppressions of nuclear weapons, nuclear power, sexism, racism, and poverty, it helps us to look at their structural underpinning—the system of patriarchy held in common by capitalism and state socialism. We don't need to argue about which came first, but we must understand how they affect our societies now. Male domination is prevalent in both capitalist and socialist ideologies, and it is oppressive to women and restrictive to men.

And yet I believe that norms of human behavior can and do change over the centuries and that sexism and racism can also be changed. We must begin to envision a society in which there is a dynamic balance interconnecting male/female, body/mind/spirit and matter. For me, ecological feminism is a hopeful perspective that integrates these concerns.

We must explain to the men in power that we are not weak, we are not meek, that we are, in fact, very angry people—angry on our own behalf because of the large and small war waged against us every day, and angry on behalf of the entire planet Earth.

We need to transform ourselves in the Western world, and we must learn to find hope and power in our bonds to each other and to the Earth. Transforming the planet also means promoting social justice, an end to the rich countries' exploiting the poor, and an end to the criminal weapons transfer from Western countries to those on the other side of the globe.

We must overcome the numbing of our innate sensibilities that makes it possible for people across this world to be dominated, oppressed, exploited, and killed. The Earth is sacred unto herself, and her forests and rivers and various creatures have intrinsic value. And we must build a political world that acknowledges these tenets.

Petra Kelly's call for political mobilization has been answered by many women, not only in Europe but around the world. The "hopeful perspective" of ecofeminism is not her vision alone, as she explains in the following excerpt,[2] which describes the efforts of ecofeminists from many nations who work to raise environmental awareness and to advance the position of women in their communities.

The World Women's Congress for a Healthy Planet, organized by brave and energetic Bella Abzug, in Florida, was proof again that we all need to listen to women for a change. Women have been in the forefront of ecological organizations and movements all over the world, but the still predominantly male media has ignored them, belittled them, and put them on the "women's pages" of the daily newspapers.

We must not only speak up louder than ever before, but we must also support each other as women struggling for nonviolent change in all parts of the world. We must know that we are not alone, that we have sisters to reach out to, to hold onto, to give support to. We must listen to one another. That's why I'd like . . . to draw your attention to just some of the women around the world who are working with much determination and courage toward these common goals.

I think of our sister, Wangari Maathai, of the Green Belt Movement International, which was inspired by the very successful Green Belt Movement of Kenya and other tree-planting programs. Her strategy is one that gives us hope and a vision for the future. "The tree is a symbol of hope and a living indicator of what needs to be done in order to rehabilitate and conserve the global environment," she says.

Her Green Belt Movement should be studied and its principles taken up by all male agriculture and environment ministers. The Green Belt Movement can arrest the degradation of nature, can encourage soil rehabilitation and reforestation, as well as the use of natural fertilizers. And it will encourage the planting of multipurpose trees for nutrition, energy, beauty, and other environmental and empowering purposes.

In the days of the Nobel Prize Award, we also came to remember again the very courageous Aung Saan Suu Kyi of Burma, who is leading her non-violent campaign under house arrest, without any contact with the outside world for over two years. Where have we women been? In solidarity with Aung Saan Suu Kyi? We have been all too silent; we have not done enough to cross the boundaries and make an effective women's campaign for our heroine in Burma.

There is an organization in Europe now, called Terre des Femmes, that will raise public consciousness about the plight of women around the world—women like Suu Kyi, like the Tibetan women suffering so terribly from forced abortions and forced sterilization in their occupied country.

We need to remember what a wealth of expertise we have through our sisters like Dr. Rosalie Bertell, expert on low-level radiation and a brave campaigner against all sources of civilian and military radiation. Or Helen Caldicott, raising the issue of children's cancer. Or Jo Valentine, campaigning against the international weapons trade in Australia.

I also want to mention our sister, Vandana Shiva, of India, who has been lecturing across the world about the dangers of the genetic industry and about the ways in which the North has exploited the South. She has become an authority on a whole range of issues, and we are blessed to be able to share her wealth of knowledge and expertise.

All these women, and of course many more, have dealt also with the issue of violence—personal, family, city, national, and global. We are all attempting to break out of that cycle of violence—we women who have opted for a nonviolent transforming of our lives and society. We are united in our efforts to become more loving and gentle human beings but, while we try, our men, our friends, our fathers, our husbands, our lovers, brothers, and sons must do the same, learning to accept their fears, their weaknesses, their mistakes and shortcomings, learning about nonviolence in everyday life and politics.

Our present path, as Rosalie Bertell wrote, is headed toward species death, whether fast, with nuclear war (perhaps with nuclear civil war) or techno-logical disaster, or slow, by poison.

We must put the feminist ecological perspective on the agenda. We must challenge male decision making and male power and power structures. We must challenge male science and male economics and male politics. Christine Milne has done so in Tasmania and Marilyn Waring has done so in New Zealand. We must demand that at least 50 percent of delegates at the UNCED (United Nations Conference on Environment and Development) in Rio will be women.

Maybe, again, I am too bold in my dreams, too hopeful in my expectations. But we women in the ecology movement need hope, need visions. We have always given early warnings that have been ignored, and we have grasped the interconnectedness of these things well before our male colleagues finally discovered them.

We must demand that women and children are put first on our priority list because the global economy, as Vandana Shiva points out, is filled with locked gates, segregated decks and policies (like the *Titanic*) that insure that women and children will be, not the first to be saved, but the first to fall into the abyss of poverty.

We must put women and children at the center of political consensus—women and children as part of the Earth, not apart from the Earth. Life creation, rather than life destruction, is our political aim. So let's listen to women for a change.

In mobilizing on environmental issues, women have empowered themselves as citizens and have promoted human rights and democratization of closed political systems. In reaching out to others, in seeing other women as members of a global sisterhood, they have begun to change world politics. How did Petra Kelly become an ecofeminist? In an address before the School of International Service at the American University in Washington, D.C., she described her life experiences and how these forged her global green vision and set her on the path to political activism.[3]

[*As a member of the German Parliament*] I have worked on issues of human rights, foreign policy, policies of neutrality, disarmament, and on the question of children's cancer and many ecological concerns. And, of course, one of my overriding principles has been that of having been a feminist for a very long time—in fact, I believe it all began here at the American University between the years 1966 and 1970 when I, for example, ran for Student Senate with quite a feminist agenda and when I initiated the first International Week in 1966–1967.

I have often stated that much of the thinking that I try to bring into the discussions with German party politics had derived from my years in the United States—between 1961 and 1970. First, I worked in Europe politically within the framework of the Social Democratic party. And then, after having been a loyal Willy Brandt voter, I had become very disillusioned with the politics of Helmut Schmidt—the politics of economic growth at all costs, the politics of pro–nuclear power, and the politics of pro–deployment of nuclear weapons in Western Europe. Thus, between 1976 and 1978, I began thinking, together with a small circle of my friends, about leaving the Social Democrats and creating an ecological, feminist, and antimilitaristic new political organization called the Green party.

At that time, many of my colleagues and friends felt that this party development would be a wrong signal, that it would be better to work *within* the existing Party and turn that green. But I, being quite stubborn and determined to find new ecological roads as the old socialist roads seemed to go crooked ways, decided to dedicate all my energy and creativity to help create a new political party. In my view, it would be an "anti-party party." And by 1979 I headed the first national list for the Green party in the European elections. We received 3.2 percent the very first time in a national election—about one million votes—and at that moment, I knew we were doing something right!

Much of that which I was taught here in Washington, D.C., about civil disobedience and about the ethics of nonviolence, I had also been able to put into practice by being an active member of the antiwar movement, of the civil rights movement, and also having become a very critical, very antiauthoritarian person, through such mentors as Dr. Abdul Said and Dr. Mott. It was Dr. Said who conveyed to me the essence of international politics as active solidarity for the poor and repressed, and for those who are exploited. And it was Dr. Said who also added an element of spirituality to all he taught about international relations—a rare combination that you usually do not find at universities. And Dr. Mott made me confront like no one else in my years in the United States my own German past. I, coming from a small Bavarian town called Gunzberg on the Danube River—the same town in which the family of the notorious Auschwitz doctor Mengele had lived—and having been raised myself in a Catholic Convent School under the influence of a very independent and radical grandmother, had come to the United States through the remarriage of my mother and had faced quite a cultural shock, having first been in Georgia, then Virginia, and then Washington, D.C.

It was through the courses with Dr. Mott that I was able to get a different perspective from that which I had left behind in Bavaria. For in my convent school, there was *no talk* about Auschwitz, *no talk* about Bergen-Belsen, *no talk* about Anne Frank, *no talk* about Buchenwald!

Now today, I feel there is quite a direct line between that which I was taught here and that which I put into green political practice! In the past ten years I have worked, laughed, and cried with someone very close to me, General and former Green member of Parliament, Gert Bastian—someone who had the courage to leave the German Army while on active duty out of protest against the deployment of mass destruction American missiles in Western Europe. Someone who set the courageous example which unfortunately other military officers have *never* followed, and someone with whom I have blockaded nonviolently military bases across Europe, as acts of civil disobedience, together with friends like Phil Berrigan and many others.

Gert Bastian and I travelled back and forth to East Germany in the 1980s. We demonstrated in the Alexanderplatz in East Berlin in 1983 and were arrested there. From that experience we had our very first dialogue with East German leader Erich Honecker later in November 1983. That critical dialogue continued with him throughout the 1980s. We made quite clear to him that we did not intend to be frightened away by his measures of not allowing us into East Germany on several occasions or by writing to us and warning us of our breaking East German law by helping East German dissidents. We made it clear that we would see our dissident friends despite the measures that he took against us.

The East German Revolution of November 1989 was led by very strong women who count among my best friends, including Barbel Bohley, Katja Havemann, Ulrike Poppe and many other brave and courageous women and men. It was these friends of ours from the independent human rights and peace groups from East Germany who had suffered oppression for many years, and had been imprisoned over and over again.

I also had the privilege to get to know courageous dissidents in the Soviet Union in the 1980s—brave women like Larissa Bogoraz, wife of Anatoly Marchenko—and I had the privilege of getting to know Andrei Sakharov and his wife Helena Bonner and talking with both in their Moscow kitchen. Through my long friendship with Lew Kopelew, the Russian writer and dissident, and through his circle of friends in Moscow, I came to know and understand what the notion of a *civil society* was all about—civil society and antipolitics, the two most important concepts that I learned from the citizens' rights movement in Eastern Europe. It does not seem so long ago when, in 1986, Anatoly Marchenko went on a hunger strike demanding the release of all political prisoners and criminal prosecution of the jailers who had beaten him. Marchenko died of a cerebral hemorrhage in prison on December 8, 1986, after spending *twenty* of his forty-eight years in the Soviet penal system. And it was not so long ago when I visited his widow in Moscow (when *perestroika* and *glasnost* were already beginning) that some bricks were thrown through our car window parked outside her apartment to warn us that our visits to her were still unwelcome.

The collapse of communist regimes in East Germany and Eastern Europe and the reforms in the Soviet Union made possible the construction of a new Europe of solidarity: a nonaligned, neutral Europe including the Soviet Union. But we in Western Europe have hardly changed. No matter what we, as West Germans and West Europeans, say about cooperation and fair play, we still believe *instinctively* in the struggle for supremacy. As an ideology, it befits our own dog-eat-dog capitalism.

Many of the former dissidents in Eastern Europe and West European peace activists, including myself, have founded the Helsinki Citizens Assembly. We recently met in Prague and tried to initiate a dialogue from below on future European cooperation. We now have a real possibility of constructing new relationships in Europe that *do not depend on the threat or use of military force.* But still, huge military infrastructures and large stockpiles of weapons are in place, and there are many major differences in the level of economic development and standards of living between East and West, North and South. Environmental degradation poses a serious threat to survival and gives rise to new conflicts. The Helsinki Citizens Assembly hopes to create a new type of security system and do away with military power blocs. We want to make sure that it is no longer necessary to maintain troops on foreign territory, that all weapons of mass destruction are eliminated, and that military spending and conventional arms be drastically reduced.

The peaceful transition of Europe is unthinkable without the full observance of all human and civil rights. This becomes all the more important because racism is now on the rise in the former Eastern bloc. The reported 12 percent rise in attacks by neo-Nazi youth gangs on synagogues, Asians, Hispanics, and others causes us grave concern. Discrimination against Africans and other Third World people is on the rise in Eastern Europe, and there is now a rejection of internationalism and support for Third World liberation movements. In their quest to return back to "Europe," there is the danger that many in Eastern Europe will throw away the values of universalism and internationalism and [*will*] promote national chauvinism instead. No event demonstrates this attitude better than the demand by miners in the Ukraine during their strike last year that *all aid to the Third World be stopped.* Here also is another statistic: There were 22,000 Africans studying in the Soviet Union and Eastern Europe up to 1988; this year [1992] there are only 5,000.

Now that people are able to open up and express themselves, the greater pluralism now erupting everywhere is also throwing up many bad things. A racist ideology is creeping out. I am afraid that the European Community may turn into a fortress, a fortress against all which is *not* European. Immigrant workers in Europe face a rising ride of racism and face the prospect of job losses and deportation. And political and economic refugees will soon feel that the doors of both Eastern and Western Europe are more tightly closed than ever. This is *not* the kind of Europe we wished for.

And there is one other worry I share much with my friend, Vandana Shiva, an Indian environmentalist and feminist. With the end of tensions between East and West, she states, the Third World will increasingly become the supplier of raw materials for the new unified North and the dump for its hazards and wastes. She uses an African proverb: "When elephants make war, the grass gets trampled. When elephants make love, the grass gets trampled." The Third World environment and the Third World communities are the ones who have paid the highest price for the superpower rivalry. The cold war in Europe had always been translated into real and burning wars in the Third

World—in Central America, in Central Asia, and in the Horn of Africa. Since 1945, 200 wars have been fought in the Third World. As the industrialized world now moves from an overarmed peace to a disarmed one, the military producers and traders merely find alternative markets in the Third World. As the superpowers withdraw from Afghanistan, the neighboring region of Kashmir goes up in flames and Pakistan and India become new markets for arms. Similarly, the United States has sold tanks, removed from Europe, to Egypt. There is now a very real danger that arms released from East-West disarmament will be dumped in the Third World.

There is, of course, much environmental devastation in Eastern Europe. Thousands of Bohemian school children must now wear breathing masks for the short walk to school. Pollution levels this winter in Czechoslovakia are soaring ten times past internationally accepted "safe" limits. The death of the Aral Sea in the Soviet Union is one other example of this destruction. The death of the Aral Sea is connected with the ecology of overirrigation and chemicalization of agriculture. But this sudden exposure of environmental problems in the East should *not* blind us to the many ecological problems also existing in the market economies in the West. Aid and expertise coming from the industrialized North continues to be the main support, unfortunately, for environmentally destructive projects in the Third World. Here I need only mention the large dam projects in India. It is the Third World that will have to bear *again* the *ecological costs* of the *new industrialism and consumerism in the North, including the cost of cleaning up Eastern Europe.* East and West Europe will increasingly use the Third World as a dump for hazards and wastes. And when the transport ways are too long for the Third World, then the West will use Eastern Europe for its dumping ground.

Europe, if it is to become a true continent of peace, ecology, and nonviolence, must begin to understand that 20 percent of the world's population has been using 80 percent of the world's resources and that the planet is already devastated. Not only Germany has to learn policies of self-restraint, but Western Europe also has to follow policies of self-restraint.

Our goal must be European unity in diversity, through policies of non-alignment, and active neutrality, and being in solidarity with the Third World. We must build a civil society, a fully demilitarized and socially just community, whose economic development will not be at the expense of the environment and at the expense of the Third World.

Germany and also, of course, Europe at the end of the second millennium have a chance of transforming themselves into a country and continent of peace, human dignity, justice, and worldwide solidarity. The hope comes from the independent citizens' rights movements that have liberated, together with President Gorbachev and his policies, Eastern Europe. Now we find ourselves, in Western Europe, learning to become dissidents so that we, too, can begin building a civil society at home. Learning from the nonviolent days of November and December 1989 must be one of our priorities. We have that "chance" of transformation *now*. Let us not spoil or lose it!

In the December 1990 elections, the Greens lost their seats in Parliament. In January 1991, the American-led coalition began to use force to drive the Iraqis from Kuwait. It was a time of personal anguish for Petra Kelly. In an open letter to the Green party, she reflected on challenges as she saw them.[4] The Greens, she wrote, had "persistently denounced the unscrupulous policy of 'legal' and illegal arms exports to countries all over the world and in particular we also revealed the criminal shipments of [*nuclear, chemical, and biological*] components to Iraq. Yet the responsible [*German*] Federal Ministries reacted with bored arrogance, and all our political demands for an immediate halt to arms exports were voted down in the German Bundestag." *The Greens had warned of ecological damage from military operations, and the Gulf War bore out those warnings. They had warned of a lifestyle that demanded a steady flow of resources from abroad that were then squandered. Kelly saw the Gulf Crisis as* "a harbinger of further crises which will arise in the future in the struggle for increasingly scarce resources." *But the Iraqi invasion was a challenge for the Greens.*

We took the victims' side, not only when the Iraqis marched into Kuwait but also during the earlier and equally criminal acts of military intervention, such as China's rape of Tibet, Morocco's occupation of the Western Sahara, the Soviet invasion of Afghanistan, the Syrian war in Lebanon, and Israeli injustice toward the Palestinians, to name just a few violations of international law. We did so because we believe that questions of international law and human rights issues have always been and will remain indivisible. They can only be judged according to immutable moral standards and must not be used by any government as instruments to further political, military, or economic interests.

The Greens, as a nonviolent political party, in the past had supported the ethical principle that injustice must not be repaid with possibly even greater injustice and that there can be no justification for military violence. Many of us wanted to introduce a bit of the Sermon on the Mount and civilism into Bonn's policies and not just save them for fine sermons at Church rallies. Yet our modest efforts to develop nonmilitary, nonviolent strategies for conflict settlement in Bonn met with nothing but weary smiles from the defense experts of the established parties. Now, in these awful February days of Desert Storm, the failure of the traditional military philosophy with its hollow phrases about a "just" war and "surgical" strikes is of course becoming apparent in the most saddening way, and the military censorship has laid a blanket of silence over the mass murder of innocent people in a bloody slaughter which cannot solve any problems but will create a host of new ones.

Why, she asked, did voters turn away from the Green party with its far-sighted, principled stance on the crucial issues? The answer, she felt, was that "eight years of self-destructive and fruitless infighting amongst the various factions and their gurus paralyzed our political activities and created an atmosphere steeped in jealousy and distrust. This proved too much even for the greenest voter." *She called on the party to use its electoral defeat as a means of learning and of recreating the political movement. But at heart, she remained committed to being in an "anti-party party."*

The term "anti-party party," which I invented, has been frequently misunderstood, and many people seem to think that it is outdated. Even so, I shall continue to use it, for to me the term denotes a party capable of choosing between morality and power, a party which uses creative civil disobedience to combat every form of repression, which combines audacious imagination with efficient working methods, and which recognizes the link between world peace and peace in every individual. And "anti-party parties" do not exercise power in the old authoritarian sense; instead, they try to transform power in order to enable people to achieve self-determination over their lives.

NOTES

1. From Petra Kelly, "Women and Global Green Politics," *Woman of Power* 20 (Spring 1991): 24–25.
2. From Petra Kelly, "Women and Children First," *Simply Living* 7 (Winter–Spring 1992): 98.
3. From Petra Kelly, "A Green View of German Reunification and Europe's Future," The American University's School of International Service Alumni dinner, November 19, 1990.
4. Petra Kelly, "Open Letter to the Green Party," Spring 1991.

12

Women in Revolutionary Movements: Cuba and Nicaragua

Margaret Randall

Cuba, mid-1970s. Milagros—a friend, poet, and radio writer—lived with her husband and two daughters in Nueva Gerona on the Isle of Youth. In this offshore community, energy was high and many of the country's social programs were first put into practice. It was easy to understand why. The island was largely populated by young people who had gone to work on the citrus farms during the revolution's first years. Many stayed, raised their own families, made a life for themselves there. Young people, it was said, take to new places and new ideas more easily.

But when Milagros published a poem criticizing men who were proud of their revolutionary affiliation but didn't understand how oblivious they were to women's needs—revolutionary men who in fact perpetrated women's oppression—many found it easier to label her provocative or troublesome than to examine the real problem she described: "Where are you, manspirit of my time / every afternoon home from work / become exactly that fountain of rude stares / reproaching me the quick lunch, / [the] pile of unwashed clothes. . . . Revolution is more than **I want** / more than Party member."[1] It would take her *compañeros*—most men, and also many women—at least a decade to catch up with these sentiments. Meanwhile, Milagros and others like her were marginalized because of their feminist consciousness. Although social revolutions express the goal of a better life for everyone, their programs have been slow to embrace a truly feminist agenda.

THE REVOLUTIONARY MOVEMENT
AS POLITICAL PHENOMENON

Until two or three decades ago, the phrase "women in revolutionary movements" would have meant the half dozen extraordinary women whose names come down to us from the histories of the French, Russian, or Chinese revolutions. If we study revolution in Vietnam, Cuba, Algeria, or other Third World countries, we learn that greater numbers of women took part. In more recent struggles in places like El Salvador, Guatemala, Southern Africa, and Nicaragua, we can document a substantial participation. Now, when we say "women in revolutionary movements," we may be talking about women being 30 or 40 percent of a movement and of women occupying some leadership positions.

What are revolutionary movements and how do they develop? When great numbers of people work in unfair conditions and still cannot provide themselves and their families with the skeletal necessities of a decent life, dissatisfaction grows. Individually, the exploited feel powerless to change their situation and often take their frustrations out on someone over whom they have a measure of control. Women frequently find ourselves on the receiving end of this injustice, in the vulnerable role of victim—compounded by the pressures meted out to us because of our gender, color, sexual identity, or the type of work we do. For this reason, poor and minority women especially constitute a powerful potential force for social change.

As inequality intensifies, the contradictions between the powerful and powerless grow sharper. This pushes people to organize. When people cannot change the conditions that affect their lives through legal means, revolutionary movements emerge and grow as a collective response to inhuman conditions. Men have generally led these revolutionary struggles. Increasingly, and particularly since the beginning of this century, women have participated in revolutionary movements that have changed their nation's history and their own lives. Here the struggle to resist gender oppression begins to intersect with battles against other types of inequality.

Karl Marx, Frederich Engels, and other intellectual architects of revolution have said that the degree of freedom enjoyed by a given society can be measured by the freedom that women have achieved within that society. A great deal may be learned from looking at the ways in which women's lives have changed (or not changed) in the context of societies that have undergone revolutionary transformation. We can also learn a lot, I believe, about the failures of certain socialist experiments—particularly the recent dramatic changes in the Soviet Union, Eastern Europe, and Nicaragua—by looking at the ways in which the new or "revolutionary" society did or did not seriously address a feminist agenda.

In this chapter, I examine revolutionary movements in Cuba and Nicaragua, two countries geographically close to the United States but about which public information here has been meager and politically manipulated. I will place the Cuban and Nicaraguan revolutionary movements, and the women who have helped make them, in their appropriate historical contexts.

I also want to ask the difficult questions that seem to repeat themselves in each new arena of struggle: How have women overcome long-embedded traditions of subservience in order to participate fully? Once involved, to whatever degree, have they managed to win and maintain any real political power? In Cuba and Nicaragua, have "women's" issues been regarded as integral to the overall struggle, or in contradiction to it? Once in power, do these movements—by this time functioning as governments—address sexism and gender bias, or do they consider other issues more important? Is there space for critical evaluation, a feminist questioning of the status quo? And finally, how do new generations of women fare in societies that purport to be more just, more democratic, more egalitarian?

The 1959 victory of the socialist revolution in Cuba preceded the most recent upsurge of feminism worldwide.[2] The 1979 Sandinista revolution in Nicaragua came to power twenty years later and, thus, was able to draw on feminist thought and practice within the context of its basically nationalist and anti-imperialist agenda. The very different historic moment gave Nicaraguan women an ideological advantage over their Cuban sisters in their efforts to change gender relations.

On the other hand, the world economic crisis sharpened considerably between 1959 and 1979. This denied women in Nicaragua the opportunity that Cuban women had of carving out an economic independence for themselves during the first two decades of their revolution. Of course, women in Cuba and women in Nicaragua also operate within their particular cultures and histories. But this twenty-year difference undoubtedly contributed to very different ways of addressing feminist issues in these two struggles.

CUBA

Cuba is a small island nation just ninety miles off the Florida keys. In the first half of the twentieth century, Cuba was almost entirely dependent upon its powerful northern neighbor. The uninvited interference of the United States in Cuba's War of Independence from Spain (which the United States called the Spanish-American War) and subsequent occupation of Cuba angered Cuban nationalists. The United States encouraged the island's one-crop economy, bought most of its sugar, and sold Cuba all manner of manufactured products. The United States also supported a series of political leaders in Cuba who could ensure "stability" for trade and tourism, usually with strong-arm tactics.

Women participated in a labor-based movement against the dictator Antonio Machado, the president in the 1930s. They did so again in the struggle against Fulgencio Batista that developed after that dictator's illegal takeover in 1952. During Batista's rule, many problems cried out for redress by the Cuban people. Most Cubans lived in extreme poverty and lacked employment opportunities and health care. Statistics from the 1950s show high rates of unemployment and a wage labor force that was 9.8 percent female.[3] Those who did find jobs had nonexistent or inadequate benefits.

In these years, women experienced unequal access to education, unequal pay when they did manage to find jobs, and degrading sexual objectification. About one-third of working women were domestic servants, whose starvation wages ranged from $8 to $25 a month. Acute poverty in the countryside forced many young girls and women to the capital, where their only possibilities for survival were as maids or prostitutes. Prostitution flourished in prerevolutionary Cuba, promoted by an active U.S.–based national crime syndicate. The big casinos were legendary; not as well publicized was their victimization of tens of thousands of women.

The opposition to Batista grew. Cuban women participated in many opposition groups, such as the old Communist party of Cuba and a student-based organization called the University Directorate. Power soon centered in Fidel Castro's 26th of July Movement (M-7-26). In this organization, women were lower- and middle-level cadre, messengers, and nurses. A few, like Celia Sanchez, Vilma Espin, and Haydee Santamaria, occupied important positions in an organization fundamentally dominated by men. In the last months of the guerrilla war (August–September 1958), some of the more active women, opposed by *machismo* in the ranks but supported by Castro's growing understanding of women as a political force, launched the country's first contingent of fighting women: the Mariana Grajales Platoon. Mariana Grajales was the mother of Antonio Maceo, a Black general in Cuba's War of Independence from Spain.

The M-7-26 led the Cuban people to victory over Batista in January 1959. When the M-7-26 took power, the guerrilla-movement-turned-government inherited an oppressive Spanish Catholicism, with its inhibition of women's freedom and social agency. But Cuba is also a predominantly Black nation with a tradition of activism in resistance to slavery.

As the Cuban revolution began to define itself as socialist (April 1961), sectors of the population looked to the communist model in other parts of the world for organizational strategies. Young children became *Pioneros* and, as they got older, members of the Communist Youth. Workers and peasants formed organizations structured to defend their rights in the new political system. In 1965, the M-7-26 became the new Cuban Communist party. Women soon organized into a broad-based movement, the Federation of Cuban Women (FMC), which had been established on August 23, 1960. Following the lead of their sisters in the Soviet Union and other socialist states, Cuban women patterned their organization on those women's movements.

So the FMC was separate from, but organically linked to, what in 1965 would be redefined as the Cuban Communist party. The federation's dual role was to mobilize around women's issues and to enlist women in support and defense of the new revolution. The traditional communist approach to the problem of women's equality was that once women's economic independence was assured, discriminatory practices and residual prejudice would disappear. Often it was Fidel Castro himself who insisted upon harnessing and channeling women's participation as women in the heated discussions of those first years.

The new revolution, largely channeling its efforts through the FMC, began to address the most urgent women's issues: education, work, health, day care, legal protection. The revolution also promoted campaigns not specifically aimed at women but that did a great deal to change their role in society. Perhaps the most important of these was the massive literacy campaign of 1961, in which 100,000 young people went out to teach reading and writing to the almost one-quarter of the adult population that was illiterate. Illiteracy was greater among women, and so those in the countryside, especially, gained access to a whole new social participation. But 56% of the young literacy *brigadistas* were also female. Most of these young girls had led previously chaperoned lives, overprotected from their own possibilities for responsibility and emotional growth. So the literacy campaign changed the lives of older women and pushed a generation of young Cuban girls toward greater personal and collective freedom, thus affecting women's social agency in future generations as well.

The revolution became stronger, in spite of ongoing threats against its sovereignty by the United States. The efforts by the United States to undermine the revolutionary process included the failed Bay of Pigs invasion, a continuing trade embargo and prohibition of U.S. citizens' travel to Cuba, and censure at international organizations like the United Nations and the Organization of American States. Many Cubans resented U.S. interference and engaged in the defense of their nation's independence. Women entered the militia that protected workplaces and other strategic areas, and they participated in night patrols (a kind of neighborhood watch) through defense committees organized on each block. They worked to become better educated, to take on a broader range of jobs, and for salaries commensurate with their labor. They also began to deal with the fact that great numbers among them had been trapped into prostitution or domestic service.

Early in the revolutionary process, through an innovative program of reeducation, prostitution was literally stamped out. This doesn't mean there were suddenly no prostitutes in Cuba, but that no Cuban woman was any longer forced by circumstance to survive by selling her body. Women who had been prostitutes were trained in other fields and placed in jobs once they were trained. Although the revolution effectively eliminated prostitution during its first three decades, more recently, with the hardships of the "special period" of austerity since 1990 when Soviet aid ended, some prostitution has reappeared.

Domestic servants, previously trapped in exploitative live-in situations and virtually on call twenty-four hours a day, went through programs leading to jobs as secretaries, bank clerks, day-care workers, interpreters, and taxi drivers. Women went into higher education in droves, competing in large numbers for positions formerly almost exclusively reserved for men. They became doctors, military officers, architects, teachers, and administrators of farming cooperatives and industrial complexes.

The Federation of Cuban Women (FMC) created a system of day-care centers. They prepared study materials and educated housewives to the new revolutionary ideas. They mobilized women in the countryside, who had previously endured lives of virtual subservience to their profoundly exploited men. Within the new project of health care for all, they focused on the special problems of women's health: adequate and fully paid maternity leaves, healthy pregnancies, contraception and abortion, a yearly pap smear to reduce the rate of cervical cancer, and special food rations for pregnant and nursing mothers.

All of these were "women's concerns." But they were also important to the entire society. The FMC became one of the new system's great mass organizations, eventually enlisting more than 80 percent of women in the country fourteen years of age or older. It was soon capable of mobilizing vast numbers of women almost instantly—whether to go door to door in the campaign for every women to have her free annual pap smear or to urge them to discuss and promote a new law, to rally in support of a new revolutionary measure, or to join with their brothers to pick potatoes or be vigilant against attacks upon the vulnerable revolutionary process.

Frequently there was no contradiction between women's needs as women and the needs of the revolution that required the support of women and other groups. But sometimes contradictions or apparent contradictions did surface. For a number of years, guided by the traditional communist analysis of women as an economically dependent sector, the priorities were seen as access to education, incorporation into the labor force, and services like day care for children or workers' dining rooms. The more radical feminism emerging in the United States and Western Europe was considered "bourgeois" by the Cuban party and seen as divisive to the revolutionary ranks. An attack on the residual ideology of sexist values was yet to come.

Sometimes the contradictions provoked situations that were ludicrous. In the early 1970s, I was stopped at a hospital gate and informed I couldn't visit a friend because I was wearing pants! I insisted on knowing why this was against the rules and was told that wearing pants "might overly excite the male patients." The rule was changed soon after. Sometimes the issue was more complex, as when one of my daughters complained at Christmas that the cowboy suit available for girls lacked the hat and gun included with the boy's version. And no, she couldn't have one of those. Toys were rationed, to make sure all children had equal access. It was hard for my daughter to understand why she was being denied the toy gun she wanted, particularly in a society where women belonged to the militia and the army and were honored for their role in defending the revolution. She was right not to understand. In time, this too was changed.

In its third of a century of survival, the Cuban revolution has endured periods in which the needs or rights of particular groups have had to be sacrificed to the revolution's elemental right to resist—and subsist. In other periods of relative prosperity, it has been possible to reexamine the needs of the different social sectors. Women's issues and rights in Cuba have moved through this spiraling process.

Midway through 1974, the Cuban party and government launched an electoral process called "People's Power" that would convene representatives at the local, provincial, and national levels. Women were found to be seriously underrepresented in this new form of popular democracy. The Cuban leadership did a double take. In a society that had loudly proclaimed the end of discrimination against women, things were not what they seemed. When the pilot project (which was tried first in a single province, Matanzas) showed under 4 percent female membership in the new governing body, an interdisciplinary group was established to try to determine why. Interviews were conducted, studies carried out. It was clear that the "second shift" (housework done after the hours of paid employment) kept many women from wanting "yet another job."

The profound concern generated by this experience led to a nationwide discussion of women's role in society. On buses and in markets, as well as in more formal meetings, women's social situation was discussed as never before. A new *Family Code* was eventually written and passed into law, with tremendous participation from women of all backgrounds and ages. The code demands that men take responsibility for 50 percent of housework, child care and rearing, and that they support their wives or sisters in their efforts to go to school or to otherwise train for more specialized work. Parts of the new code were written into the civil marriage ceremony, to be read aloud to men and women who then publicly committed themselves to upholding these more egalitarian tenets.

Although much has been accomplished, Cuban women still have a long way to go. Some progress has been made in addressing sexuality in general and homosexuality in particular. Oppression of gays and lesbians was intense during the mid-1960s and early 1970s, when many were sent to "reeducation" camps for undesirables because of a presumed "deviancy." Since then, life for Cuban gays and lesbians has gotten progressively better. But a comprehensive program of sex education in the schools came late, and lesbian rights are still little discussed, at least publicly.[4] Women continue to be underrepresented in positions of political power, though there are slightly more each year. The FMC continues to be an organization capable of mobilizing great numbers of women but has not played the vanguard role it might have in women's examination of the cultural or ideological aspects of discrimination: *machismo* or male chauvinism, misogynist attitudes, or the development of feminist theory and practice within the Cuban context.

In fact, frequently it has been women in other organizational structures or areas—the trade unions, the army, intellectuals and artists—who have led the debate in the area of feminist discourse. Sometimes it has been men, most notably Castro himself. The Cuban film industry has addressed so-called women's issues in a number of important films, such as *The Catcall* (*El piropo*) and *Portrait of Teresa*. The late 1970s saw an explosion of poetry and other writing by women, much of it fueled by a specifically feminist passion. Artistic creativity and feminist discourse have come together in particularly exciting ways in the area of popular theater. For example, in the *Teatro Escambray*, a group of professionals from Havana went to live in the Escambray mountains, did long-range studies of the problems there and then wrote plays with the people themselves, who acted in them and participated in other ways, for example, in heated postperformance debates. These have provided places for addressing feminist concerns not raised by the FMC.

There is no doubt, however, that the Cuban revolution has changed women's lives in fundamental ways. In 1991 women were 38.7 percent of the salaried labor force. Nearly half of them work outside the home, compared to 13.6 percent when the revolution took power. Women constitute 57.3 percent of university students, 55.3 percent of university graduates, and 58.3 percent of middle-level technicians. And women who work earn salaries comparable to men's and have job security and excellent benefits. Almost 34 percent of the national legislative body is now female.[5] Cuban girls grow up in a system that supports their right to be educated, to work, to make their own reproductive decisions, and to aspire to real power. These are extraordinary achievements in a society that inherited abysmal underdevelopment and has had to battle unrelenting U.S. aggression at all levels simply to survive.

The current disintegration of socialism among the countries that most effectively supported the Cuban process clearly raises problems in the social as well as the economic spheres. The "special period" of austerity has made the life of all Cubans harder—and has made "women's work," such as putting food on the family's table and washing clothes with a scarcity of soap, particularly difficult. Some women feel that the "special period" has further socialized the household, since men are now forced to help more. Others see it as having pushed women back into more traditional roles. In any case, it seems likely that although specifically feminist issues are more and more a topic of debate in Cuba, official examination of feminist concerns will not be a priority as long as the survival of the revolution itself is in danger.

In the past thirty-five years, Cuban women have undergone a deep shift in consciousness about the ways in which they can expect society to meet their needs—as Cubans and also as women. If this is a period that will most likely not provide the context for more than the daily task of holding on, changes have nevertheless been made that have acquired their own momentum. The collective memory is changing. Cuban women have learned to ask questions and look for answers in a process that is ongoing. Rather sooner than later, that process must embrace the issues still to be addressed.

NICARAGUA

Where Cuba's population has its roots in Spanish colonialism that virtually eliminated the indigenous population and the important influx of African slave trade, Nicaragua's people inherit an Indian ancestry that survived. Women achieved a unique level of participation in Nicaragua before the Spanish conquest; they were engaged in commerce and controlled part of the economy. They also participated in opposition to Spanish rule. During the 1920s and 1930s when a nationalist named Augusto C. Sandino led the country's peasants and workers against the first of the Somoza dynasty, women like Teresa Villatoro and María Altamirano were guerrilla leaders. This gives Nicaraguan women an unusually strong history of economic and political participation.

By the 1960s, when the Sandinista National Liberation Front (FSLN) continued where Sandino's war of liberation left off, a new wave of feminist thought and practice had emerged internationally. The revolutionary movement that would finally oust the younger son of that first Somoza and bring about a successful revolutionary process in Nicaragua was able to draw on this new feminism in a variety of ways.

The founders of the new movement were all men. And the nine-member National Directorate (DN) that eventually oversaw the victory was also entirely male. But women participated in the FSLN in ways previously unparalleled in the history of people's struggle. Many were exceptionally young women—eighteen, fifteen, even twelve years of age. A woman member of the local government in the northern city of Ocotal, whose fifteen-year-old daughter had been killed in the guerrilla war, told me: "We should have been capable of giving our sons and daughters this new nation; they shouldn't have had to give it to us!"[6]

Some Nicaraguan women came to revolutionary consciousness from the ranks of a changing Christian movement.[7] A number of Catholic sisters were active on the front lines. Some of the women in the FSLN were university students who had gone from their tiny Central American country to study abroad and were touched by the feminist movements surfacing in Europe and the United States. Women struggled with their male *compañeros* and demanded a political space for themselves. This space produced more than a few leaders who were women, and these women continued to ask complex questions about their political participation and its meaning.

Amada Pineda is a peasant woman whose husband was involved in the early struggles against the Somoza dictatorship. She participated as well, eventually surviving widowhood, capture, torture, and ongoing repression. Later, in the first years of the new government, Pineda—who knew the suffering of Nicaraguan farmers because it was her own experience—was appointed to a commission set up to hear the complaints of large property owners whose lands had been confiscated and given to those who worked them. This creative turnabout was typical of Sandinista justice.

Women were credited with extraordinary feats of political and military prowess in the war against Somoza. The liberation army, at the time of its victory, was approximately one-third female. The first free territory of Nicaragua, the city of León, was liberated by guerrilla forces commanded by Dora María Téllez, a woman then in her early twenties. Dora was in her second year of medical school when she went underground with the FSLN. After the victory, she served as Minister of Public Health during most of the years of Sandinista government. She was also the vice-president of the new legislature.

The story of Nora Astorga is worth telling here. She was from a wealthy family and had an excellent education. She worked as an attorney for a large construction company during the last years of Somoza's rule. One day, she was sexually approached by Reynaldo Pérez Vega, nicknamed "The Dog," a general who was notorious for his torture and humiliation of women. She had already begun to aid the FSLN in various ways and alerted her contact in the organization to the fact that this man was interested in her.

With FSLN encouragement, Nora Astorga embarked on the plan to take Pérez Vega hostage and obtain the release of political prisoners. It was March 8, 1978, International Women's Day. Astorga invited the torturer to her home. She managed to disarm and undress him. But the original plan had to be dropped when he offered excessive resistance. The revolutionaries were forced to shoot their hostage.

Thousands of Nicaraguan women received the news of Pérez Vega's death with the emotion only those who have suffered at the hands of such a torturer can know. To evade capture, Astorga was forced to leave her life in the city and join the guerrilla forces active in the southern mountains. Much later, when asked how it felt to have to leave her own children behind, she always spoke of her conviction that she was part of a struggle that would free all Nicaraguans.

As a result of her training and her outstanding participation in the revolutionary movement, Nora Astorga became Special Attorney General of the new Nicaragua, prosecuting the more than 7,000 cases of ex–National Guardsmen who were tried for crimes against the people.[8] Later, the Sandinista government appointed her ambassador to the United States, but the United States refused to accept her credentials, citing the 1978 action against Pérez Vega (who, it turned out, had been on the payroll of the CIA).

Eventually, Astorga headed Nicaragua's delegation to the United Nations. In the most difficult years of the war with the Contras, already fatally ill with cancer, her brilliance, skill, and what many have called her particular womanist spirit, enabled her to represent David in that world arena of Goliaths. She made it through one last General Assembly, then returned to Nicaragua where she died of cancer in February 1989. Her story is extraordinary, but—among Nicaraguan revolutionary women—not unusual.

These women and many others took part in the liberation army and in the postwar process of transformation. This attests to the degree to which women's lives changed in the Nicaraguan revolution as in no previous struggle. Still, a "glass ceiling" did persist insofar as none of these women ever made it to the top echelons of party politics.

During twenty years of consolidation, the Nicaraguan revolutionary forces made several different attempts to organize women. AMPRONAC (The Association of Nicaraguan Women Facing the Nation's Problems) was the group that would finally prove successful. In the late 1970s, AMPRONAC called to women across class lines and throughout the country and played a decisive role in the strategy that led to victory.

In war time, AMPRONAC mobilized women around issues such as hunger, repression in the countryside, and release of political prisoners. Mothers of revolutionaries staged hunger strikes and occupied the local United Nations office and the Managua cathedral. Sons and daughters politicized their mothers, who then often assumed their own militancy.[9] In the context of full-scale armed struggle, AMPRONAC saw winning the war as the priority, as the most important feminist issue.

Once the war was won, AMPRONAC became AMNLAE: the Luisa Amanda Espinosa National Women's Association. Luisa Amanda Espinosa was the first woman killed in the ranks of the FSLN. There was a great deal of debate about how best to organize women—both for the compelling tasks of reconstruction and structural change and around the issues that confronted them as women. One of the Sandinista government's first decrees banned the use of women's bodies in commercial advertising, a move that signaled a singular feminist consciousness, but enforcement fluctuated throughout the Sandinista administration. However, to the credit of the FSLN as well as Nicaraguan women, feminist issues were on the agenda from the beginning of the revolutionary experience.

Nicaraguan revolutionaries could count on the solidarity and generosity of the Cuban revolution; Cubans came to Nicaragua to help in all areas of transformation. Nicaraguan women looked to the Cuban model of a mass organization of women, and AMNLAE's first year or year and a half did in fact draw heavily on the Cuban experience. AMNLAE established transnational connections with the Cuban Federation of Women (FMC) as well as with other women's groups, such as the Association of Women of El Salvador (AMES).

Nicaraguan women soon began to question this model that seemed to duplicate the efforts of other mass organizations and had trouble concentrating on the unique challenge of problems specific to women. A woman might be encouraged to join her neighborhood defense committee, the Sandinista youth organization or the FSLN, and perhaps also her labor union if she worked outside the home. Much work was necessarily duplicated in these different venues, weakening the effect of a place where women could get together as women, and as women address both the revolution's needs and their own.

After less than two years, a first national conference was held. Women came to Managua from remote regions as well as from the cities to assess their experiences and to share opinions and questions. As a result, the mass organization model was abandoned. AMNLAE began to conceive of itself as a movement, operating small groups in workplaces, neighborhoods, schools—wherever there was a significant female presence. In this way, it was able to focus on issues of particular relevance for women, within the general context of social change—and, of course, the by-now familiar hostility from the United States.

It should be noted that as far as the Cuban and Nicaraguan revolutions were concerned, the United States targeted women in its campaign to undermine the revolutions. Through economic blockade, a succession of U.S. administrations targeted the buying power of the household, making scarce such articles as food, cleaning supplies, refrigerators, stoves, and other kitchen aids. Articles traditionally associated with women's beauty and recreation, such as makeup, nylon stockings, dress fabric, shoes and the like, also disappeared from the market. It was whispered that religion would disappear and that women who had used it especially in times of trial would be deprived of that solace. Other rumors were disseminated, threatening the dissolution of the family, with children sent away to schools in the countryside or abroad and husbands and providers forced by circumstances to defense posts that were also often distant from their homes.

If, in Nicaragua, the historic moment was more conducive than it had been in Cuba to the inclusion of a feminist agenda, the world economic situation was also much worse in 1979 than it had been twenty years earlier. On top of a much more acute global crisis, Nicaragua's war of liberation left a country ravaged by two years of wholesale death and destruction, an agricultural country without a harvest, widespread hunger, and massive unemployment.

AMNLAE could not try to address the predominantly female problems of prostitution and domestic service through programs of reeducation and relocation as the FMC had done in Cuba, because this time there were no jobs available for women who wanted to change their lives. So the women's movement worked differently in Nicaragua. AMNLAE joined forces with labor to help domestic servants unionize and demand a ten-hour day, elemental benefits, and effective redress for incidents of abuse. In the urban centers where prostitution flourished, sewing cooperatives were established in which at least some prostitutes were able to take up another line of work. Here, again, the remedies in Nicaragua utilized people's homes and were makeshift arrangements that could not hope to attack the problems at their roots.

As had been the case in Cuba, service remained a woman's sphere. In Nicaragua, women engaged in public health projects, mass literacy and educational reforms, and programs to deal with the large numbers of orphans and mutilated persons left by the war. But the fact that so many Nicaraguan women had fought alongside men also energized the struggle for women's rights. Feminist issues were debated in broad forums, with a range of opposing opinions in newspapers and other media.

One of the most serious problems faced by Nicaraguan mothers has always been the high percentage of men who father their children and then leave them to support those children by themselves. The revolution instituted Women's Offices that, among other things, helped abandoned families get economic support from absentee fathers.

Sex education was introduced into public education much sooner and more completely than it had been in Cuba. A consciousness of the rights of homosexuals existed within the FSLN, and Sandinista Nicaragua managed to avoid the level of abuse that had taken place in Cuba. On the other hand, in an essentially Catholic country, and one in which the Church would quickly split along class lines, abortion was never legalized during the ten years of revolution. During the Sandinista administration, the official women's movement never engaged in open debate or frontal struggle over the abortion issue. Legalizing it would have risked further alienating the hierarchical Church. But more and more women were dying from the growing number of illegal abortions being performed. Most women in FSLN leadership now feel that not pushing for legalization during the Sandinista period was a mistake.

When the war against the Contras created the need for a compulsory draft, AMNLAE's delegation to the National Assembly demanded that women be included. The FSLN argued that the country's current conditions still left women essentially responsible for home and child care and that it was premature to give women the "equality" of compulsory military service. This provoked a heated debate on the floor of the nation's legislative body. AMNLAE lost. But splits in this and other struggles showed that in Nicaragua, unlike Cuba, the revolutionary women's movement had its moments of rebellion even if it never proposed autonomy.

At this writing, the Cuban revolution lives. Although deeply affected by the disintegration of socialism in the Soviet Union and Eastern European countries, it is one of the few socialist experiments remaining. In spite of enormous problems of all kinds, Cubans continue to enjoy a higher standard of living and broader access to education, work, shelter, health care, culture, and recreation than most other Latin American peoples.

Nicaragua is another story. Although the ten years of Sandinista rule cannot be erased from popular consciousness, the loss of the 1990 elections has affected absolutely every revolutionary project and program, including those specifically benefiting women. The United States would not permit the vibrant, promising, and truly pluralist experiment of a mixed economy with state and collective ownership in which Christian as well as nationalist and socialist values coexisted. When the war waged by the Contras failed and "Contragate" was exposed, the National Endowment for Democracy and other specialized U.S. agencies funneled $17.5 million into an opposition electoral campaign to place in power a pro-American figurehead, Violeta Barrios de Chamorro, who is discussed in chapter 2.

For the Nicaraguan people, the end of the Sandinista administration has been a terrible loss. Driven by hunger and anguish over the mounting death toll from an ongoing fratricidal war, many voted against the Sandinistas. Women, and particularly mothers, suffered real anguish during the last years of a thoroughly undermined and attacked Sandinista government. Too many of their sons and daughters had been killed in the war with the Contras. An economy in crisis gravely affected every household. The draft had been a sore point. It was difficult to know whether the need for an ample defense or the continued loss of young lives was the more urgent issue. The people believed the lavish promises of peace and prosperity made by Chamorro and her hastily formed coalition of fourteen conservative parties. Three years later, none of those promises had been kept. Economic aid from the United States has only been partially forthcoming, and almost none of what has arrived has filtered down to the people who so desperately need it. The ordinary Nicaraguan is in much worse shape than before.

But the Sandinistas, now once again in a struggle to gain state power, have had the opportunity to evaluate their ten years in government: an impressive range of achievements, but also errors of judgment, internal and external pressures, arrogance on the part of some of the leadership, and instances of corruption and/or isolation from the rank and file. In the intensity of the survival struggle that accompanied the Sandinistas' last years in office, many feminist issues, like abortion, were pushed aside. Although the electoral loss has been a terrible blow to the revolution, it has also provided the context for some much needed debate. In the long run, feminism in Nicaragua, as well as other issues of people's power—race, ethnicity, gay rights—may well gain from this temporary defeat.

After almost two years of exhaustive discussion, from grassroots to leadership levels, the FSLN held its first congress in July 1991. Along with ideological and policy issues, one point on the agenda was that of reelecting or changing the National Directorate (previously the highest level of party authority). One member of this all-male group had died, another could no longer serve because there was a conflict of interest in that he still headed the army. There were those who felt the organization needed the continuity of reelecting the original body and then filling its two empty seats. Others wanted the opportunity to hold some members of the National Directorate accountable for what they perceived as less than revolutionary attitudes during the Sandinista administration; they favored addressing each member's election individually. Linked to all this was the possibility, promoted by some, of Dora María Téllez's filling one of the two empty seats.

This did not happen then. The slate was reelected as a body, and the two new members were men who, it was argued, were well deserving of those positions. The National Directorate was no longer proclaimed the party's highest governing body, superseded both by the party congress (scheduled for every four years) and by a ninety-eight–person Sandinista assembly elected by congress delegates. Then, in the summer of 1994, the FSLN held an extraordinary congress, from which the National Directorate emerged enlarged to fifteen seats, five of them held by women. This directorate, with one-third female representation, resulted from a heated debate in which some favored half of all leadership positions to be held by women. This position lost. It is clear, however, that women are making their presence felt—in the FSLN, in its leadership, and in the country as a whole.

Dora María Téllez, who is a member of the new directorate, had this to say after her unsuccessful bid for the same position in 1991:

It's not a matter of putting in token women. . . . It's not gender which defines the qualities of a leader. Margaret Thatcher is a politician, and is only a woman in addition, in other words, in second place, coincidentally; her presence insofar as she is female doesn't determine anything. I think that in a party like the FSLN the only way to stop or decrease discrimination against women is through our effective involvement in the struggle for our rights.[10]

This perspective is from a woman whose personal and collective experience gives credence to her point of view. As women we can only guarantee our eventual equality by not losing sight of feminist issues, even—or especially— within the struggle for the liberation of all peoples. Movements that cannot or will not include us will ultimately fail to survive. And they will betray the women who fought to bring them to power.

NOTES

1. Milagros González, "First Dialog," in Margaret Randall, ed. and trans., *Breaking the Silences: 20th Century Poetry by Cuban Women* (Vancouver: Pulp, 1982). Reprinted by permission.

2. The women's rights movement of the nineteenth century is considered the "first wave" of modern Feminism. The Feminist movement that emerged in the industrially developed countries at the end of the 1960s and gained momentum in the early 1970s is referred to as the "second wave" of Feminism.

3. Data are from my works entitled *Cuban Women Now* (Toronto: Canadian Women's Educational Press, 1974) and *Women in Cuba: Twenty Years Later* (New York: Smyrna, 1981).

4. See Lourdes Arguelles and B. Ruby Rich: "Homosexuality, Homophobia, and Revolution: Notes Toward an Understanding of the Cuban Lesbian and Gay Male

Experience," in Martin Duberman, Martha Vicinus, and George Chauncey, Jr., eds., *Hidden from History: Reclaiming the Gay and Lesbian Past* (New York: New American Library, 1989).

5. Gail Reed, "The Media on Women: Caught Napping," *Cuba Update* 12:3 (Summer 1991): 17.

6. From an interview in my book entitled *Sandino's Daughters: Testimonies of Nicaraguan Women in Struggle* (Vancouver: New Star, 1981).

7. The Second Vatican Council had been called by Pope John XXIII in 1962, and Latin American bishops met in Medellín, Colombia (1968) to talk about its implications for their Church. Two concepts emerged that profoundly affected Latin American Christians and helped break down the barriers that had previously made it difficult for them to work with Marxists and other revolutionaries: the idea that the Church was a part of history (not outside history, as was previously assumed) and the acceptance of a *preferential option for the poor.*

8. Unlike Cuba and other revolutionary experiences, the Sandinistas abolished the death penalty in one of their first decrees. These criminals were tried, and if found guilty given sentences ranging from six months to thirty years. Many were subsequently amnestied. Some stayed in Nicaragua; many others left to join ranks with the Contra forces that were financed and trained by the CIA in Honduras and Costa Rica.

9. Interestingly, this appeared much more common than fathers' being influenced by their offspring. And women frequently also separated from husbands who feared political confrontation or who fled the demands of revolution.

10. *Barricada Internacional* 11:340 (August 1991).

Conclusion: An End and a Beginning

Peter R. Beckman and Francine D'Amico

We started out this book by asking, Where are the women? We conclude it by asking, Where do we go from here? Now that you have started looking for women in world politics and thinking about what we mean when we say "world politics," there are a number of steps you might take. We are going to present some specific projects that occurred to us during the writing of this book. The projects begin with women who seem most visible in world politics and then turn to harder-to-see women and conceptions of gender. You now know that part of the difficulty in seeing women comes from the perspective or lens that we sometimes consciously or unconsciously adopt when we think about world politics. Part of the difficulty is also that women have been marginalized in some aspects of world politics. Women's participation in world politics, however, is changing as you read these words. For you, therefore, finding women in world politics will be both easier and more interesting. We invite you to consider working along with us on these projects, or to design your own.

FINDING WOMEN AT THE TOP—AND ELSEWHERE

One project that you should consider is to enhance your understanding of the arguments raised in the chapters you have just read. There is a growing body of scholarly literature devoted to the question, Where are the women? and to the analysis of the intersection of gender and world politics. Cynthia Enloe's *Bananas, Beaches, & Bases* has quickly become a classic guide for the discovery of harder-to-see women.[1] She has expanded her analysis in *The Morning After: Sexual Politics at the End of the Cold War.*[2] V. Spike Peterson and Anne Sisson Runyan's *Global Gender Issues* would also make an especially good follow-up to this text for people new to gender analysis and the study of world politics, as would our companion volume, *Women, Gender, and World Politics.*[3] Two recent anthologies entitled *Gender and International Relations*, edited by Rebecca Grant and Kathleen Newland, and *Gendered States*, edited by V. Spike Peterson, as well as J. Ann Tickner's *Gender in International Relations*, and Christine Sylvester's *Feminist Theory and International Relations* would be useful for more advanced study.[4] You might also watch for two forthcoming books: Sandra Whitworth's *Feminism and International Relations* and Jan Jindy Pettman's *Worlding Women.*[5] Consult the bibliography at the back of this book for other recommended sources.

Where are the women? should be a question that sticks with you for the rest of your life. Ask it in all your surroundings. The daily newspaper and television or radio news broadcast are places to look for women in world politics. Media reports tend to focus on leaders. Periodically, women such as Tansu Ciller of Turkey or Kim Campbell of Canada will become prime ministers or presidents of their nations, reminding us that some women are central participants in the making of foreign policy. Close attention to their decisions and behavior and to how they are perceived and portrayed by their peers and the media will add to the information about women leaders that we have begun to assemble here.

Another project would be to look for patterns in the analyses presented here. What are the similarities and differences regarding women in world politics in Harvey Williams' discussion of Violeta Chamorro, Mary Carras' discussion of Indira Gandhi, Kenneth Harris' discussion of Margaret Thatcher, and Vincent Boudreau's discussion of Corazon Aquino? You might also ask how these authors have seen their subjects. How does each conceptualize gender? How does each see world politics? How might different perspectives or lenses provide us other ways of understanding the political participation of these women leaders?

The following are some questions that occurred to us in reading these four chapters.

1. The element of newness stands out in the experiences of women leaders: Here are pathbreaking women. Harris argues that Thatcher used her gender for political effect and that men found it difficult to respond to her. Perhaps as more women enter policy-making positions, gender difference will have less of an effect. Or you may find just the reverse: Could it be that the pathbreaking women may have had *fewer* gender differences (which may have allowed them to advance in a world dominated by men)? Once the door is open to women, however, more women with those gender differences may enter into positions of power. It may also be the case that the first encounter between a woman leader and men subordinates may indefinitely foreclose leadership positions for women. For instance, the British Conservative party leadership—mostly men—may be reluctant to elect a

woman leader in the near future. No nation that has had a woman as its elective leader since 1945 has subsequently been governed by another woman. How might you account for this?

2. Some women leaders, such as Thatcher and Gandhi, get the label "Iron Ladies." How does a leader get a particular label, especially in the realm of world politics? How do such labels reveal gender-as-difference? gender-as-power? For example, Patricia Lee Sykes found that Margaret Thatcher's reputation as an "Iron Lady" was based on the gendered perceptions of (men) cabinet ministers and political analysts: "Most accounts of Thatcher and her cabinet describe a leader who bullied her ministers, one who governed through fear and intimidation. . . . During interviews that I conducted . . . cabinet members frequently and surprisingly turned to the subject of their mothers. . . . Thatcher apparently evoked the image of the only other female authority figure they knew: mother (and perhaps nanny)."[6] How do perceived gender differences affect how other women are perceived, portrayed, and evaluated? Compared to men's perceptions, do women, either as scholars, political leaders, or citizens see women leaders differently?

3. Will women leaders make feminist or women's issues clearly their own? Gandhi tried to distance herself from feminists, as did Thatcher. Is this likely to be the case for the first women leaders in a nation? Why or why not? You might consider by way of contrast Gro Harlem Brundtland in Norway or Mary Bourke Robinson in Ireland, both of whom have made explicit their commitment to the advancement of women.[7] Will such leaders seek to promote their agendas across as well as within the borders of their nations?

Other types of projects are also possible. Francine D'Amico provides a list of contemporary women leaders in chapter 1. You might select one and develop the kind of analysis that Williams, Carras, Harris, and Boudreau have done for their subjects. For more on contemporary women leaders, you might examine a recent anthology, *Women as National Leaders*, compiled by Michael Genovese, or biographical sources on a wide range of historical rulers, such as *Women Who Ruled*, by Guida Jackson.[8]

Thinking about women as leaders brings us to other questions about gender and leadership. How do *men* policy makers respond to perceived gender differences? How does gender shape or constrain the behavior and policy choices of *men* national leaders?

Some prominent men policy makers appear to think gender differences are important. Just after taking office as secretary of state in 1993, Warren Christopher expressed support for increasing gender and racial diversity within the Department of State. He then remarked:

I don't like to attend meetings where there are not some women or minorities in attendance. I think they've got a lot to contribute. They have a distinctive point of view. They educate us. They bring new and different insights. So it isn't just that I have a commitment to [diversity] on a moral basis, it is because I think it's essential to carrying out American foreign policy.[9]

What kinds of differences do men policy makers *expect* when women are added? The "new and different insights" women may bring might be appreciated, but they may set women policy makers apart from men. Men policy makers might therefore look to women for ideas and comment, but still rely on men for "leadership" in making decisions. Alternatively, the "distinctive point of view" that women are thought to have may be seen as just something else that men policy makers have to contend with in the already complex process of making foreign policy.

Or does the very *process* of policy making begin to change as women become key participants? For example, in the United States, the number of women enrolling in higher education programs has increased from 1.2 million in 1960 to 6 million in 1980, according to *The Statistical Abstract of the United States*. By 1990, 7.5 million women were enrolled, for the first time exceeding the number of men enrolled (6.5 million). The *Abstract* also reports that the proportion of women in professions associated with politics and public service is increasing. For example, in 1983, women were 15.3 percent of lawyers and judges, 36.3 percent of college and university teachers, and 37.9 percent of economists. By 1992, women were 21.4 percent, 40.9 percent, and 43.3 percent of these professions, respectively.[10] More women are thus entering the pool of individuals from which policy makers and foreign policy bureaucrats are typically drawn. This trend suggests that women may become increasingly active direct participants in policy making.

The policy process itself may begin to change as women participate in greater numbers. "A lone woman in a room of 10 men speaks differently than she does in a room of 10 women. But add more women to the mix and take away men, and soon, whether they know it or not—or resent it or not—it is the men who start changing the way they talk. In other words, you don't need a majority to make things change."[11] Moreover, if women tend to emphasize cooperation and problem solving over conflict and domination seeking, we would expect to find those tendencies increasing within the process of policy making as more women enter the ranks of policy makers.

If the process changes, will the *content* of policy change as well because women are participants in the policy making? Are the agendas of foreign policy changing because women bring different interests into play? Questions about agendas have usually been asked regarding domestic politics. The Center for the American Woman and Politics at Rutgers, for instance, found that women state legislators in the United States were more likely to emphasize women's rights policies and policies such as health care, children and families, education, and housing.[12] Will women make such concerns more prominent in world politics as well?

Men leaders, of course, are familiar with these issues. The question may be, will women policy makers get their concerns higher on the agenda and translated into policy as their numbers increase? Will men now hear familiar things (old arguments, let's say), but with a new urgency or emphasis and a new political clout? Or will they see the familiar issues in new ways—that foreign aid policies, for instance, will not promote economic development unless women are made central in planning strategies?[13]

We can also ask how gender might shape the policy options considered by men leaders. For example, why is violence—armed troops, air strikes— the policy of choice in Bosnia or in Somalia? Can gender help us understand why alternative policies such as embargoes are so soon discarded—if adopted at all?

All well and good, you might be saying. How am I supposed to find out if women make a difference regarding the process of making decisions and the content of those decisions? How can I investigate the connection between gender and leadership? Some of you may be able to interview policy makers or officials of the diplomatic corps. You may be able to serve as an intern in a policy-making organization, in which you can become participant-observers of the effect of women. Or you may work with autobiographies and biographies of women and men in policy-making positions. And there is the possibility of creating laboratory-type experiments. For instance, you might simulate foreign policy making with an explicit concern for the effect of gender.[14]

In proposing projects thus far, we have concentrated on leaders and policy makers—women and men occupying formal positions of political power. Women have also been connected to world politics in other, less visible, ways. You might discover women in world politics by beginning with men in power and studying their spouses or lovers. Eleanor Roosevelt and Chiang Ch'ing are examples that come to mind. What connection did each have with world politics? Women might serve a number of different roles in association with men leaders: confidante; advisor; policy advocate; emissary; provider of support, encouragement, and love; conduit for others seeking to influence the leader. Each of those roles—as well as others waiting for you to dis- cover—may have a significant effect on world politics. In some circum- stances, you may find such women making crucial decisions. Edith Gault Wilson, for instance, may have wielded great powers when her husband, Woodrow Wilson, was incapacitated by a stroke. You might consult a study by Rita Mae Kelly and Mary Boutilier, who examined twelve "political wives" or First Ladies as well as ten "political achievers" (elected leaders) and four- teen revolutionaries.[15] Once again, you will have discovered more women connected to world politics who merit attention.

Events of the past—even from what seem to be the dry, dusty pages of history—are a good place for your inquiries as well. Sybil Oldfield found Jane Addams to be worthy of study because Addams engaged in and un- derstood the connections between local and global political conditions. What other women of the past can you discover? In *The Warrior Queens*, Antonia Fraser examines both historical and contemporary women legends and leaders.[16] *The Continuum Dictionary of Women's Biography*, compiled and edited by Jennifer Uglow, sketches the lives of prominent women in many different professions, cultures, and time frames.[17]

Finding women at the interiors of bureaucracies and staffs is a difficult proposition, as Kristen Timothy's chapter in this book discusses for the United Nations. Nancy E. McGlen and Meredith Reid Sarkees' book, *Women in Foreign Policy*, suggests what can be done with the American foreign policy bureaucracy.[18] Similarly, finding women in other international organizations and transnational corporations may be difficult. A good place to begin your search is in a new anthology edited by Anne Winslow titled *Women, Politics, and the United Nations*.[19]

As we move away from people "at the top" in official positions or near official positions, how do we find harder-to-see women in world politics? The perspectives on world politics that we explored in this book's introduction provide a clue. The traditional theories of world politics (Realism, Pluralism, and Critical Theory) tend to connect people to world politics through their part in or efforts to have influence upon governments. From these perspectives, women are participants in world politics to the extent that they voice their opinions to or make demands on governmental leaders or officials. (Granted, some of the theories argue that individuals are not particularly important, but none deny that at least some individuals or groups attempt to shape world politics.) Thus, for instance, women who wrote letters or took part in demonstrations for or against the North American Free Trade Agreement (NAFTA) participated in world politics.

You might identify a foreign policy issue (such as NAFTA or the debate between Britain and France during the 1930s over how to respond to Nazi Germany) and read scholarly and media accounts, looking for women participants and evidence of gender. Indeed, certain general issues have historically interested women, and you might concentrate on them: peace, war prevention, justice, human rights, and those labeled as "women's issues" regarding political, social, and economic rights. You might also look for women in public service organizations and clubs, such as Zonta or Hadassah, who may routinely try to influence policy decisions, as might women affiliated with political parties.

Ole Holsti and James Rosenau suggested in chapter 8 that you might use a survey to explore individuals' attitudes and opinions regarding world politics. They identified several issues on which there were gender-based differences of opinion. Can you find others? Can you suggest what creates the differences in some areas, and little to no difference in others? Alternatively, you might analyze their survey data in different ways. For example, do *all* women share a similar view about the threat that other nations pose to national security? We would be surprised if you did not find some variation even among the women "opinion leaders" whom they surveyed. What might account for that variation: education, expressed interest in world politics, social class, race/ethnicity? How might the opinions of other women—working-class women, women living in poverty, single heads of households—compare to those of the opinion leaders surveyed in the United States? How might their opinions compare to those of women (and men) from different nations, cultures, classes, races, peoples? You might conduct your own survey, much as Holsti and Rosenau did, to address these questions.

Other perspectives would lead our search for women not only to those who sought to influence government leaders or policies, but also to those who sought to establish alternatives. You might begin with the women who have stood outside usual processes of politics and demanded entrance, a hearing, or a radical reconstruction of the whole endeavor. This book's representatives are Oldfield's study of Jane Addams, Petra Kelly's account of her ecofeminism, and Margaret Randall's story of the women of the Cuban and Nicaraguan revolutions. How did women, for instance, in the Russian and Chinese revolutions come to shape world politics?

One place to look for these harder-to-see women is in the histories of women's movements, as Deborah Stienstra has done in her chapter, for these movements were specifically organized to challenge so-called politics as usual. Where else might we look for women who are organizing for change? Kumari Jayawardena describes historical women's movements in a number of Third World states, and she analyzes the intersection between feminist and nationalist movements in each.[20] Jane Jaquette has edited an anthology looking at the same theme and the trend toward democratization in Latin America in the 1980s.[21]

Another project might be to look to literature to discover women who are engaging in world politics. For example, Rigoberta Menchú of Guatemala and Alicia Partnoy of Argentina tell their stories of human rights abuse in autobiographic testimonies and in a collection of poetry, fiction, and personal narrative that gives voice to other victims.[22] They have helped to organize transnational networks of survivors of human rights abuse and of expatriates forced to live in exile because of their political beliefs. Their works not only illustrate the particular ways in which women experience human rights abuse but also explore how such abuse is gendered. They also describe how people in the local community and around the globe connect to challenge such abuse.[23]

You might also observe operations in your local government or student government. Granted, their decisions and policies are not what would traditionally be considered as world politics, but other perspectives see them differently. For example, local decisions about waste management and disposal may have consequences that affect other communities and countries. Remember the "garbage barge" that couldn't find a port? From less traditional perspectives, local governments and businesses engage in world politics in a variety of ways, such as "sister city" arrangements with municipalities in other nations, and transnational production and purchase contracts. We know from various studies that women's formal political participation is greatest at local levels; if we see world politics expansively, we understand women's participation differently.[24]

FROM WOMEN TO GENDER

Once we have identified individual women as participants in world politics, we are ready to ask what their participation signifies. How and why do they have an effect on world politics? Do women make world politics in a distinctive way because they are women? Is world politics itself a gendered enterprise—a patriarchal system that is grounded in and that reproduces men's domination of women?

We come to one of the central questions regarding women and world politics. Are there gender differences that are relevant for world politics? How might you go about exploring this question? Gender has long been a subject for psychology and sociology, as reflected in the journal *Sex Roles*. Other journals that focus on gender analysis include *Signs*, *Gender and Society*, *Women & Politics*, *Women's Studies Quarterly*, *Women's Studies International Forum*, and *Feminist Studies*. Browsing through an issue of each may suggest a number of questions about women, gender differences, and world politics. For a more systematic approach, you might consult *Women Studies Abstracts* in the reference department of your library. This indexes articles from a variety of publications.

These existing studies are important building blocks for our understanding of the connections among women, gender, and world politics. How specifically might you investigate gender differences? Let's begin with the presumption that there *may* be differences between men and women that are relevant for world politics. Take a recent article by Doreen Kimura on gender differences.[25] She argues that "men's and women's brains are organized along different lines from very early in life." As a consequence, men and women tend to have different abilities when it comes to certain kinds of perceptual and reasoning tasks.

For instance, Kimura suggests that men tend to have a greater spatial sense, understanding connections between geographic points, while women tend to be better with recognizing and working with distinct landmarks. That suggests to us that perhaps men "see" maps differently than women do. Maps with political boundaries might be read by men in terms of the spatial distribution of power: where power is, who threatens it, and who benefits from it. Women may see political boundaries more in terms of location: France is west of Germany. We are not claiming that there is such a difference; rather, we are saying that here is a possible feature of world politics that *you* might think of testing.

Similarly, Kimura notes that women tend to be more effective than men in matching items or determining what is missing from an array of items. That suggests that men tend to be more likely to ignore differences, to generalize in ways that miss important differences between events. We are reminded of President Lyndon Johnson and Secretary of State Dean Rusk who put the war in Vietnam in the same category as Hitler's wars of aggression—and felt they had no choice but to respond to Vietnam as if they were confronting a Hitler. Can you think of a way to explore whether men and women generalize about world politics differently?

Feminist perspectives have a different vision of women and world politics. Through a Feminist lens, we see women engaged in world politics when they are struggling for their political rights, when they are working to prevent rape and to end female circumcision and dowry deaths, and when they are organizing to influence how development aid is allocated. Women who provide sexual services to foreign soldiers or businessmen are also part of world politics. That is, these actions—traditionally thought of as either "domestic politics" or not politics at all—are a part of world politics. Women (and men) are, from these perspectives, important participants in world politics, day after day.

Feminist theory's expanded notion of world politics allows us to look for women in different ways, and in looking for women, to find gender. For example, if we see the economy as global in scope, then women take part in world politics both as *producers* and as *consumers*. As *producers*, women work for multinational corporations, particularly in communications, food processing, textiles, and light manufactures. As workers their decisions about whether or not to unionize, their wages, and their productivity affect and are affected by changes in the global economy. In many nations, women make export agriculture possible both by assisting in the production of cash crops and by taking responsibility for subsistence crops to feed the family. Many nations depend upon the foreign exchange earnings created by women farmers.

As *consumers*, women are responsible for much of the purchasing done by a family, whether from a street vendor or a supermarket. Individual choices about what goods to consume often have a cumulative effect on production decisions and government policy, on international trade and the political relations between nations. The consumer tuna fish boycott and subsequent appearance of "dolphin safe" tuna demonstrate this. How women "spend the sixpence" is a part of world politics.[26]

You can look for women and find gender in the media. Where are the women here, especially when what is traditionally called "world politics" is being discussed? A careful reading of the world's press might be a fascinating way to watch for the appearance of "nonofficial" women in world politics and to see how gender shapes world politics. Your library may have an index for the *New York Times, Globe and Mail, London Times*, or another daily newspaper with an international focus. Try putting on some Feminist lenses and asking, How are these news reports gendered? Are women described as agents who make things happen or as passive victims who have things done to them? That is, are they depicted as *participants* in world politics, or are they portrayed as "womenandchildren," as Cynthia Enloe has put it?[27]

Here is one example. A recent Associated Press news report was titled: "Rips in the Social Fabric: Mother Tries to Keep Family from Unraveling Amid Chaos."[28] The article focuses on the daily struggle for survival of Amela Muratovic, a woman with two small children in Sarajevo, Bosnia-Hercegovina. The interviewer asked her questions about the availability of food and other necessities, yet did not ask her opinion about the conflict. We hear only *part* of her story. The children's father, Edin, is also in the home with his family, but his part in struggling to "keep the family together" was not discussed. Why did the report take this focus? What perspective, what conception of gender, lies behind this particular report?

What are we told about other women in Bosnia or in Gaza or in Haiti? What would these women themselves tell us about their lives? How would knowing their stories change our ideas about the scope of world politics and about the policies of governments, international organizations, and multinational corporations and our own role in world politics? We cannot find answers to these questions until we listen to their stories and at least consider other perspectives.

In recent years, statistical studies have appeared that tell us about women as a group. These studies include *Women in the World: An International Atlas*, edited by Michael Kidron; *Women of the World: A Chartbook for Developing Regions*, compiled by Ellen Jamison, and *Women . . . a World Survey*, compiled by Ruth Leger Sivard.[29] Each of these studies presents data on such things as women's employment, education, and health, as well as on the legal and political status of women in different nations. Leger Sivard's study also provides information on the content and ratification status of seven international treaties on the rights of women.

The United Nations has compiled an even more up-to-date and complete set of statistics about women—including unwaged labor by women—as a part of its Decade for Women commitment. *The World's Women: Trends and Statistics, 1970–1990* includes data on women, families, and households; education and training; health and childbearing; housing, settlements, and environment; women's work and the economy; and public life and leadership. Annexes to the statistical data include the complete texts of the UN Decade for Women's "Nairobi Forward Looking Strategies for the Advancement of Women" (1985) and the "Convention on the Elimination of All Forms of Discrimination against Women" (1981).

The UN's *World's Women* report identifies a number of "gaps" between the life situations of men and of women. For example, the report contains the following information. Although more girls than boys are born each year and women's average life expectancy is longer than men's, there are fewer women than men in the world today because of social and cultural factors like sex-selection abortion of female fetuses, female infanticide, widow burning and dowry deaths, denial of adequate nutrition and health care to female family members, and high maternal mortality rates (p. 11). There continues to be a "gender gap" in basic literacy: In 1985, 352 million men and 597 million women were determined to be illiterate (p. 45). While much of the work women do is unpaid production in the home, the UN report finds a "wage gap" in that "even when women do the same work as men, they typically receive less pay—30 to 40 per cent less on average world-wide" (p. 3). Further, the UN report states that women "are poorly represented in the ranks of power, policy-, and decision-making" and "make up less than 5 per cent of the world's heads of State, heads of major corporations, and top positions in international organizations" (p. 6). Women make up less than 20 percent of midlevel managers and less than 10 percent of parliament and legislative representatives, on average, worldwide (p. 6).

In *Global Gender Issues*, V. Spike Peterson and Anne Sisson Runyan argue that data like these confirm the existence of a ubiquitous pattern of gender inequality. That is, the numbers offer evidence of *gender-as-power*. But the numbers also suggest that change is possible: The literacy gap is shrinking in most nations, as is the wage gap. Change will come not only when more women get into formal leadership positions—as in the UN's still unfulfilled pledge to increase the number of women in upper posts—but also when conscious efforts are made to change the structural basis of gender inequality in all areas, as in the gendered division of labor and of access to and control over community resources.[30]

Feminist perspectives urge us to think about how gender has shaped the discourse—the very language used to discuss—world politics. For instance, President Lyndon Johnson characterized his critics regarding the Vietnam war as "Nervous Nellies." You might examine the comments that Kaiser William jotted in the margins of diplomatic messages, or Hitler's table talk, or the transcripts of Richard Nixon's Oval Office conversations to see how gendered images shaped their considerations of world politics. In cultures where men's actions in world politics are disparaged by characterizing them as "feminine," we would suspect that people would be resistant to having women in positions of influence in foreign policy.

Feminist perspectives also encourage us to ask how gender shapes world politics at the "systemic" level—the level of analysis focused on from the "Realist" perspective. In chapter 1, D'Amico argues that conceptualizations of gender have been used to legitimize historical colonization and the current hierarchial world order, with colonized and Third World peoples depicted as "feminine"—dependent, emotional, irrational. Gender hierarchy underlies and authorizes international hierarchy. To illustrate: Japan was accused of a failure to "take responsibility in world affairs" when its leaders refused to join in the use of military force in the Gulf War. That is, Japan "wimped out" because it refused to adopt the militarized masculinity that defines "power" in the Realist world vision. Nationalists in Russia cast their critique of the post-Soviet leadership in gendered terms: The leaders have "sold out" (prostituted themselves and Russia) to the West; the nationalists will restore the vigor (virility) of the feminized homeland. These examples illustrate how even our language about world politics is gendered.

A BEGINNING

Our request of you has been both simple and profound: Look for women, and once found, ask how they and the ideas of gender that define them and men shape world politics. Only by our common efforts—yours and ours—will we come to some better understanding of the role that gender plays in world politics. How does gender interface with other factors said to shape world politics, such as nationalism, class, and race?[31]

We've suggested that there are many places to look for women in world politics. Where you look and how you see them will depend upon the lens that you use. A particular lens also colors the vision of others who report on world politics, be they academics, journalists, or political leaders. When you hear or read those visions, ask what lens is being used. Then try substituting a different lens to see if the vision—and your understanding—changes.

Once we find where women are, the next questions are: Why are they there? What are they doing there? How did they get there? How do we explain discrepancies in rates of literacy, life expectancy, and formal education for women versus men? Why do more men than women participate in certain aspects of world politics? What might be done about these discrepancies? How do the policies of our governments and our own decisions and actions in our daily lives help to eliminate or to sustain patterns of gender inequality? In other words, now that we have started looking for and counting women, we have to think about what the numbers mean, how they came to be, whether or not they should be changed, and how we might go about changing them. These questions lead us to an analysis of not only gender-as-difference but also gender-as-power.

At the close of *Global Gender Issues*, Peterson and Runyan suggest a *political* project: the "ungendering" of world politics. They say this task is "twofold—adding women to the existing world politics power structures *and* transforming those very power structures, ideologically and materially."[32] Further, they state that

ungendering world politics requires a serious rethinking of what it means to be human and how we might organize ourselves in more cooperative, mutually respectful ways. We would have to reject gendered dichotomies: male versus female, us versus them, culture versus nature. Ungendering world politics also requires a reconceptualization of politics and a shift from power-over to power-to. We would have to recognize power in its multiple forms and be willing to imagine other worlds.[33]

What can *we* imagine for the future of world politics? What "new" world order can we create? How do we get there from here? That's our challenge and yours.

NOTES

1. Cynthia Enloe, *Bananas, Beaches, & Bases: Making Feminist Sense of International Politics* (Berkeley: University of California Press, 1990).

2. Cynthia Enloe, *The Morning After: Sexual Politics at the End of the Cold War* (Berkeley: University of California Press, 1993).

3. V. Spike Peterson and Anne Sisson Runyan, *Global Gender Issues* (Boulder, CO: Westview, 1993); Peter Beckman and Francine D'Amico, eds., *Women, Gender, and World Politics: Perspectives, Policies, and Prospects* (Westport, CT: Bergin & Garvey, 1994).

4. Rebecca Grant and Kathleen Newland, eds., *Gender and International Relations* (Bloomington: Indiana University Press, 1991); V. Spike Peterson, ed., *Gendered States: Feminist (Re)Visions of International Relations Theory* (Boulder, CO: Rienner, 1992); J. Ann Tickner, *Gender in International Relations: Feminist Perspectives on Achieving Global Security* (New York: Columbia University Press, 1992); Christine Sylvester, *Feminist Theory and International Relations in a Postmodern Era* (Cambridge: Cambridge University Press, 1994).

5. Sandra Whitworth, *Feminism and International Relations* (London: Macmillan, forthcoming); Jan Jindy Pettman, *Worlding Women: Gender and International Politics* (London: Allen & Unwin, forthcoming).

6. Patricia Lee Sykes, "Women as National Leaders: Patterns and Prospects," in Michael Genovese, ed., *Women as National Leaders* (Newbury Park, CA: Sage, 1993), 226.

7. See Sykes, "Women as National Leaders," 219–29.

8. Genovese, ed., *Women as National Leaders*; Guida M. Jackson, *Women Who Ruled* (Santa Barbara, CA: ABC-Clio, 1990).

9. Warren Christopher, Remarks to Employees of the Department of State, January 25, 1993.

10. "Employed Civilians by Occupation, Sex, Race, and Hispanic Origin," *Statistical Abstract of the United States* 113 (1993): 405, see Table 644.

11. Allison Adato and Melissa G. Stanton, "If Women Ran America," *Life* 15 (June 1992): 46.

12. Center for the American Woman and Politics, *Reshaping the Agenda* (New Brunswick, NJ: Rutgers/Center for the American Woman and Politics, 1991).

13. See the chapters by Nüket Kardam, Geeta Chowdhry, and Birgit Brock-Utne in Beckman and D'Amico, eds., *Women, Gender, and World Politics*.

14. Harold Guetzkow's classic *Inter-Nation Simulation* (Chicago: Science Research Associates, 1966) might make an interesting project with a conscious exploration of gender. A second version is available for computers: Bahram Farzanegan and Ronald

Parker, *Inter-Nation Simulation II* (Raleigh: North Carolina State University Software, 1985).

15. Rita Mae Kelly and Mary Boutilier, *The Making of Political Women: A Study of Socialization and Role Conflict* (Chicago: Nelson-Hall, 1978).

16. Antonia Fraser, *The Warrior Queens* (New York: Knopf, 1989), originally published as *Boadicea's Chariot: The Warrior Queens* (London: Weidenfeld & Nicolson, 1988).

17. Jennifer S. Uglow, comp. and ed., *The Continuum Dictionary of Women's Biography*, new ed. (New York: Continuum, 1989).

18. Nancy E. McGlen and Meredith Reid Sarkees, *Women in Foreign Policy: The Insiders* (New York: Routledge, 1993).

19. Anne Winslow, ed., *Women, Politics, and the United Nations:* (Westport, CT: Greenwood, 1995). See also the chapters by Margaret Galey and by Geeta Chowdhry in Beckman and D'Amico, eds., *Women, Gender, and World Politics*.

20. Kumari Jayawardena, *Feminism and Nationalism in the Third World* (London: Zed, 1986).

21. Jane S. Jaquette, ed., *The Women's Movement in Latin America: Feminism and the Transition to Democracy* (Boston: Unwin Hyman, 1989).

22. Rigoberta Menchú, *I, Rigoberta Menchú: An Indian Woman in Guatemala*, edited and with an introduction by Elisabeth Burgos, translated by Ann Wright (London: Verso, 1984); Alicia Partnoy, *The Little School: Tales of Disappearance and Survival in Argentina* (San Francisco, CA: Cleis, 1986); and Alicia Partnoy, ed., *You Can't Drown the Fire: Latin American Women Writing in Exile* (San Francisco, CA: Cleis, 1988).

23. See also Amnesty International, *Women in the Front Line: Human Rights Violations against Women* (New York: Amnesty International, 1990).

24. See, for example, Malcolm Jewell and Marcia Lynn Whicker, "The Feminization of Leadership in State Legislatures," *PS: Political Science and Politics* 26:4 (December 1993): 705–12.

25. Doreen Kimura, "Sex Differences and the Brain," *Scientific American* 267 (September 1992): 118–25.

26. Virginia Woolf, *Three Guineas* (New York: Harcourt Brace Jovanovich, 1938).

27. Cynthia Enloe, "Womenandchildren: Making Feminist Sense of the Persian Gulf Crisis," *The Village Voice* 35 (September 25, 1990): 29–32.

28. This AP report appeared in *The Press and Sun-Bulletin* (Binghamton, NY) January 16, 1994, 10A.

29. Michael Kidron, ed., *Women in the World* (New York: Simon & Schuster, 1986); Ellen Jamison, *Women of the World* (Washington, DC: U.S. Department of Commerce/USAID, 1985); Ruth Leger Sivard, *Women . . . a world survey* (Washington, DC: World Priorities, 1985).

30. Peterson and Runyan, *Global Gender Issues*, 149–66.

31. See Joan Smith, Jane Collins, Terence K. Hopkins, and Akbar Muhammed, eds., *Racism, Sexism, and the World-System* (Westport, CT: Greenwood, 1988); Paul Lauren Gordon, *Power and Prejudice: The Politics and Diplomacy of Racial Discrimination* (Boulder, CO: Westview, 1988); Hugh Tinker, *Race, Conflict, and the International Order: From Empire to United Nations* (New York: St. Martin's, 1977); James N. Ro-

senau, *Race in International Politics: A Dialogue in Five Parts* (Denver: University of Denver Press, 1970).

32. Peterson and Runyan, *Global Gender Issues*, 150.

33. Ibid., 165.

Selected Bibliography

Adamson, Nancy, Linda Briskin, and Margaret McPhail. *Feminist Organizing for Change: The Contemporary Women's Movement in Canada*. Toronto: Oxford University Press, 1988.

Addams, Jane. *Peace and Bread in Time of War*. 1922. Reprint, with an introduction by John Dewey. Boston: Hall, 1960.

———. *Twenty Years at Hull House*. New York: Macmillan, 1910.

Addams, Jane, Emily Balch, and Alice Hamilton. *Women at The Hague*. New York: n.p., 1915.

Arnold, Bruce, *A Study in Power* (Thatcher). London: Hamilton, 1984.

Barry, Kathleen, Charlotte Bunch, and Shirley Castley, eds. *International Feminism: Networking against Female Sexual Slavery*. New York: International Women's Tribune Centre, 1984.

Baxter, Sandra, and Marjorie Lansing. *Women and Politics: The Invisible Majority*. Ann Arbor: University of Michigan Press, 1980.

Bhutto, Benazir. *Daughter of Destiny: An Autobiography*. New York: Simon & Schuster, 1989.

Blake, Robert. *The Conservative Party from Peel to Thatcher*. London: Methuen, 1985.

Boserup, Ester. *Women's Role in Economic Development*. New York: St. Martin's, 1970.

Boulding, Elise. *Women: The Fifth World*. New York: Foreign Policy Association, 1980.

Bulbeck, Chilla. *One World Women's Movement*. London: Pluto, 1988.

Bunch, Charlotte, and Roxanna Carrillo. "Feminist Perspectives on Women in Development." In *Persistent Inequalities: Women and World Development*, ed. Irene Tinker. New York: Oxford University Press, 1990.

Bunch, Charlotte, and Shirley Castley. *Developing Strategies for the Future: Feminist Perspectives*. Report of the International Feminist Workshop held at Stony Point, New York, April 20–25, 1980. New York: International Women's Tribune Centre, 1980.

Buvinic, Mayra, and Sally Yudelman. *Women, Poverty, and Progress in the Third World.* Washington, DC: Foreign Policy Association, 1989.

Bystydzienski, Jill, ed. *Women Transforming Politics: Worldwide Strategies for Empowerment.* Bloomington: Indiana University Press, 1992.

Carras, Mary C. *Indira Gandhi in the Crucible of Leadership.* Boston: Beacon, 1979.

Chamorro Cardenal, Jaime. *"La Prensa": The Republic of Paper.* New York: Freedom House, 1988.

Chowdhry, Geeta. *International Financial Institutions, the State, and Women Farmers in the Third World.* London: Macmillan, forthcoming.

Cole, John. *The Thatcher Years.* London: BBC Books, 1987.

Confronting the Crisis in Latin America: Women Organizing for Change. Santiago, Chile: Isis International and DAWN (Development Alternatives with Women for a New Era), 1988.

Conover, Pamela Johnston. "Feminists and the Gender Gap." *Journal of Politics* 50:4 (November 1988): 985–1010.

Constantino, Renato. *Demystifying Aquino.* Quezon City, Luzon: Karrel, 1989.

Cooke, Miriam, and Angela Woollacott, eds. *Gendering War Talk.* Princeton: Princeton University Press, 1993.

Daly Heyck, Denis Lynn. *Life Stories of the Nicaraguan Revolution.* New York: Routledge, 1990.

Davis, Allen F. *An American Heroine: The Life and Legend of Jane Addams.* New York: Oxford University Press, 1973.

Duberman, Martin, Martha Vicinius, and George Chauncey, Jr., eds. *Hidden from History: Reclaiming the Gay and Lesbian Past.* New York: New American Library, 1989.

Elshtain, Jean Bethke. *Women and War.* New York: Basic, 1987.

Elshtain, Jean Bethke, and Sheila Tobias, eds. *Women, Militarism, and War.* Savage, MD: Rowman & Littlefield, 1990.

Enloe, Cynthia. *The Morning After: Sexual Politics at the End of the Cold War.* Berkeley: University of California Press, 1993.

———. *Bananas, Beaches, & Bases: Making Feminist Sense of International Politics.* Berkeley: University of California Press, 1990.

Farrell, John. *Beloved Lady: A History of Jane Addams' Ideas on Reform and Peace.* Baltimore: Johns Hopkins University Press, 1967.

Ferguson, Kathy. *The Feminist Case against Bureaucracy.* Philadelphia: Temple University Press, 1984.

Fraser, Antonia. *The Warrior Queens.* New York: Knopf, 1989. Originally published as *Boadicea's Chariot: The Warrior Queens.* London: Weidenfeld & Nicolson, 1988.

Fuentes, Annette, and Barbara Ehrenreich. *Women in the Global Factory.* Boston: South End, 1983.

Genovese, Michael A., ed. *Women as National Leaders.* Newbury Park, CA: Sage, 1993.

Gilligan, Carol. *In a Different Voice.* Cambridge: Harvard University Press, 1982.

Government of India, Ministry of Information and Broadcasting. *Indira Gandhi: Selected Speeches and Writings.* New Delhi: n.d.

Grant, Rebecca, and Kathleen Newland, eds. *Gender and International Relations.* Bloomington: Indiana University Press, 1991.

Harding, Sandra, ed. *Feminism and Methodology.* Milton Keynes, England: Open University Press, 1987.

Harris, Kenneth. *Thatcher.* London: Weidenfeld & Nicolson, 1988.

———. *The Queen.* London: St. Martin's Press, 1994.

Hennessy, Peter, and Anthony Selon. *Ruling Performance* (Thatcher). Oxford: Basil Blackwell, 1987.

Higonnet, Margaret Randolph, Jane Jenson, Sonya Michel, and Margaret Collins Weitz, eds. *Behind the Lines: Gender and the Two World Wars.* New Haven: Yale University Press, 1987.

Holsti, Ole R., and James N. Rosenau. "The Domestic and Foreign Policy Beliefs of American Leaders." *Journal of Conflict Resolution* 32:2 (June 1988): 248–94

———. "The Foreign Policy Beliefs of Women in Leadership Positions." *Journal of Politics* 43:2 (May 1981): 326–47.

Howes, Ruth H., and Michael R. Stevenson, eds. *Women and the Use of Military Force.* Boulder, CO: Rienner, 1993.

Hurwitz, Edith. "The International Sisterhood." In *Becoming Visible: Women in European History,* ed. Renate Bridenthal and Claudia Koontz. New York: Houghton Mifflin, 1977.

Jackson, Guida M. *Women Who Ruled.* Santa Barbara, CA: ABC-Clio, 1990.

Jane Addams: A Centennial Reader. New York: Macmillan, 1960.

Jaquette, Jane S., ed. *The Women's Movement in Latin America: Feminism and the Transition to Democracy.* Boston: Unwin Hyman, 1989.

Jayawardena, Kumari. *Feminism and Nationalism in the Third World.* London: Zed, 1986.

Jenkins, Peter. *Mrs. Thatcher's Revolution.* London: Cape, 1987.

Jones, Kathleen B., and Anna G. Jonasdottir, eds. *The Political Interest of Gender.* London: Sage, 1988.

Kardam, Nüket. *Bringing Women In: Women's Issues in International Development Programs.* Boulder, CO: Rienner, 1991.

Karl, Marilee, and X. Charnes, eds. *Women, Struggles, and Strategies: Third World Perspectives.* Rome: Isis International, 1986.

Kelly, Petra Karin. *Nonviolence Speaks to Power.* Edited by Glenn D. Paige and Sarah Gilliatt. Honolulu: Matsunaga Institute for Peace, University of Hawaii, 1992.

———. *Fighting for Hope.* Translated by Marianne Howarth. Boston: South End, 1984.

Kelly, Petra Karin, and Jo Leinen. *Life Principle: Ökopax: The New Strength.* Berlin: Olle & Wolter, 1982.

Kelly, Rita Mae, and Mary Boutilier. *The Making of Political Women: A Study of Socialization and Role Conflict.* Chicago: Nelson-Hall, 1978.

Keohane, Robert O. "International Relations Theory: Contributions of a Feminist Standpoint." *Millennium: Journal of International Studies* 18:2 (Winter 1989): 245–53.

Klein, Ethel, *Gender Politics.* Cambridge: Harvard University Press, 1984.

Lancaster, Roger. *Life Is Hard: Machismo, Danger, and the Intimacy of Power in Nicaragua.* Berkeley: University of California Press, 1992.

Lasch, Christopher, ed. *The Social Thought of Jane Addams.* New York: Bobbs-Merrill, 1965.

Levine, Daniel. *Jane Addams and the Liberal Tradition.* Madison: State Historical Society of Wisconsin, 1971.

Linn, James Weber. *Jane Addams* (family memoir). New York: Appleton, 1935.

Macdonald, Sharon, Pat Holden, and Shirley Ardener, eds. *Images of Women in Peace and War: Cross-Cultural and Historical Perspectives.* Madison: University of Wisconsin Press, 1987.

Mansingh, Surjit. *India's Search for Power: Indira Gandhi's Foreign Policy, 1966–1982.* New Delhi: Sage, 1984.

Martinez Cuenca, Alejandro. *Sandinista Economics in Practice: An Insider's Critical Reflections.* Boston: South End, 1992.

McGlen, Nancy E., and Meredith Reid Sarkees. *Women in Foreign Policy: The Insiders.* New York: Routledge, 1993.

Mies, Maria. *Patriarchy and Accumulation on a World Scale: Women in the International Division of Labor.* London: Zed, 1986.

Minogue, Kenneth, and Michael Biddis, eds. *Thatcherism, Personality, and Politics.* London: Macmillan, 1987.

Mitter, Swasti. *Common Fate, Common Bond: Women in the Global Economy.* London: Pluto, 1989.

Mohanty, Chandra Talpade, Ann Russo, and Lourdes Torres, eds. *Third World Women and the Politics of Feminism.* Bloomington: Indiana University Press, 1991.

Morgan, Robin. *Sisterhood Is Global: The International Women's Movement Anthology.* Garden City, NY: Anchor, 1984.

Norsworthy, Kent. *Nicaragua: A Country Guide.* Albuquerque, NM: Inter-Hemispheric Education Resource Center, 1990.

Oldfield, Sybil. *Women against the Iron Fist: Alternatives to Militarism, 1900–1989.* Oxford: Basil Blackwell, 1989.

———. *Spinsters of the Parish.* London: Virago, 1984.

Peterson, V. Spike, ed. *Gendered States: Feminist (Re)Visions of International Relations Theory.* Boulder, CO: Rienner, 1992.

Peterson, V. Spike, and Anne Sisson Runyan. *Global Gender Issues.* Boulder, CO: Westview, 1993.

Pettman, Jan Jindy. *Worlding Women: Gender and International Politics.* London: Allen & Unwin, forthcoming.

Pouchpadass, Emmanuel. *Indira Gandhi: My Truth.* New York: Grove, 1980.

Randall, Margaret. *Sandino's Daughters Revisited: Feminism in Nicaragua.* New Brunswick, NJ: Rutgers University Press, 1994.

———. *Gathering Rage: The Failure of Twentieth Century Revolutions to Develop a Feminist Agenda.* New York: Monthly Review Press, 1992.

———, ed. and trans. *Breaking the Silences: 20th Century Poetry by Cuban Women.* Vancouver: Pulp, 1982.

———. *Sandino's Daughters: Testimonies of Nicaraguan Women in Struggle.* Vancouver: New Star, 1981.

———. *Women in Cuba: Twenty Years Later.* New York: Smyrna, 1981.

———. *Cuban Women Now.* Toronto: Canadian Women's Educational Press, 1974.

Randall, Vicky. *Women and Politics: An International Perspective.* 2d ed. Chicago: University of Chicago Press, 1987.

Riddell, Peter. *The Thatcher Decade.* Oxford: Basil Blackwell, 1989.

Riley, Denise. *"Am I That Name?": Feminism and the Category of "Women" in History.* Minneapolis: University of Minnesota Press, 1988.

Robbins, Pauline Frederick. "People in Glass Houses." *Ms.* 3:7 (January 1975): 48.

Rosenau, James N., ed. *Global Voices: Dialogues in International Relations*, with contributions by James Der Derian, Jean Bethke Elshtain, Steve Smith, and Christine Sylvester. Boulder, CO: Westview, 1993.

Ruddick, Sara. *Maternal Thinking*. Boston: Beacon, 1989.

Runyan, Anne Sisson, and V. Spike Peterson. "The Radical Future of Realism: Feminist Subversions of IR Theory." *Alternatives* 16:1 (Winter 1991): 67–106.

Rush, Ramona, and Donna Allen, eds. *Communications at the Crossroads: The Gender Gap Connection*. Norwood, NJ: Ablex, 1989.

Sargent, Lydia, ed. *Women and Revolution: A Discussion of the Unhappy Marriage of Marxism and Feminism*. Boston: South End, 1981.

Sen, Gita, and Caren Grown. *Development, Crises, and Alternative Visions: Third World Women's Perspectives*. New York: Monthly Review, 1987.

Shapiro, Robert Y., and Harpeet Mahajan. "Gender Differences in Policy Preferences." *Public Opinion Quarterly* 50:1 (Spring 1986): 42–61.

Sherrick, Rebecca L. "Toward Universal Sisterhood." *Women's Studies International Forum* 5:6 (1982): 655–61.

Shiva, Vandana. *Staying Alive: Women, Ecology, and Development*. London: Zed, 1989.

Sivard, Ruth Leger. *Women . . . a world survey*. Washington, DC: World Priorities, 1985.

Skidelsky, Robert, ed. *Thatcherism*. London: Chatto & Windus, 1988.

Smith, Geoffrey. *Reagan and Thatcher*. London: Bodley Head, 1990.

Snyder, Paula, ed. *The European Women's Almanac*. New York: Columbia University Press, 1992.

Spender, Dale, ed. *Men's Studies Modified: The Impact of Feminism on the Academic Disciplines*. Oxford: Pergamon, 1981.

Staudt, Kathleen. *Women, Foreign Assistance and Advocacy Administration*. New York: Praeger, 1985.

———, ed. *Women, International Development, and Politics*. Philadelphia: Temple University Press, 1990.

Stiehm, Judith Hicks, ed. *Women and Men's Wars*. Oxford: Pergamon, 1983.

Stienstra, Deborah. "Gender Relations and International Organizations: The Role of International Women's Movements in the League of Nations and the United Nations System." Ph.D. diss., York University, North York, Ontario, 1992.

Sylvester, Christine. *Feminist Theory and International Relations in a Postmodern Era*. Cambridge: Cambridge University Press, 1994.

———, ed. "Feminists Write International Relations." *Alternatives: Social Transformation and Human Governance*, Special Issue (February 1993).

———. "Feminist Theory and Gender Studies in International Politics." *International Studies Notes* 16:3/17:1 (Fall–Winter 1992): 32–38.

Tannen, Deborah. *You Just Don't Understand: Men and Women in Conversation*. New York: Ballantine, 1990.

Tavris, Carol, and Carole Wade. *The Longest War: Sex Differences in Perspective*. San Diego: Harcourt Brace Jovanovich, 1984.

Taylor Edminston, Patricia. *Nicaragua Divided: "La Prensa" and the Chamorro Legacy*. Pensacola: University of West Florida Press, 1990.

Terborg-Penn, Rosalyn, Sharon Harley, and Andrea Benton Rushing, eds. *Women in Africa and the African Diaspora.* Washington, DC: Howard University Press, 1987.

Thatcher, Margaret. *The Downing Street Years.* New York: Harper-Collins, 1993.

————. *In Defence of Freedom (Speeches).* London: Aurum, 1986.

Tickner, J. Ann. *Gender in International Relations: Feminist Perspectives on Achieving Global Security.* New York: Columbia University Press, 1992.

————. "Hans Morgenthau's Principles of Political Realism: A Feminist Reformulation." *Millennium: Journal of International Studies* 17:3 (Winter 1988): 430–37.

Tinker, Irene, ed. *Persistent Inequalities: Women and World Development.* New York: Oxford University Press, 1990.

Uglow, Jennifer S., comp. and ed. *The Continuum Dictionary of Women's Biography.* New ed. New York: Continuum, 1989.

United Nations. *The World's Women: Trends and Statistics, 1970–1990.* New York: United Nations, 1991. ST/ESA/STAT/SER.K/8.

————. *Nairobi Forward-Looking Strategies for the Advancement of Women.* New York: United Nations Division for Economic and Social Information, April 1986.

Vilas, Carlos M. *The Sandinista Revolution: National Liberation and Social Transformation in Central America.* New York: Monthly Review, 1986.

Walker, Thomas, ed. *Revolution and Counterrevolution in Nicaragua.* Boulder, CO: Westview, 1991.

Weed, Elizabeth. *Coming to Terms: Feminism, Theory, Politics.* New York: Routledge, 1989.

Whitworth, Sandra. *Feminism and International Relations.* London: Macmillan, forthcoming.

————. "Gender in the Inter-Paradigm Debate." *Millennium: Journal of International Studies* 18:2 (Summer 1989): 265–72.

Wiltsher, Anne. *Most Dangerous Women: Feminist Peace Campaigners of the Great War.* London: Pandora, 1985.

Winslow, Anne, ed. *Women, Politics, and the United Nations.* Westport, CT: Greenwood, 1995.

Wurfel, David. *Filipino Politics: Development and Decay.* Quezon City, Philippines: Ateneo de Manila University Press, 1988.

Young, Hugo. *The Iron Lady: A Biography of Margaret Thatcher.* New York: Farrar, Straus, Giroux, 1989.

Index

AAWORD (Association of African Women for Research and Development), 151

Abzug, Bella, 173

Addams, Jane, 12, 155–66, 203, 205

Adiseshiah, Malcolm, 98

Afghanistan, 179–80

Africa, 16–17, 179. *See also Individual country names*

Africans, 178

Albright, Madeleine Korbel, 105

Americans Talk Security surveys, 118, 121, 137

American University, 175

AMES (Association of Women of El Salvador), 193

AMNLAE (Luisa Amanda Espinosa National Women's Association), 193–94

Andrei, Florica, 143

Androcentrism, 27

Angell, Norman, 151

Angola, 100–101, 134

Anstee, Margaret Joan, 7, 11, 95–102

Anti-Communist, 50, 65–66, 78, 80–81

Aquino, Benigno "Ninoy," 71–75

Aquino, Corazon Cojuangco, 11, 22, 25, 27, 71–83, 134, 139, 200; compared to Violeta Barrios de Chamorro, 39

Arab Women's Solidarity Association, 147

Argentina, 18, 205; Falklands/Malvinas War with the United Kingdom, 25, 54, 67; Mothers of the Plaza de Mayo, 171. *See also* Martínez de Perón, María Estela "Isabelita" Cartas

Arms control, and political beliefs of U.S. opinion leaders, 117–18, 122, 125, 128–32, 134, 136. *See also* INF (Intermediate-range Nuclear Forces) Treaty; Nuclear weapons

Asia, 16–17, 50, 52, 145, 147, 179. *See also* Aquino, Corazon Cojuangco; Bhutto, Benazir; *Individual country names*

Astorga, Nora, 192–93

Aung Saan Suu Kyi, 174

Austria, 8, 95, 101–2

Bandaranaike, Sirimavo Ratwatte Dias, 18, 48, 103

Bangladesh, 18, 25, 27, 48, 50–53, 96

Barrios de Chamorro, Violeta, 1, 2, 10, 22, 24, 27, 31–43 196, 200; compared to Corazon Aquino, 39

Bastian, Gert, 176–77

Bastista, Fulgencio, 185–86

Beatrix, Queen of the Netherlands, 16
Belgium, 68, 144, 158
Ben-Gurion, David, 111
Bernardino, Minerva, 86
Bertell, Rosalie, 174
Bhutto, Benazir, 11, 18, 22, 24–26, 48, 95, 102–5
Bhutto, Nusrat, 103–4
Bhutto, Zulfikar Ali, 18, 102–4
Boernstein, Diana, 91
Bolivia, 96, 97, 98
Bonner, Helena, 177
Bosnia, 203, 208
Boutros-Ghali, Boutros, 92, 100
Brazil, 8, 175
Brundtland, Gro Harlem, 26, 201
Bulgaria, 171
Bureaucracy: feminist critique of, 91–92; at the UN, 85; women in, 204
Burma, 174
Bush, George, 28, 39, 40, 42, 63

Caldicott, Helen, 174
Campbell, P. Kim, 22, 200
Canada, 7, 8, 15, 22, 27, 95, 151, 200
Castro, Fidel, 186, 190
Catholic Church: in Cuba, 186; in Nicaragua, 34, 36, 191; in the Philippines, 75
Chamorro, Violeta Barrios de. *See* Barrios de Chamorro, Violeta
Chamorro Cardenal, Pedro Joaquín, 33–35
Chamorro family, 33–34, 36–41
Chiang Ch'ing, 203
China, 136–37, 146, 203, 205; and India, 50–52; and Tibet, 180
Chipko Movement, 171
Christopher, Warren, 201
Churchill, Winston, 59, 159
Ciller, Tansu, 22, 200
Clinton, Hillary Rodham, 16
Clinton, William (Bill), 28, 42
Cohn, Carol, 28
Cojuangco family, 71–72, 82
Colombia, 96, 97, 150
Colonization, 28, 209
Communist party: in Cuba, 186, 188–89;

in Eastern Europe, 177; in Nicaragua, 31; in the Philippines, 73, 77–78, 80. *See also Individual country names*; revolutionary movements
Congress party of India, 45, 47, 48
Conservative party: in Nicaragua, 31, 34, 38; in the United Kingdom, 59, 61, 63, 68
Contras, 36–41, 136, 192, 195–96
Costa Rica, 34, 35, 36
Critical theory, 6, 8–9, 204
CSW. *See* United Nations Commission on the Status of Women
Cuba, 9, 12; and the United States, 184–87, 190–91; and the USSR, 186–87, 195; women and revolution in, 183–91, 193–95, 205
Czechoslovakia, 171, 178–79

Dahl, Robert, 17–22
DAWN (Development Alternatives with Women for a New Era), 148, 151
Decolonization, 16–17
Defensor-Santiago, Miriam, 82
Denmark, 16
Dequalification, 11, 106
Development, 45, 51, 52, 96–99, 178, 179; women and/women in, 54–55, 90, 144–45, 148–49, 151, 166. *See also Individual development organizations* (AAWORD, DAWN, UNCTAD, UNDP, UNIDO)
Dewey, John, 164
Diplomats, 2, 7, 10–11, 13, 88–89. *See also* Anstee, Margaret Joan; Kirkpatrick, Jeane Duane Jordan; Meir, Golda Mabovitch (Meyerson); Pandit, Vijaya Lakshmi
Disengagement, as political strategy, 144–45, 148–53. *See also* Mainstreaming, as political strategy
Dominica, 23

Ecofeminism, 169, 173–74, 205. *See also* Green: movement
EDSA (Epifanio de los Santos Avenue), 74–75, 77–79, 81
Egypt, 179

Elizabeth II, Queen of the United Kingdom, 16, 105
El Salvador, 131, 134, 193
Engels, Friedrich, 184
Enloe, Cynthia, 13, 199, 208
Enrile, Juan Ponce, 75, 80
Espin, Vilma, 186
Essentialism, defined, 10
European Community, 7, 178; and the United Kingdom, 61, 65, 66–68

Feminine, 3–5, 18, 24, 27–28, 42, 53, 56, 62, 67, 71, 78–79, 88, 101, 209. *See also* Gender; *Individual leader names*
Feminism: in Cuba, 188–90; debated, 149–51, 188; global, 185; indigenous, 172; Nicaragua, 191, 196–97; and policy making, 25–26, 85. *See also* Ecofeminism; *Individual leader names*; Women: national leaders
Feminist, 22, 56–57, 85, 91, 145; agenda, 15, 56, 82, 85, 175, 183, 194, 197; consciousness, 146, 183, 193; critique, 85, 91–92, 98, 185; discourse, 92, 189–90; movement, 149–50, 191; networks, 144–45, 148–53; organizing, 143–54, 176; pacifist, 159; politics, 41, 56–57, 92–93, 98, 144, 153, 171, 185; radical, 159, 188; social, 165; women leaders as, 25–26, 41, 54–57, 66, 82, 109–10, 201
Feminist perspectives on world politics, 6, 9–10, 13, 26–29, 207–11
Feminization, of Third World peoples, 28, 209
Ferraro, Geraldine, 17
Finland, 143
FINRRAGE (Feminist International Network of Resistance to Reproductive and Genetic Engineering), 152
First ladies, 16, 203
FMC (Federation of Cuban Women), 186–88, 190, 193–94
Foreign policy: and gender, 24–29, 45, 53–54, 56–57, 59–68, 77–81, 200; and political beliefs of U.S. opinion leaders, 125–34. *See also Individual country names; Individual leader names*
FPLP (Foreign Policy Leadership Project), 113; survey results, 113–39
Framework. *See* Lens; Perspective
France, 114, 159, 204
FSLN (Sandinista Front for National Liberation), 31, 35–42, 191–93, 195–97. *See also* Sandinistas

Gandhi, Indira Nehru, 10, 18, 22, 45–58, 103, 200–201. *See also* India
Gandhi, Maneka, 171
Gandhi, Mohandas Karamchand (Mahatma), 45, 47, 58 n.1, 172
Gandhi, Rajiv, 18, 22, 47
Gender: bias, 89–90; defined, 2–3; differences, 3–5; and foreign policy, 24–29, 45, 53–54, 56–57, 59–68, 77–81; hierarchy, 5–6, 28, 209; and leadership, 15–29, 57, 78–79, 81–82, 106–7, 111, 200–205; and opinion leaders, 113–39; as social construction, 3–4; and world politics, 210–11. *See also Individual leader names*; Patriarchy
Gender-as-difference, 2–5, 10, 13, 23, 26–28, 201, 210; defined, 2–3
Gender-as-power, 3, 5–6, 10, 13, 26–29, 201, 209–10; defined, 3
Gender gap: in literacy, 209; in political beliefs of American opinion leaders, 114–15, 117, 121, 125, 128, 131, 137–38
Germany, 28, 160–61, 163, 169–81, 204
Gilligan, Carol, 57
Glass ceiling: in Nicaraguan politics, 193; at the UN, 11, 85, 90, 93
Global Gender Issues (Peterson and Runyan), 199, 209, 210–11
Godoy, Virgilio, 39, 40–41
González, Milagros, 183
Gorbachev, Mikhail, 66–67, 121, 125, 130, 137, 138, 179
Grajales, Mariana, 186
Great Illusion, The (Angell), 157
Green: movement, 9, 169–75; party (Germany), 169, 175–76, 180–81
Grenada, 131

Guatemala, 205
Gueiler Tejada, Lidia, 43 n.1
Gulf War, 28, 63, 180–81, 209

Habachy, Susan, 89
Hamilton, Alice, 159–60
Hammarsjköld, Dag, 88
Harding, Sandra, 3
Helsinki Citizens Assembly, 177–78
Henderson, Sir Nicholas, 65–66
Hierarchy: gender, 9–10, 28, 209; in
    world politics, 9, 28, 57, 209. *See also*
    Patriarchy
Hobbes, Thomas, 107, 157
Homosexuality, 189, 195
Hungary, 155, 171

Ileto, Reynaldo Clemeña, 76
ILO (International Labour Organization),
    88
IMF (International Monetary Fund), 74
India, 10, 17–18, 24, 28, 45–57, 98, 103,
    114, 151, 171–72, 179; and the United
    Kingdom, 45, 49; and the United
    States, 50–52. *See also* Gandhi, Indira
    Nehru
INF (Intermediate-range Nuclear Forces)
    Treaty, 130, 134–38
International Alliance of Women, 146
International Council of Women, 143,
    146
International Federation of Business and
    Professional Women, 143, 146
International Feminist Network against
    Forced Prostitution and other forms
    of Female Sexual Slavery, 151
International Interdisciplinary Con-
    gresses on Women, 151
Internationalism: cooperative vs. mili-
    tant, 121–25, 139; of Jane Addams,
    163–66
International organizatons, 11–12, 118,
    166, 187, 208. *See also* NGOs (non-
    governmental organizations)
International relations. *See* World poli-
    tics
International Tribunal on Crimes against
    Women, 144

International Union of Women's Suf-
    frage Associations, 155
International Year for the Advancement
    of Women (1975), 143, 144, 145, 146
Iran, 134
Iraq, 28, 63, 180
Ireland, 23, 201
Iron Lady, 11, 26, 50, 56, 62, 66, 107,
    201. *See also* Gandhi, Indira Nehru;
    Thatcher, Margaret Roberts; Women:
    national leaders
Isabella, Queen of Spain, 105
Isis (International Women's Information
    and Communication Network), 149
Islam, and women, 26, 102–4, 149
Israel, 8, 11, 22, 95, 108–11, 114, 128,
    180; Israeli women for peace, 152,
    172. *See also* Meir, Golda Mabovitch
    (Meyerson)
IWTC (International Women's Tribune
    Centre), 149

Jacobs, Aletta, 159–60
JAJA (Justice for Aquino, Justice for All),
    73
Japan, 96, 100, 151, 162, 209
Johnson, Lyndon, 50–51, 105, 207, 209
Jordan, 16

Kashmir, 24
Keen, James, 98
Kelly, Petra Karin, 12, 169–81, 205
Kenya, 152, 173–74
Kimura, Doreen, 206–7
King, Anthony, 63
Kirkpatrick, Jeane Duane Jordan, 7, 11,
    95, 105–8
Kissinger, Henry, 50, 52, 106
Komisaruk, Katya, 171
Korea, People's Democratic Republic
    (North Korea), 28
Korea, Republic of (South Korea), 128,
    132, 151
Korean, war, 137
Kuwait, 17, 63, 180

Lacayo, Antonio, 39, 41
La Prensa, 33–39, 42

Latin America, 17, 98, 101, 150; women in, 37; women leaders in, 31, 43 n.1. *See also* Barrios de Chamorro, Violeta; Martínez de Perón, María Estela "Isabelita" Cartas

Latin American feminist meeting, 150

Leaders: apprentice pool, 19, 23, 202; categories/types, 17–22; national leaders, 1, 4–5, 15–29, 200–203; U.S. opinion leaders, 12, 113–39, 204–5

Leadership style, 4, 10, 15, 24–28, 56, 99–100

League of Nations, 88, 163

Lens, 1–2, 6–10, 13, 27, 199–200, 207, 210. *See also* Perspective

Liberal party in Nicaragua, 31, 33, 38

Liberia-Peters, Maria, 23

Libya, 134

Maathi, Wangari, 173–74

Maceo, Antonio, 186

Mainstreaming, as political strategy, 144–48, 153

Major, John, 2

Malawi, 114

Marchenko, Anatoly, 177

Marcos, Ferdinand E., 71–82, 134, 139, 171

Marcos, Imelda Romualdez, 73, 82

Margarethe II, Queen of Denmark, 16

Marquand, David, 64

Martínez-Cabañas, Gustavo, 98

Martínez de Perón, María Estela "Isabelita" Cartas, 18, 43 n.1

Marx, Karl, 184

Marxist political party, 38

Marxist theory, 8

Masculine, 3–4, 5, 28, 53, 62, 79, 88. *See also* Gender

Meir, Golda Mabovitch (Meyerson), 11, 22, 54, 95, 105, 108–11

Menchú, Rigoberta, 205

Mexico, 7, 55, 98, 103, 149

Milne, Christine, 175

Mitterrand, François, 65

MNCs (multinational corporations), 7, 208

Mongella, Gertrude, 93

Morocco, 96, 98

Ms., 90

Mujibur, Sheik, 18

Muratovic, Amela, 208

Muslim faith, and women, 102–4; Women under Muslim Laws network, 149

NAFTA (North American Free Trade Agreement), 7, 204

NAMFREL (National Movement for Free Elections), 74

Nansen, Fridtjof, 163

Nehru, Jawaharlal, 45–52, 56

Netherlands, the 16, 158–60

Networking, 148–52

Newer Ideals for Peace (Addams), 157

NGOs (nongovernmental organizations), 2, 7, 12, 86–88; and the United Nations, 143–54

Nicaragua, 9, 10, 12, 17, 24, 27, 31–43; political beliefs of U.S. opinion leaders, 114, 131, 134, 136; U.S. policy toward, 31, 33, 37–40, 42, 184, 191–92, 194–96; women and revolution in, 184–85, 191–97. *See also* Barrios de Chamorro, Violeta

Nicholson, Sir Harold, 88

Nixon, Richard, 52, 105, 209

Noor al Hussein, Queen of Jordan, 16

Norton, Eleanor Holmes, 23

Norway, 114, 200. *See also* Brundtland, Gro Harlem

Nuclear weapons, 17, 25, 53, 169, 171–72, 174, 176

Ogata, Sadako, 96, 100

Oman, 17

Opinion leaders, 113–39, 204–5

Ortega Saavedra, Daniel, 36–41

Ortega Saavedra, Humberto, 41

Owen, David, 98

Pacifism. *See* Peace movements

Pacifist, 15, 24–25, 114, 159. *See also* Addams, Jane; Kelly, Petra Karin

Pakistan, 11, 18, 24, 25, 28, 48, 50, 52–

53, 95, 96, 102–5, 114, 179. *See also*
Bhutto,Benazir
Pakistan People's party, 103–4
Palestine, 108–9, 128
Palestinian groups, 25; women for
peace, 152, 172
Panama, 27
Pandit, Vijaya Lakshmi, 48
Paquet-Sévigny, Thérèse, 95
Partnoy, Alicia, 205
Pasyon and Revolution (Ileto), 76
Paths to power, 15, 17–19, 47–48, 53;
and gender, 22–24
Patriarchy, 85, 172, 206; defined, 10. *See
also* Gender: hierarchy
Patrician, 17–18, 22, 48
Peace and Bread (Addams), 163
Peace movements, 9, 152, 171, 179–81;
in the United States during World War
I, 155–66
Pérez Vega, Reynaldo, 192
Perspective: defined, 1–2; perspectives
on world politics, 1–2, 6–10, 82, 204.
See also Lens
Peterson, V. Spike, 199–200, 209, 210–
11
Philippines, 11, 39, 71–82, 96; military
factions, 74–75, 79; and the United
States, 73–75, 77–81, 114, 134, 139;
women in, 71, 82, 171. *See also*
Aquino, Corazon Cojuangco
Pineda, Amada, 191–92
Pluralism, 6, 7–8, 204. *See also* Perspec-
tive
Poland, 131, 171, 172
Policy making: feminism, 25–26, 85; and
gender, 1–5, 24–29, 200–203. *See also*
Individual policy makers
Political beliefs: and gender, 113–39;
and ideology, party, occupation, gen-
eration,134–37
Political Realism, 6–7, 8, 10, 13, 51, 53,
116–17, 158, 165, 204, 209, 210. *See
also* Perspective
Political surrogate: 22–23, 42, 47–48, 53,
82; defined, 22
Political system, and leader selection,
15–16

Power: conceptions of in perspectives
on world politics, 6–8, 10–11, 58, 210;
paths to, 15, 17–19, 22–24, 47–48, 53;
politics, 25
Prostitution, 18, 41, 145, 187, 194
Proxy, 82. *See also* Political surrogate
Purdah, 103

Qatar, 17

Rahman, Ziaur, 18
Ramírez, Sergio, 37
Ramos, General Fidel V., 75, 82
Reagan, Ronald, 38, 63, 65–67, 74, 107,
114, 125, 130–34, 136
Reagan and Thatcher (Smith), 67
Realism. *See* Political Realism
Reproductive issues, 145, 151–52, 174,
188,195
Revolutionary movements, 9, 12–13; in
Cuba, 183–90; in Eastern Europe,
177–78, 184; in Nicaragua, 184–85,
191–97; and women, 183–85, 203
Robelo, Alfonso, 35–36
Robinson, Mary Bourke, 23, 201
Romania, 143, 171
Room of One's Own, A (Woolf), 107
Roosevelt, Eleanor, 86, 203
Roosevelt, Theodore, 159
Routinization of politics, 11, 81
Runyan, Anne Sisson, 199–200, 209,
210–11
Russia, 28, 108, 120, 164, 205, 209. *See
also* USSR

Sadik, Nafis, 92, 95
Said, Abdul, 176
Sakharov, Andrei, 77
Sanchez, Celia, 186
Sandinistas, 31, 35–38, 42–43, 185, 191–
93, 195–97
Santamaria, Haydee, 186
Saudi Arabia, 17, 48, 114, 134
Schwimmer, Rozika, 159–60
Senegal, 151
Sex tourism, 151
Sexual harassment, at the UN, 91
Shastri, Lal Bahadur, 47–48

Shevardnadze, Eduard, 65
Shiva, Vandana, 174, 175, 178
Silpia, Helvi, 143
Smith, Geoffrey, 67
Smith, Margaret Chase, 18
Social movements, 9
Somoza family, 17, 22, 33–36, 40–41, 191–92
South Africa, 131, 132, 136
Soviet Union. *See* USSR
Sri Lanka, 18, 103, 114. *See also* Bandaranaike, Sirimavo Ratwatte Dias
Steinem, Gloria, 150
Survey research, 204–5
Surveys, of public opinion: Americans Talk Security, 118, 121, 137; Chicago Council on Foreign Relations, 125; Foreign Policy Leadership Project, 113–39
Sweden, 166
Switzerland, 143, 158
Sykes, Patricia Lee, 201

Taiwan, 128
Tanzania, 93
Téllez, Dora Maria, 192, 197
Terre des Femmes, 174
Thatcher, Margaret Roberts, 1, 11, 22, 23, 25–27, 50, 54, 59–69, 105, 114, 200–201. *See also* United Kingdom
Theory, of world politics, 6–10, 204; defined, 6
Third World, 54, 57, 118, 122, 178–79; feminized, 28, 209; women in, 145, 147–51; women leaders in, 47–48. *See also* Aquino, Corazon Cojuangco; Bhutto, Benazir; Gandhi, Indira Nehru; *Individual country names*
Thorsson, Inga, 166
Tribalism (vs. internationalism), 157–58, 166
Tsien, Patricia, 90
Turkey, 22, 200
TW MAE W (Third World Movement against the Exploitation of Women), 151

Ukraine, 28
UNCED (United Nations Conference on Environment and Development), 8, 175
UNCTAD (United Nations Conference on Trade and Development), 146
UNDP (United Nations Development Programme), 86, 92, 96, 98, 146
UNEP (United Nations Environment Programme),146
UNESCO (United Nations Education, Social, and Cultural Organization), 98, 131, 145
UNFPA (United Nations Fund for Population Activities), 86–87, 92, 96, 146
UNHCR (United Nations High Commission on Refugees), 96, 100
UNICEF (United Nations Children's Fund), 88
UNIDO (United Nations Industrial Development Organization), 146
UNITAR (United Nations Institute for Training and Research), 89
United Arab Emirates, 17
United Kingdom, 16, 17, 22, 28, 95, 98, 152; and Falklands/Malvinas war with Argentina, 25, 54, 67; Greenham Common, 152; and India, 45, 48, 56; and Palestine, 109–10; Thatcher government, 59–68; and the United States, 61–63, 66–67. *See also* Anstee, Margaret Joan; Thatcher, Margaret Roberts
United Nations, 7, 8, 11, 48, 187; and international women's movements, 143–54; and political beliefs of U.S. opinion leaders, 125, 131, 136, 139; statistics on women, 208–9; women personnel in, 48, 85–93, 95–102, 105–8, 166, 192–93, 204, 209. *See also* Anstee, Margaret Joan; Astorga, Nora; Kirkpatrick, Jeane Duane Jordan; Pandit, Vijaya Lakshmi
United Nations Ad Hoc Group on Equal Rights for Women, 90–91
United Nations *Charter*, 85–86, 88–89
United Nations Commission on the Status of Women, 88, 90, 143
United Nations Conference on Human Rights, 8

United Nations Conferences on Women, 55, 92–93, 102, 103, 144, 146, 149, 208
United Nations Decade for Women (1975-1985), 55, 85, 93, 103, 144, 146, 148, 153, 208
United Nations *Declaration of Human Rights*, 86
United Nations Secretariat, 86–92 passim
United States, 7, 12, 15, 17, 34, 39, 48, 95, 151–52; and Cuba, 184–87, 190–91; foreign policy of, 8, 105, 107; and India, 50–52; and Nicaragua, 31, 33, 37–40, 42, 184, 191–92, 194–96; and the Philippines, 74–75, 77–81; political beliefs of opinion leaders, 113–39, 204–5, and the United Kingdom, 61–63, 66–67; women in, 18, 19, 27–28, 57. *See also* Addams, Jane; Kirkpatrick, Jean Duane Jordan
UNO (National Opposition Union), 31, 38–42
Uruguay, 96
USSR, 51, 89, 108; dissidents in, 177; and political beliefs of U.S. opinion leaders, 115, 118–21, 130–32, 136–38, 152, 164. *See also* Russia

Valentine, Jo, 174
Vietnam, 50, 135, 137, 145, 207, 209

Wajid, Sheik Hasina, 18
Waltz, Kenneth, 117
Waring, Marilyn, 175
Whitworth, Sandra, 12, 200
Who (World Health Organization), 88
Who Governs, 17
Who's Who in America, 113
Who's Who of American Women, 113
WIC (Women's International Congress), 158–60, 162, 165
WIDF (Women's International Democratic Federation), 143, 147–48
Widow's walk, 10, 18, 47. *See also* Political surrogate

WILPF (Women's International League for Peace and Freedom), 8, 162, 165
Wilson, Edith Gault, 203
Wilson, Woodrow, 160–62, 164, 165, 203
WIN (Women's International Network), 149
WMS (Women for Mutual Security), 152
Women: diplomats, 2, 7, 10–11, 13, 88–89; national leaders, 1–2, 4–5, 7, 10–11, 15–29, 200–203; participants in world politics, 1–6, 12–13, 15, 171, 207–8; paths to power, 15, 17–19, 22–24, 47–48, 53; in peace movements, 177, 205; policy makers, 3, 50, 201–4; in revolutionary movements, 3, 76, 177–78, 183–97, 203. *See also Individual country names; Individual names*; United Nations
Women, Gender, and World Politics: Perspectives, Policies, and Prospects (Beckman and D'Amico, eds.), 6, 200
Women at The Hague (Addams), 165
Women's Encampment for Peace and Justice, 152
Women's Peace party, 158, 162
Women under Muslim Laws networks, 149
Woolf, Leonard, 165–66
Woolf, Virginia, 107
World politics: and gender, 4–5, 210–11; as gendered, 28–29, 206–11; perspectives on, 1–2, 6–10
World War I, 155–62, 165
World War II, 16, 19, 59, 88, 108
World Women's Congress for a Healthy Planet, 173

Young, Hugo, 66
Yugoslavia, 114. *See also* Bosnia

Zardari, Asif Ali, 104–5
Zia, Khalida, 18, 48
Zia, ul-Haq, 26, 103–4
Zionist, 108–10

About the Editors and Contributors

MARGARET ANSTEE is head of the United Nations Angola Verification Mission (UNAVEM II) peacekeeping and transition force in Luanda, Angola.

PETER R. BECKMAN is Professor of Political Science at Hobart and William Smith Colleges, Geneva, New York.

VINCENT G. BOUDREAU is Assistant Professor of Political Science and Chair of the MA Program in International Relations at City College, New York, New York.

MARY C. CARRAS is Professor of Political Science at the State University of New Jersey–Rutgers at Camden, New Jersey.

FRANCINE D'AMICO is Visiting Research Fellow for the "Women and the Military" project of the Peace Studies Program, Center for International Studies, Cornell University, Ithaca, New York.

KENNETH HARRIS is a journalist with the (London Sunday) *Observer* and Director, Associate Editor, and Chairman of its holding company, George Outram, London, England.

OLE R. HOLSTI is George V. Allen Professor of Political Science at Duke University in Durham, North Carolina.

PETRA KELLY was a pacifist and ecofeminist and representative of the Green party in the German *Bundestag* (Parliament), 1983–1992.

SYBIL OLDFIELD is Lecturer in English and Chair of Women's Studies at the School of Cultural and Community Studies, University of Sussex, Brighton.

MARGARET RANDALL is an independent scholar, poet, photographer, editor, journalist, and translator, who lived and worked in Latin America for more than twenty years and now lives in Albuquerque, New Mexico.

JAMES N. ROSENAU is University Professor of International Affairs at George Washington University in Washington, D.C.

DEBORAH STIENSTRA is Assistant Professor of Political Science at University of Winnipeg, Manitoba.

KRISTEN TIMOTHY is a political economist, has been with the United Nations since 1970, and has served as President of the UN Group on Equal Rights for Women, 1989–1990.

HARVEY WILLIAMS is Professor of Sociology, Anthropology, and International Studies at University of the Pacific, Stockton, California.

ISBN 0-89789-410-3

EAN

9 780897 894104

HARDCOVER BAR CODE